DOWNSIZING DEFENSE

DOWNSIZING DEFENSE

Edited by
Ethan B. Kapstein

Written under the auspices of the
John M. Olin Institute for Strategic Studies
Harvard University

1993

Congressional Quarterly Inc.
Washington, D.C.

Copyright © 1993 Congressional Quarterly Inc.
1414 22nd St., N.W., Washington, D.C. 20037

Printed in the United States of America

Jacket design: Tina Chovanec

Library of Congress
Cataloging-in-Publication Data

Downsizing defense / edited by Ethan B. Kapstein.
p.   cm.
Includes bibliographical references and index.
ISBN 0-87187-945X
1. United States--Defenses.   2. United States--Armed Forces-
-Appropriations and expenditures.   3. Defense industries-
-United States.   4. Economic conversion--United States.
I. Kapstein, Ethan B.
UA23.D69   1993
355'.0335' 73-dc20   93-5636
                                                              CIP

Contents

Tables and Figures

Tables

Figures

Preface

J ust as the rapid rise in defense spending during the early Reagan years sparked widespread national debate about its effects on the economic and security environments, so too the sharp fall in defense outlays that began in 1986 has sparked debate today. Americans are never quite satisfied with their peacetime defense budget; it is always too big or too small. Since the collapse of the Soviet threat in 1989, many have called for cuts in defense spending far beyond those currently projected in official documents. Soldiers and Pentagon bureaucrats, in turn, speak of the need to retain a base force that is strong enough to fight brush-fire wars around the world today and of the need to reconstitute, if necessary, to meet any emerging threat tomorrow.

Clearly, the debate over how the United States should proceed with downsizing its defense establishment is in flux, and one of the greatest challenges confronting the Clinton administration will be to maintain a military that is able to do its job (the nature of that job, of course, is central to the debate) despite greatly reduced resources. Can the Pentagon scale back yet retain a force structure and defense industrial base that are ready to meet the next crisis? Or will the current downsizing lead to a military characterized by inexperience and poor morale and a defense industry that is no longer at the cutting edge of research and development? In a world that lacks a monolithic threat, should the budget focus on developing technologies for the future or on the continued production of proven systems? These and other questions are being hotly debated in Washington and in the thousands of communities that are feeling the effects of lower defense spending owing to base and plant closings.

Downsizing Defense was written in the hope of illuminating the current debate over defense cutbacks. It is unique in that it brings together distinguished analysts from government, industry, and academia. Furthermore, it provides a comparative perspective on the issues by examining how Europeans and Russians are coping with lower levels of defense spending. While it is intrinsically valuable to understand how these debates are playing out overseas, the members of this project would also agree that a comparative perspective can help sharpen our understanding of critical issues at home.

Although the book does not go into any detailed discussion of the history of defense downsizing in the United States or other countries, a few words may be in order here to provide some perspective on the contemporary debate. After all, it should be recalled that the United States has significantly reduced defense spending several times during the past fifty years, including at the ends of World War II, the Korean War, and the Vietnam War.

One might think that public officials would have learned something of value from these earlier experiences. Unfortunately, the lack of institutional memory in Washington is legend, and the version of the historical record that lingers is often incorrect. This is certainly the case with respect to economic conversion. Today, many in Congress and the defense establishment believe that the United States has successfully transformed guns into butter at the end of its major conflicts. Even worse, many Russian officials, whose country confronts a conversion problem several times bigger than our own, also seem to accept this view of history. The record, however, does not support this conclusion.

At the end of World War II, the U.S. government held title to a significant portion of the country's industrial base, including 90 percent of the synthetic rubber, aircraft, and magnesium industries and over 50 percent of the aluminum and machine tool industries. This gave the government tremendous power over the future direction of the American economy. Its conversion programs were of direct consequence not only to the communities in which defense plants were located, but to the country as a whole. Indeed, the importance of the conversion program was signaled by President Franklin D. Roosevelt's appointment in 1943 of his trusted aid Jimmy Byrnes to oversee the process of industrial transformation.

Between 1943 and the war's end, Byrnes dispatched teams of engineers across the country to study the defense industrial base and its best alternative uses in a civilian economy. What most of these studies revealed was the difficulty of turning guns into butter. Indeed, rather than convert, the United States ended up dumping billions of dollars' worth of machine tools in the ocean and rebuilding the economy anew. Of course, with the outbreak of the Korean War in 1950, a large part of the defense industrial base that had been preserved was mobilized.

What ultimately saved the post-World War II American economy was not conversion at the plant level but macroeconomic policies that encouraged economic growth. Economic conversion was really an economic transformation in which the factors of production—labor and capital—flowed from defense to their next best use. This transformation was not always easy, and for many communities it meant the end of the boom years. We should also remember that in the process of conversion, returning veterans displaced women and minorities who had found good industrial jobs in the wartime economy. Thus, although economic growth would prove buoyant after 1948, not all Americans partook of this bounty.

Perhaps of more relevance to contemporary circumstances is the post-Vietnam experience. After the Vietnam conflict drew to a close, defense firms had a difficult time. On the macroeconomic level, the American economy was performing badly in the 1970s, suffering from that fatal mix of inflation and stagnation dubbed "stagflation." Scrambling for new niches in this dismal environment, defense companies entered a variety of businesses, from building buses (Grumman) to bathtubs (Boeing). For its part, General Dynamics went on to lose money in shipbuilding and mining.

Overall, the record of defense industries in commercial enterprise has not been a good one. Government advocates of defense industry diversification would do well to recall that a booming commercial sector already exists in the United States, always seeking new demands to be met. Awarding contracts for civilian work to defense firms in an effort to "force" them to convert, as some officials and policy analysts have proposed, would hurt the existing commercial firms that are already serving those needs.

In short, there is little in the American experience to give us optimism about the potential for turning guns into butter at the plant level; what "saved" the United States each time in the past was the renewal of economic growth. This suggests that, in the short run, defense downsizing will be painful to many of those who have given their careers to the military and its supporting industries. In order to help these workers transfer to new careers, the government should help with retraining programs and perhaps some direct financial assistance. But the government should not give false hopes to the American (or Russian) people that jobs and plants can be maintained and converted. The historical record suggests that this simply does not happen.

Given that historical record, we open this volume with an overview of the macroeconomics of defense spending reductions, prepared by Dr. Roger Brinner of DRI/McGraw-Hill, one of the nation's leading economic consulting firms. Brinner makes the important point that while the projected overall reductions in defense spending are small from a macroeconomic perspective, they can have large effects if the government fails to adopt appropriate policy measures. Specifically, should economic growth continue to lag, the Federal Reserve must be prepared to provide an economic stimulus in one form or another as this key element of government spending declines. In the absence of such a stimulus, the drop in defense spending could cause a prolonged drag on the American economy.

The volume then provides a number of perspectives on policy issues that are currently facing the United States as it contemplates defense downsizing. In his contribution, David Blair of the Air War College suggests that the Pentagon's cold-war system of budgeting and procurement (the famed PPBS system, developed in the early 1960s by then secretary of defense Robert McNamara and his "whiz kids"—Les Aspin among them) will require radical changes in the years to come. The ability to make those changes, however, will require not just sound policy analysis but also significant transformation by long-entrenched bureaucracies.

Moving to domestic and local politics, the contributions by Kenneth Mayer of the University of Wisconsin, Peter Trubowitz of the University of Texas, and John Lynch and Bill Dickens, both of whom have worked in the Pentagon's Office of Economic Adjustment, focus on different aspects of the contemporary debate over defense downsizing.

Mayer examines how relations between Congress and the Pentagon may be expected to evolve and suggests that both bodies have been incapable, as yet, of processing the strategic changes brought about by the end of the cold war. In this regard, it is interesting to note that one of the sharpest critics of the Reagan-Bush defense policy, Les Aspin, is now guiding the nation's military. Mayer suggests that we should not be surprised if Congress and the Pentagon agree on a series of defense cuts that are less dramatic than those contemplated following the collapse of the Berlin Wall, as we continue to debate the nature of the new strategic environment.

Trubowitz argues that the response to defense downsizing by members of Congress will be largely a function of regional economic politics. Based on a sophisticated reading of roll-call votes, Trubowitz shows how the defense budget is now a focus of significant political conflict. It is not so much the level of defense cuts that is of concern to Congress, but rather their allocation across districts. Given this finding, we should expect rampant logrolling as members of Congress try to maintain weapons programs or win new commercial projects in the jurisdictions they represent.

Lynch and Dickens follow Trubowitz's work with an overview of the specific cutbacks to be made and where they are likely to be sharpest. They go beyond this, however, by describing the role of the federal and local governments in working with communities once cutbacks have been made. The important lesson to be derived from their chapter is that the experience of communities that have suffered the loss of military facilities has been surprisingly variable, and in several cases the regional economy has improved as better uses are made of land and labor.

The book then takes a microperspective on the downsizing debate by focusing on industrial outlooks. Richard Minnich, who brings to his contribution many years of experience inside the defense industry, casts a critical eye on the prospects for defense conversion at the plant level in the United States. He argues from a corporate standpoint that many firms will be able to transform themselves into competitive enterprises over time. However, Minnich suggests that once defense plants are closed and firms transformed, we should not expect them to be able to "reconstitute" defense capabilities should they be needed to do so in the future. Bud Udis of the University of Colorado, writing about the future of Western Europe's defense industries, reports that conversion is not generally viewed as a realistic possibility by most firms on the continent. Indeed, based on detailed field research he shows that governments have done surprisingly little in the way of conversion planning. Instead, a variety of policies are being adopted to ensure the maintenance of a defense and high-technology industrial base. The success of these policies in terms of efficiency may be open to debate, but thus far Europeans have been willing to pay the costs associated with this approach. Whether such policies can endure over the long term is an important question for Europe's future.

In his contribution, Yevgeny Kuznetsov of Cornell describes the gloomy situation inside the defense industries of the former Soviet Union. He argues that, given the centrality of the defense industry in the former Soviet Union, we really cannot speak about conversion as a policy solution; the problems require much stronger medicine. Kuznetsov outlines a number of models of economic reform and addresses the costs and benefits associated with each one. In so doing, he renders two important services to American and other foreign observers: first, he reminds us that the manner in which we downsize defense is subject to debate and is a matter of choice; second, he notes that Russian conversion and reform efforts pose a dilemma for the West. If Russia fails, the implications for the security environment are grave; but if Russia succeeds, the West may face a formidable competitor for world markets.

Murray Weidenbaum, a long-time observer of the defense industrial base and former chairman of the Council of Economic Advisers, details in Chapter 9 an "acquisition policy for a new era." Weidenbaum describes the changes that must be made if the United States is to maintain a cost-effective and credible defense in the 1990s and beyond. He clearly analyzes the shortcomings of the present system and the certain failure of any "quick-fix" remedies. His analysis will find a place at the center of the contemporary debate over defense policy and acquisition strategy. Finally, in the concluding chapter, I provide an overview of our findings and identify some implications for policymaking.

This volume has been a collective venture. We at Harvard's Economics and National Security Program and John M. Olin Institute for Strategic Studies would like to thank the authors who took time from their busy schedules to attend meetings, write drafts, and prepare final chapters. They did so with grace and humor. We would also like to thank the Pew Charitable Trusts for supporting this project and wish to express our gratitude to Kevin Quigley and Steve Del Rosso of the Trusts for their tremendous assistance at every step of the way. The debate over the relationship between economics and national security may be expected to rage for many years to come, both in the United States and abroad, and the Pew Charitable Trusts has done as much as any foundation to bring the critical issues to public attention. We hope this volume contributes to wider understanding and analysis of current and future reductions in defense spending.

Ethan B. Kapstein

1

Impact of Defense Reductions on the U.S. Economy in the 1990s

Roger E. Brinner

The economic repercussions of defense reductions are a source of pervasive anxiety because of the industry's substantial role in the U.S. economy. However, the current downsizing is not unprecedented, and it would be a mistake to project broad national distress as a necessary consequence. It would be equally incorrect to underestimate the adjustments required of government and business to achieve a successful transition.

The size of this sector tends to follow "long wave" patterns because it is driven by policy judgments on major national security needs. These judgments may change abruptly, as they have recently, but related plans and contractual obligations necessarily span relatively long periods. Therefore cycles of scaling up and scaling down typically stretch five-to-ten years.

These long time frames allow for adjustments to be made, as they must be now. The affected businesses are shifting their labor and capital away from defense production. They are also seeking productive civilian applications of their core competencies. In the end, these firms will shed vast resources; the defense-specific attributes of the released pool of skills, technologies, and facilities will be devalued, perhaps sharply, to their next closest application values in other industries.

On a national basis, significant employment and income will be lost until other sectors can take up the slack. This cyclical weakness will be shorter in duration and shallower in magnitude if the Federal Reserve loosens its credit policy. Construction activity, investment in capital equipment, and consumer spending for durable goods would all rise substantially in response to lower interest rates. To date, however, the Federal Reserve has not shown that it comprehends the magnitude of the adjustment it must make. Either that or it has elected to permit slow growth in order to achieve its target of zero inflation.

Roger E. Brinner is executive director at DRI/McGraw Hill.

The size of the federal deficit makes easier credit the preferred policy but, if the Federal Reserve fails to act, Congress cannot allow defense reductions to lead to a five-year recession. Congress also could alleviate the cyclical weakness, by expanding nondefense government spending or cutting taxes. Congress seems aware that an explicit short-term choice can be made to increase employment and income through interest-sensitive private spending or with public spending.

The compensating policy choices hold long-run implications for national living standards. Only if private or public investment is stimulated to offset the defense retrenchment will long-run benefits offset the short-run costs. There is broad recognition of this implication among citizens and elected officials; thus the "peace dividend" is likely to be dedicated to federal deficit reduction. Failing this, it will be used to fund federal programs that can be justified as building human capital or government-owned infrastructure. Indeed, President Bill Clinton explicitly proposed education, job training, and infrastructure programs as core ingredients of his economic policy.

Directing the savings to deficit reduction is particularly appropriate because the defense expansion from 1979 to 1987 was debt financed, not tax financed. In other words, future generations are already obligated to pay for the Reagan administration's heavy defense spending; it is proper that the termination of these programs opens the way to fund the investments to generate the income to service the debt.

This study will elaborate and quantify these themes of adjustment. Illustrations will be drawn from alternative simulations of the DRI Model of the U.S. Economy, a large-scale, econometric model designed to portray both cyclical and secular phenomena. The study will contrast economic developments flowing from the current long-run defense budget and DRI extrapolations through 2002 for two alternative cases: very significant reductions (the reduced-defense case); and an economy driven by constant, inflation-adjusted defense outlays (the flat-defense case).

The key conclusions are:

1. The current retrenchment that began in 1988 may last a decade. Cyclical and permanent losses will occur in regions and industries that grew strongly in the 1980s as the defense industry expanded. However, the national losses can be held to a temporary increase of approximately 0.5 percentage point in the unemployment rate if the Federal Reserve loosens its credit policy. The income and employment losses during the first years of defense reductions will result in a slight reduction in inflation.

2. There is no "peace dividend" because the defense buildup was produced with borrowed funds, not tax revenues. The federal

deficit, excluding the temporary funding for the deposit insurance crisis, was about $300 billion in 1992 even after three years of restrained defense expenditure. In the absence of defense cutbacks, tax increases, or unexpected nondefense program reductions, the deficit will probably expand to $500 billion in ten years. On the other hand, the projected defense cutbacks are sufficient to bring the deficit below $200 billion by the end of the century. Of this possible deficit reduction, $180 billion comes from lower defense outlays; the remainder is the net result of lower interest payments offset by lower nominal tax revenues because average prices are lower. (Prices are lower because unemployment is anti-inflationary.) Indeed, more than $200 billion per year eventually accrues from decreased interest expenses on a smaller debt financed with lower interest rates.

3. Substitution of private investment for defense outlays, in response to substantially lower capital costs, will expand national output if defense outlays are significantly reduced (the reduced-defense case). Today, large pools of labor, capital, and materials are dedicated to producing "security," which is not counted in GNP or other official measures of national output. The defense goods and employment costs are counted as the federal funds are spent, but no stream of security benefits is later evaluated. In the future, these pools will be employed in producing nondefense goods and services that are measured.

4. The international competitiveness of U.S. goods and services will be enhanced in industries not tied to defense technologies. Greater private capital spending should accelerate the retooling of America. In addition, the foreign exchange value of the dollar will likely be reduced as U.S. interest rates decline relative to those in Germany and Japan. Just as our policy shift to large deficits and tight credit led to a progressively overvalued dollar until 1985, a policy reversal will tend to produce devaluation. Moreover, defense purchases have far lower import content than almost any other domestic spending; thus, a weaker dollar will be necessary to balance international flows.

5. Losses in the defense industry will be offset by gains in dozens of smaller industries. Assuming the reduced-defense case, by the turn of the century industry output will be only 65 percent of that likely with a flat budget (the flat-defense case). Communications and aircraft output will be trimmed by perhaps 10 percent. The largest beneficiaries, with gains of 5-7 percent, are likely to be lumber, other construction materials, office equipment, instruments, and production machinery. Total manufac-

Figure 1-1 Long Waves in Real Defense Spending (per capita federal spending, 1987 dollars)

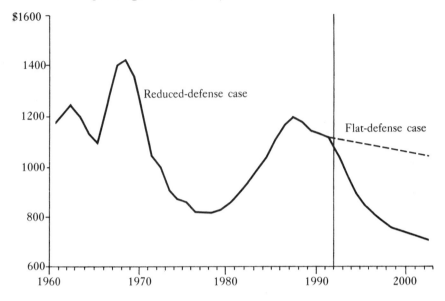

turing output and employment would not be materially different, but the composition of these totals would be.

The Policy Choices

The Defense Budget in Perspective

In 1987 per capita federal defense purchases reached $1,200 (1987 dollars). Pressures to reduce the federal deficit thereafter eliminated growth in spending in excess of inflation, implying a slight $89 reduction in per capita outlays between 1987 and 1991. Today, the diminished military threat and inensfied U.S. budget problems have prompted an accelerated decline in defense outlays. By 1995 per capita real spending is assumed to be trimmed to $830 (see Figure 1-1); defense purchases are assumed to decline at a 5.4 percent compound annual rate while population should grow at a 0.7 percent rate.

The current eight-year (1987-1995) reduction is quite similar to that of two decades ago when the United States scaled back from its Vietnam expenditures (see Table 1-1). In 1968 federal defense purchases were $1,400 per capita; by 1976 the burden had been trimmed to $800. The surprising similarity in the magnitudes may suggest minimum and maximum tolerances of defense commitment by the electorate or may be coinci-

Table 1-1   Two Downsizing Waves in Defense Spending

Wave 1: Post-Vietnam	1968	1976	1980	Change 1968-76	Subsequent Change 1976-1980
Real GDP ($, billion)	2,801	3,381	3,776	580	395
Population (million)	201	218	228	17	10
Defense outlays ($, billion)	285	180	194	−105	14
Real, per capita dimensions of the federal budget (1987 dollars)					
Defense outlays ($)	1,418	824	853	−594	29
Nondefense purchases	323	359	398	36	39
Interest payments	177	235	323	58	88
Transfer payments	755	1,428	1,542	673	114
Total spending	1,779	1,183	1,250	−596	67
Income taxes	1,245	1,284	1,568	39	284
Total taxes	2,776	2,979	3,384	203	405
Deficit	74	463	368	389	−95

Wave 2: Post-Reagan	1987	1995	2000	Change 1987-95	Subsequent Change 1995-2000
Real GDP ($, billion)	4,540	5,384	6,052	844	668
Population (million)	243	261	270	18	9
Defense outlays ($, billion)	292	216	194	−76	−22
Real, per capita dimensions of the federal budget (1987 dollars)					
Defense outlays ($)	1,202	830	719	−372	−111
Nondefense purchases	382	412	398	30	−14
Interest payments	562	766	790	204	24
Transfer payments	1,697	2,052	2,116	355	64
Total spending	1,584	1,242	1,117	−342	−125
Income taxes	1,650	1,746	1,943	96	197
Total taxes	3,763	4,115	4,650	392	405
Deficit	625	712	472	87	−240

dental. Regardless, it illustrates that the current downsizing cycle is not unique; therefore, past experience may be a reliable guide in estimating prospective effects.

The per capita comparison places this vast industry on a comprehensible scale. These are the per person commitments made on behalf of the federal government. For reference, real GNP in 1968 was $14,000 per capita, real after-tax household income was $9,000, and real federal spending was $3,000; at the beginning of the 1992 down-cycle, GNP was $19,000 per capita, income was $14,000, and federal spending was $4,000.

An alternative presentation, outlining defense purchases relative to total national output, reveals the current shift to be a smaller reduction than that of two decades ago. The economic pain of dislocation may be no less, however, because both population and income growth were more rapid in the prior episode. Labor and capital resources that migrated out of the defense sector had a slightly easier time finding productive new opportunities.

An important technical and conceptual point is that this study of defense reductions focuses only on the period in which real defense purchases are actually declining, that is, from 1992 onward. The small decline in per capita spending from 1987 to 1991 was entirely due to rising population; total spending adjusted for inflation was actually stable. The maximum calendar year total was $292 billion; the minimum was $281 billion.

Early in the 1980s budgets had called for annual growth of 5 percent or more beyond inflation, but budget pressures and diminished perceptions of Soviet military prowess eliminated such growth. These initial 1987-1991 cuts in planned spending presented substantial problems to the industries and employees serving the military, but the consequences are not directly addressed by this study.

The Nondefense Budget

The October 1990 budget summit temporarily prevented defense savings from being used to bolster civilian programs. The economic scenarios compared here generalize this partitioning rule.

Although programs are held fixed, many dimensions of government spending do vary. First, the lower inflation of the reduced-defense case carries over to all federal purchases and tax bases. This follows the standard convention of comparative fiscal policy analysis that real (that is, inflation-adjusted), not nominal, purchases are assumed to represent the program objective. Second, unemployment and welfare programs vary in predictable ways with the cyclical level of unemployment, and such automatic changes are allowed to play out. Third, interest payments are defined by the level and maturity of debt and the interest rates prevailing in financial markets at the date of each debt issue.

The assumption that defense reductions have no impact on real civilian program content or scale is central to this study. Any alternative assumption would have required an arbitrary specification of which federal programs would be increased or which taxes cut and by how much. The popular contenders are national health insurance, aid to education, highway and infra-structure improvements, and an array of tax cuts. Each contender has a

Table 1-2   Budget Reactions to Lower Defense Spending and its Economic Consequences

	Flat Defense		Reduced Defense		Percent Difference	
	1995	2002	1995	2002	1995	2002
Federal Budget Dimensions ($, billion, National Income and Product Accounts basis, FY)						
Total taxes	1,361	2,182	1,321	2,039	−3.0	−6.6
Total spending	1,755	2,762	1,649	2,329	−6.0	−15.7
Defense purchases	370	517	283	338	−23.4	−34.6
Nondefense purchases	144	203	144	197	−0.5	−2.7
Transfer payments	693	1,018	696	983	0.4	−3.4
Grants to state/local governments	237	432	235	414	−0.5	−4.2
All other programs	34	48	34	48	0.0	0.0
Subtotal: programs	1,478	2,217	1,392	1,981	−5.8	−10.7
Interest payments	278	545	257	348	−7.3	−36.1
Selected Economic Measures						
National income (GNP)	7,138	11,027	7,009	10,613	−1.8	−3.8
GNP deflator	1.31	1.76	1.30	1.69	−0.4	−4.2
Real GNP	5,449	6,263	5,375	6,291	−1.4	0.4
Unemployment rate[1]	5.29	5.60	5.81	5.68	0.52	0.09
90-day Treasury bill rate[1]	7.13	8.83	6.17	5.91	−0.96	−2.92
30-year T-bond yield[1]	9.48	11.06	8.28	7.75	−1.20	−3.31

[1] Differences shown as percentage points, not percent.

Figure 1-2   Lower Interest Rates Produce Higher Asset Prices: Standard & Poor's 500 Stock Market Index (adjusted for inflation, 1992 GDP prices)

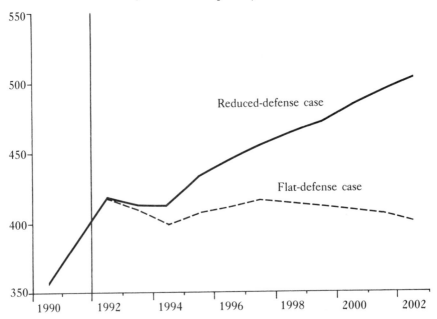

particular market that would benefit most in the short run; each contender also has a different impact on long-run national growth potential. The assumption made here is that all saved funds would be devoted to deficit reduction, thus leaving the reallocation choice implicitly to citizens following historic market response patterns.

This scenario also follows from the observation that Congress and administrations have stated a desire to balance the budget every year since 1985, when the Gramm-Rudman-Hollings legislation was enacted. This image was reinforced in the winter of 1992 when, despite the impulse to hand out pre-election benefits, neither party had a majority willing to transfer defense savings to nondefense programs or even to tax cuts.

The Federal Reserve's Reaction to Reduced Defense Spending

The Federal Reserve is nearly certain to change its policies in response to accelerated defense reductions. The nation's central bank is charged with maintaining price stability and supporting economic growth, always a difficult balancing act. The Federal Reserve seeks to avoid either an overheated or a sluggish economy; thus it must offset major shifts in private sector spending or in government fiscal policy.

Figure 1-3   The Federal Government Would Borrow Less at Home and Abroad ($, billions)

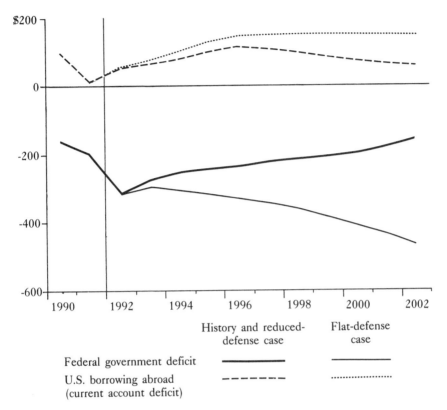

	History and reduced-defense case	Flat-defense case
Federal government deficit	————	————
U.S. borrowing abroad (current account deficit)	– – – – –	··············

Statistical analysis at DRI and other institutions has identified regular response patterns of the Federal Reserve to variations in inflation and unemployment during the postwar period. Credit is reduced when inflation is high or rising; credit is expanded and interest rates are cut when unemployment is rising. Equations that codify or quantify these patterns are called "reaction functions," and their use in policy analysis is broadly accepted.

In the current context, the DRI Federal Reserve reaction function was used to estimate the response to alternative defense spending policies. The speed and the magnitude of this response are pivotal elements in the discussion to follow. Forecasts of the speed and the magnitude are based on a statistical evaluation of the average historical reactions of the Federal Reserve. All of the conclusions should thus be understood as average tendencies and not as guarantees. The qualitative conclusions about the changing sectoral composition of the economy are not sensitive to the particular

Figure 1-4   Progressively Cheaper Credit from Better Budget Balance

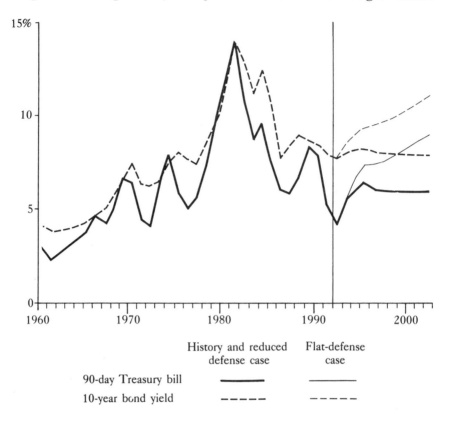

	History and reduced defense case	Flat-defense case
90-day Treasury bill	——————	————
10-year bond yield	– – – –	– – – –

assumptions made but, as noted in the introductory paragraphs, the timing and depth of the cycle are.

The cyclical sluggishness produced by lower military spending increases unemployment and this reduces inflation. The central bank therefore has a double incentive to cut interest rates, and does so gradually. As military spending is cut an estimated $104 billion between 1991 and 1996, the key short-term interest rate (the "federal funds rate") would be cut gradually 1.2 percentage points if traditional patterns prevailed; by 2002 the annual difference in military spending is $180 billion, and the funds rate would be 3.0 percentage points lower. The five-year difference in the U.S. government ten-year bond rate would be 1.4 percentage points, and foreign bond rates would be down an estimated 0.7 points. After ten years, the bond rate differentials are estimated to be 3.2 points for the U.S. and 1.4 for the average of the other major industrial nations' bonds.

Table 1-3   Credit Costs and Savings-Investment Balances (average annual values)

Selected Economic Measures	1960s	1970s	1980s	1990s-Constant Defense[1]	1990s-Reduced Defense[1]
90-day bill rate	3.98	6.29	8.82	7.44	5.86
Core inflation	2.46	6.48	6.08	4.08	3.73
Real short-term rate	1.52	−0.19	2.75	3.37	2.14
10-year bond rate	4.67	7.50	10.59	9.73	7.91
Core inflation	2.46	6.48	6.08	4.08	3.73
Real long-term rate	2.22	1.01	4.52	5.65	4.18
Private savings/GNP (%)	12.6	14.9	13.4	12.3	11.8
Federal deficit/GNP (%)	0.2	1.7	3.6	4.3	2.8
Net funds available[2]	12.4	13.2	9.8	8.0	9.0

[1] Average values in the defense scenarios, 1993-2002
[2] The surplus of domestic private savings over federal borrowing is available for domestic housing and capital spending. State/local governments and foreign sources are potential additional lenders or borrowers.

The inflation rate is projected to be cut slightly more than one-half percentage point on a sustained basis after the first five years; therefore, the real cost of borrowed funds is eventually more than 2 percent lower. Most of the drop in interest rates reflects a better global balance among government deficits and private investments (as demands for funds) and private savings (as sources of funds). (See Figure 1-4.) Moreover, not only is the Treasury borrowing less but the Federal Reserve can be a more active buyer of U.S. government securities because monetary stimulus is required to offset fiscal restraint. Conceivably, the Federal Reserve could be even more generous given the improved inflation outcome, but the historical record suggests it would behave otherwise.

During the debates in the 1980s on the growing U.S. deficits, senior representatives of the Federal Reserve and private analysts were often asked how much credit markets would change if federal borrowing were to be cut. The rule of thumb offered then was that a credible, permanent reduction of $50 billion would bring forth a 1 percentage point reduction in bond yields. (See Table 1-3.) The reaction function results cited above suggest almost 50 percent less interest rate relief than this mid-1980s testimony. However, the fiscal savings are in the context of a global economy that will have approximately doubled in size. The assumed monetary policy reaction used in this analysis thus has the support of its own historical, statistical analysis and the testimony of respected independent authorities.

The Economy in Transition and Back in Balance

The Short-Run Pain

The assumed sequence of presumed cuts in real military spending over the first five years is: $8, $32, $50, $65, and $72 billion. These begin at a scale equal to 0.2 percent of GNP and rise to 1.3 percent by 1996.

If the Federal Reserve does not ease credit, these shocks would multiply through the economy to losses of about two-and-one-half times the direct reductions. For every dollar of lower defense spending, there would be approximately another $1.50 lost in lower retail sales, capital spending, and housing as the defense industry employees and firms cope with lower income. Instead, with the assumed conservative yet positive Federal Reserve reactions, the total GNP loss is held to one-and-one-half times the military spending cutback in the first two years and then trimmed to about three-fourths the military reduction by the fifth year. In other words, by year four (1995) the feedback effects have been neutralized in the aggregate, but the total national output is still lower by the amount of the defense reductions. The composition of the nondefense economy, however, shifts significantly.

The prime beneficiary is the residential construction industry (see Table 1-4). New home construction is tied to affordability and to consumer confidence. With regard to affordability, the benefits of lower mortgage rates outweigh the detrimental effects of the initial reductions in personal income. The ratio of the full cost of homeownership to income progressively improves by 1 percent per year relative to a flat-defense case (see Figure 1-5). The fear of job losses in the restructuring initially blunts these benefits, but by 1994 the affordability gains are quite strong and confidence is rebuilt. Housing starts in the reduced-defense scenario could be expected to exceed those in the flat-defense case by 3-4 percent in 1994 and continue improving in relative terms thereafter.

Nonresidential building construction would follow a similar but slightly less improved path (see Figure 1-6). Changes in such activity are driven by changes in capacity requirements and by financing costs. The greater the industrial and commercial square footage requirements, the greater is new construction; the lower the financing costs, the earlier the replacement or rehabilitation spending occurs and the lower the required occupancy rate to meet normal profit objectives. Initially, a softer economy works in both directions, reducing space demands and necessary occupancy rates; as growth comes back and interest costs keep declining, commercial and industrial building activity can be expected to exceed the level of the flat-defense case.

Spending on durable equipment is driven by motivations similar to those for business construction but the shorter lifetime of machinery, autos, and computers implies less sensitivity to financing costs and greater ties to

Table 1-4   Medium-Term Cyclical Shifts in Spending
(Reduced-defense scenario vs. constant-defense scenario,
changes in major spending components, 1987 dollars,
billions)

	1992	1993	1994	1995	1996
Defense purchases	−14	−36	−55	−67	−73
Real GNP	−19	−55	−73	−72	−61
Housing construction	0	0	3	7	10
Nonresidential construction	0	−1	−1	0	2
Producer durable equipment	0	−5	−8	−3	3
Consumer durables	−2	−6	−7	−5	−3
Other consumer purchases	−3	−11	−19	−25	−28
Goods exports	0	−1	−1	0	3
Goods imports	−1	−8	−13	−12	−9
Net service exports	1	4	8	13	16
Real incomes					
Compensation	−13	−33	−52	−61	−62
Interest	−1	−5	−16	−28	−39
Profits	−4	−12	−11	−6	−4

short-term capacity utilization. Moreover, production of military hardware is capital-intensive. For both reasons, the particular type of policy shift examined in this study (lower interest rates and eased credit) would tend to be harder on durable equipment manufacturers than, for example, a slump that was produced by higher income taxation or cuts in social security benefits. DRI analysis thus suggests an initial decline in spending on durable equipment, followed by a convergence toward the flat-defense case in 1996.

Consumer durable purchases—of cars, furniture, and appliances—are driven by income, confidence, and wealth. Lower interest rates raise confidence and wealth, but the income loss from lower defense employment probably initially overrides these positive effects. In 1992 durable spending is cut by an estimated 0.5 percent, followed by 1.3 percent and 1.2 percent losses in the next two years. As the economy converges back to the baseline, the medium-term loss is trimmed to 0.5 percent or $3 billion. Other components of consumer spending are almost totally driven by income and demographics. The demographics do not change; thus, these sectors remain depressed below those of the flat-defense case. This reflects not only the interim reduction in GNP but also a redistribution of national income from the household to the business sector, given lower interest rates. Households are net lenders to the business community and government; therefore a decline in real interest rates reduces the household share of total income.

Figure 1-5   Housing Gains from Cheaper Credit

Housing Starts (millions of units)

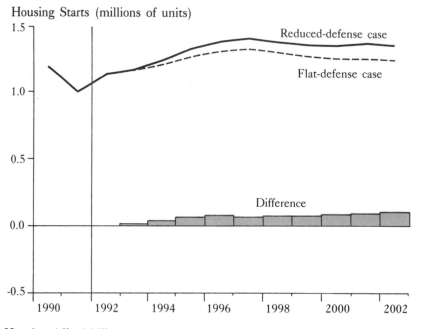

Housing Affordability (housing expenses relative to income, percent)

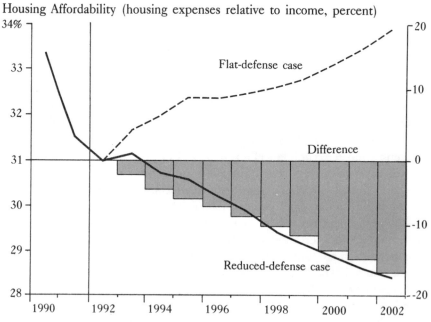

Figure 1-6   Capital Spending Eventually Rises Substantially as Federal Budget Pressures Recede (1987 dollars, billions)

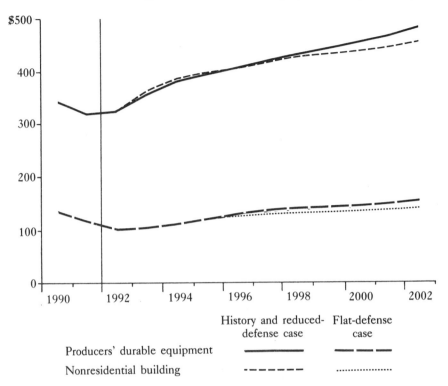

	History and reduced-defense case	Flat-defense case
Producers' durable equipment	▬▬▬▬	▬ ▬ ▬
Nonresidential building	‐‐‐‐‐‐	⋯⋯⋯⋯

However, this does not mean that families are losers: as the nation's ultimate asset owners, they benefit substantially from the projected substantial appreciation in home prices (and greater home ownership), stock prices, and other assets. The national economy is eventually stronger, and the associated service, earnings, and other portfolio income streams therefore have higher discounted present values, particularly in a low interest rate environment.

Another noteworthy redistribution of income and ownership pertains to foreign investors. As the federal budget approaches balance (rather than greater imbalance), the need to borrow abroad proportionately decreases. The balance of payments improves because domestic spending is initially lower, the real exchange value of the dollar falls with the decline in U.S. rates relative to those of Germany and Japan, and the nation's debt service on past borrowing decreases. After the first five years of adjustment, military spending has been cumulatively reduced by $330 billion, federal borrowing has been cut by $250 billion, and borrowing abroad has been trimmed by $95 billion. (During the first five years, the reduction in federal borrowing is less than the military cutbacks because the weaker economy initially depresses tax revenues and raises unemployment compensation.)

The Long-Run Gain

The beneficial changes are expected to expand, many exponentially, as the military savings accumulate during the rest of the period of analysis extending to 2002 (see Figure 1-7). In that final year, real military spending is assumed to be only two-thirds that of 1991, $190 billion versus $280 billion. The cumulative reduction in nominal defense spending is $1.2 trillion. The cumulative reduction in federal borrowing is $1.5 trillion, and capital required from overseas has been cut $0.5 trillion.

As noted earlier, the government deficit is eventually reduced by much more than the military savings. In the year 2002, an $8.2 trillion national debt is financed with Treasury bond rates at 8 percent and bill rates at 6 percent in the reduced-defense case, rather than a $9.5 trillion debt financed at rates 3.00-3.25 percent higher in the flat military spending case. By this arbitrary endpoint, annual federal interest payments are an estimated $210 billion lower, making a 20 percent greater contribution to budget balance than the direct annual defense cut of $180 billion. (This cannot be a precise estimate because the maturity structure of the current and future debt is not known; the interest savings could be as great as $300-350 billion if the federal debt could be rolled over more rapidly than assumed here.)

The national economy can make considerable progress in this environment. As noted earlier, business investment is first weaker and then progressively stronger as investment hurdle rates (the minimum rate at which an investment can be profitable) are cut in line with market rates. Annual spending on producer durable equipment achieves a 4 percent relative gain by 2002; nonresidential construction is 9 percent higher. The value of all in-place equipment and structures (the capital stock) is 2 percent higher, and this offers an almost 1 percent gain in potential GNP. In simpler terms, potential real output per capita could be enhanced by $200 as of 2002, and the prospective medium-term growth in living standards would be raised from about 1.5 percent to 1.7 percent per year.

These are the estimated improvements in measured GNP. If the same level of national security can be obtained with two-thirds the current defense expenditures, then this stated gain is fully legitimate. If the global risks are not so far reduced, then these GNP gains overstate the national advantage of lower military spending.

Of course, the same transformation to a more productive, capital-intensive economy could be accomplished in alternative ways. If the military outlays are justified to maintain global security, then either U.S. or foreign taxpayers should pay for them. U.S. citizens could pay through higher taxes

Figure 1-7   As Defense Cutbacks Accumulate, the Interest Savings
Compound

Annual Federal Spending ($, billions)

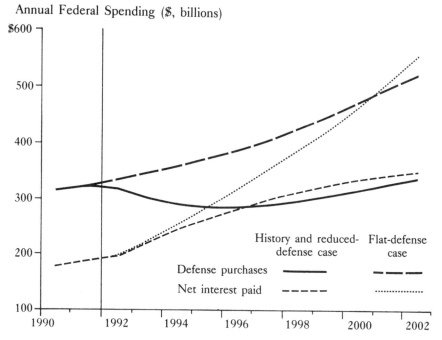

Annual Change in Federal Spending between Scenarios ($, billions)

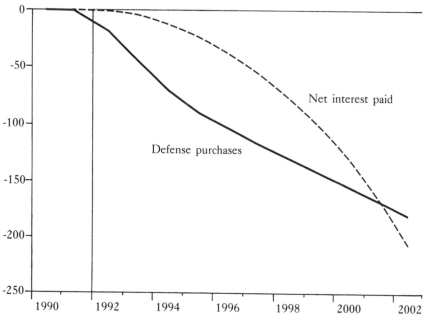

Figure 1-8   Rising Capital Spending Means Rising Living Standards
(percent difference between scenarios)

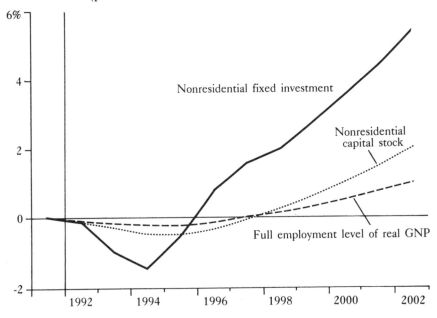

or reductions in benefit programs. Foreign citizens could pay directly, as they did during operations Desert Shield and Desert Storm, or by expanding their defense budgets, or by counting the extraordinarily high defense contribution of the U.S. against our payments due the United Nations. These foreign options are far-fetched in political terms, but they are realistic economic assessments. The United States is sacrificing potential capital formation and income to provide a global service.

Qualifications and Conclusions

Alternative Means to Balance the Budget

A substantial number of the economic benefits described are due simply to a more balanced budget, an outcome that is achievable through other reasonable means; however, other benefits are unique to the case of defense reductions. To understand better the specific effects of defense spending, consider an alternative scenario in which the same dollar savings are achieved by raising federal taxes (personal income, corporate profits, and payroll) and reducing all noninterest expenditures (purchases, entitlements, and state grants) by a common proportion. This adjustment, over the same period

Table 1-5   Shifts in the Economy Under Alternative Budgets
(Defense-cut scenarios vs. flat-defense scenario, changes in
major spending components, 1987 dollars, billion)

	Original Reduced-Defense Case			Across-the-Board-Cut Case		
	1992-1995	1995-1998	1999-2002	1992-1995	1995-1998	1999-2002
Defense purchases	−43	−76	−91	−6	−10	−11
Real GNP	−55	−59	−1	−27	−30	−9
Housing construction	2	10	19	1	5	9
Nonresidential construction	−1	3	13	−1	2	8
Producer durable equipment	−4	4	18	−2	2	7
Consumer durables	−5	−3	6	−8	−12	−14
Other consumer purchases	−14	−29	−36	−18	−43	−65
Goods exports	0	5	18	1	7	14
Goods imports	−9	−11	−11	−8	−15	−22
Net service exports	7	19	40	4	14	32
Real incomes						
Compensation	−40	−63	−63	−15	−26	−35
Interest	−12	−46	−116	−13	−44	−101
Profits	−8	−6	0	−8	−12	−11

from 1992 to 2002, matches the scale of the earlier-evaluated military reductions. Because, coincidentally, the deficit is approximately the same size as interest obligations, this approach requires nearly equal tax increases and expenditure reductions relative to the flat-defense case. The comparative results are displayed in Table 1-5.

The initial cyclical losses in GNP are only half as great when tax increases and entitlement cuts, instead of cuts in direct government purchases, provide most of the budget savings. This is the standard macroeconomic result in which changes in income produce smaller multiplier effects on the economy than do changes in purchases: private savings and private spending are both immediately reduced in response to a tax or entitlement change, while (government) spending is, by definition, fully cut when purchases are reduced.

Higher payroll taxes are higher costs to business and, therefore, tend to lead to higher prices. This inflationary impetus is almost neutralized by the slightly weaker economy of the balanced-cut case relative to the flat-defense case. With no improvement in inflation (relative to the flat-defense case) and a smaller short-term unemployment problem (relative to the reduced-defense case), the Federal Reserve is not likely to reduce interest rates as much as if defense bore the whole burden. Compared to the case with rising federal deficits, interest rates are about a half percentage point lower after three years and 2 full points lower after ten. This is only two-thirds the improvement found earlier.

More expensive credit and lower after-tax income and profits (due to higher tax rates) imply that the gains in housing construction and capital spending are not as great under this new scenario, but they still increase and expand through 2002. The scale of the added investment is approximately half that of the pure defense cut case.

Losses Difficult to Measure: Technology and Security

An important dimension, quite difficult to quantify, is the spillover from military research and production to civilian applications. The official R&D portion of the defense budget does not count much of the technology development and production experience implicitly paid for in production contracts with suppliers of all goods and many services. It is quite likely that this benefit, and the explicit expenditures on military R&D with civilian applications, are larger than will be provided by the expanded scale of construction and other industries benefiting from rapid downsizing of the military.

DRI's research on national productivity clearly identifies commercial R&D outlays as a prime mover of economic growth. We and other researchers discern a significant correlation between the growth of such outlays and the effectiveness of American labor and capital. When R&D grows rapidly, the knowledge base expands, permitting more output to be produced by the same number of labor hours or machines or computers. In fact, a marked decline in R&D during the late 1970s and 1980s is a logical explanation for as much as a third of the deceleration of output per hour, from an approximate norm of 2.5 percent annually before 1973 to 0.8 percent thereafter.

The impact of technology lost due to defense reductions can only be guessed, but the potential scale is substantial. For example, in 1992 total federal defense spending of $318 billion included $192 billion in purchased goods; the rest was compensation of employees. By 2002, goods purchases would be cut to $179 billion in current prices, and the cumulative reduction would be approximately $650 billion. Even if just 25 percent of the goods purchases, or $160 billion, are assumed to generate technology developments and production experience akin to private-sector R&D, the national loss would be very substantial as the defense curtailment proceeded. As a point of reference, in 1992 private industrial R&D expenditures will only slightly exceed $80 billion.

Final Thoughts

Of course, the reduction of military spending could end within five years, followed by stability or a new long wave of higher spending. It is unlikely that permanent peace will break out after millennia of human conflict. U.S. citizens may opt to buy greater security. With some imagination, the medium-term analysis above can be applied to sketch out the implications. In comparison to the extended-defense-cut case, such a reversal should be thought of as the injection of fiscal stimulus and the likely provocation of monetary restraint in response. In other words, the compositional changes described earlier would soon stop (if defense outlays flattened) or be reversed (if a new upward wave began).

Reversing course is a bad option. Cutting military spending too deeply and then reversing course would be highly wasteful in its interruption of technology development, corporate planning, and employee careers. It would also be apt to breed significant political problems, because the public would be temporarily led to believe they could afford more private consumption and government benefits than they were able to.

The recognition that major cycles of military spending have persisted throughout the postwar era should make Congress and the administration more careful about hasty and exaggerated reductions during this current cycle. There is no doubt that the present level of total federal spending cannot be afforded with the present level of taxes. The federal deficit must be reduced and the domestic investment climate must be vastly improved. But the military may be too attractive a target and thus may be called upon to bear a disproportionate burden.

2

Can We Plan the U.S. Defense Industrial Base?
David Blair

The most recent edition of the public document that lays out the president's national security strategy lists reconstitution (along with nuclear
deterrence, forward presence, and crisis response) as one of the principles
guiding the U.S. defense agenda for the 1990s.[1] Reconstitution is defined as
the "ability to generate wholly new forces" if a major threat to the United
States arises.[2] But fundamental changes in the whole U.S. acquisition system, both in government bureaucratic processes and in the structure of private contractors, will be required if the United States is to prepare seriously
to reconstitute forces in, say, the years 2000-2005.

In order to reconstitute forces it is necessary to maintain the physical
capital, human skills, and manufacturing and research organizations needed
to produce new weapons within a relevant time frame. But neither the Planning, Programming, and Budgeting System (PPBS), the Department of Defense (DoD) "milestone" acquisition process, nor the structure of the defense industry is designed to allow the DoD to plan the defense industrial
capital stock over the long term. The U.S. acquisition system is based on a
"competitive model" that is designed to acquire as efficiently as possible a
specific system to meet a specific military need. It is not designed to plan
capital stocks.

What are the options for dealing with this dilemma? The two polar types
of weapons acquisition policy are (1) the kind of competitive market system
that the United States has sometimes strived for over the last twenty years, and
(2) a quasi-nationalized defense industry similar to that of France. Of course,
it is tempting to try to compromise, to take the best from the competitive
model and the French model. However, the two systems are so incompatible
that an intermediate system is likely to be worse than either pole.

David Blair is professor of deterrent strategy and defense economics at the Air War
College of Air University. Views presented here are those of the author and do not
necessarily reflect those of the U.S. Air Force or the U.S. government.

In the face of looming defense budget cuts that will greatly affect the defense industrial base, the United States now has to make fundamental choices about the nature of its acquisition system. These choices may be as important as the obvious choices about the size and type of force structure. The real problem is that we do not know enough about reconstitution of the defense industrial base to judge whether being able to plan the defense industrial capital stock justifies very fundamental changes in the planning and acquisition systems.

The DoD seems to have concluded that defense industrial capital stock considerations will not significantly affect its decisions about how it will go about making choices about what should be cut in the defense budget. This makes some sense in light of the vast changes in the system that would be needed if we are to "plan" the defense industrial base. But this hands-off course means that long-term defense capital stock considerations will not be an explicit, rational criterion in DoD decisions.

This chapter is not about general industrial planning. There is a large, though generally tendentious, literature on the national security argument for protecting certain industries that produce basic inputs for weapons systems. For instance, it is often argued that the United States needs to protect its semiconductor and machine tools (or leather, textiles, or fill in the blank) industries because they are needed for national security.[3]

Often, however, government planning of industrial investments is wasteful and unproductive, and the national security argument for protectionism is usually a canard. It is possible, however, to be an advocate of planning the defense industrial base without being an advocate of government planning of wider industry. The general argument that laissez-faire is the best way to allocate capital does not automatically apply to defense industry since the government is the sole U.S. customer of the defense industry, and the whole raison d'être of the defense industry is to fulfill a government strategy.

This study goes into some detail about the DoD process for deciding which weapons are procured and which contracts are let. Then it looks at the effect of this process on the structure of the defense industry and on the defense industrial capital stock. All this may seem like paying attention to minute detail while missing the big picture. But the bottom line is that the principal, almost the only, way the DoD can affect the defense industrial base is through contracts. People can do all the studies and issue all the policy guidance they want, but if these steps do not affect the process through which the DoD decides which contracts will be let, they have little or no effect on the defense industrial base.

No outside study can determine the long-term strategy of the United States, the weapons needed to implement that strategy, or the industrial base needed to build those weapons in the long run. Rather, the Department of

Defense must have a formal institutional structure that can continuously examine these issues, link the industrial base to strategic planning, and implement decisions about the defense industrial base. The only way it can implement these decisions is by affecting the contracts that are let. Industrial base planning is not now part of either the PPBS, which is designed to link budgetary decisions to planned strategy, or of the milestone process used in developing and procuring individual weapons. Furthermore, there are fundamental reasons why it will be very difficult to introduce such planning into the American weapons acquisition system.

The Competitive Model Versus the French Model of Defense Acquisition

In a recent editorial, the *New York Times* argued that: "There's a better way to preserve vital defense industries as the Pentagon budget shrinks. Careful planning can choose exactly which skilled workers and plants are essential." [4] This is much easier said than done. There are fundamental systemic reasons why such planning will be very difficult to institute in the United States.

The key to reconstitution is capital—physical, human, and organizational. Any attempt to reconstitute U.S. military force structure will depend on the capital stock that is available at the time the decision is made to begin the reconstitution. The most worrisome aspect of the current defense downsizing is that decisions are being made that will have the effect of scrapping billions of dollars worth of capital and there is no systematic procedure for determining which capital will be most essential in a reconstitution effort and which can be safely discarded. [5]

The lack of such a systematic procedure is not the result of any incompetence or lack of understanding of the problem on the part of officials in the DoD. The United States's competitive acquisition model is particularly inappropriate when the goal is to plan capital stock rather than to procure well-defined weapons in the near future. In short, the competitive acquisition system was appropriate for the 1980s but is not appropriate for the very different environment of the 1990s.

At least since David Packard was deputy secretary of defense in the early 1970s, the United States has been guided by the competitive model of defense acquisition. [6] The competitive acquisition model implies that the DoD holds a competition and chooses the company that is best at producing a particular weapons system. The key element here is that, in every competition, the company that can produce that particular weapons system most effectively and cheaply will win the competition. The government is concerned primarily with the product it receives rather than with the maintenance of any capabilities of the producer. In this model, it is the final product that matters.

On the other hand, any "planning" of the defense industry will involve making a choice on the basis of which company has capital the DoD wants to preserve in the long term. If "reconstitution capital" were to be the decision criterion, a company could lose a competition even though it was the best and cheapest producer of the weapons system being bid upon. It is hard to imagine what "competition" would mean in such circumstances. The DoD would have to choose which companies it wanted to preserve and treat them as regulated monopolies. This is especially true in a time when production runs will be too short to support more than one producer of many types of weapons systems.

It is a great exaggeration but an informative analogy to say that the goal of the competitive model of acquisition is for the DoD to have a relationship with weapons producers that is similar to the relationship of a car buyer with a car producer. A car buyer does not worry about the production facilities or the long-term capital capabilities of each producer. He or she simply tries the product and decides whether to buy. Of course, nothing like this extreme goal was ever achieved on major military development projects, but the analogy illustrates the idea that the DoD wanted to leave capital investment decisions to the contractors. Proponents of competitive acquisition also wanted the contractors to bear much of the risk involved in the investment.[7]

The principal external manifestations of this competitive acquisition strategy were: an increase in the portion of contracts that were let on a fixed price basis; the DoD's insistence that there be flyoffs late in the development process; and the use of dual-sourcing with multiple production lines for weapons that were produced in quantity.[8] The theoretical benefits of this strategy are obvious and the DoD in practice has been able to achieve significant price reductions and quality improvements. However, the downside is that the strategy will not work if production runs are low. More fundamentally, the competitive model has shaped the decision-making structure and the decision criteria within DoD in a way that makes it difficult for the DoD to have any kind of direct control over the capital investments of competing companies.

This competitive model falls apart if the decision criterion is some industrial base consideration rather than the best producer of an individual product. Once the government decides that it needs to protect the existence of a particular company, that company becomes de facto a government-owned or government-controlled company. No free market company can compete for a government contract with such a government-preferred company. If there is no competition between defense contractors, there will, ipso facto, be a need for an industrial policy to choose which firms are worth keeping alive and which are not. In essence, the defense contractors will become regulated monopolies.

It is useful to contrast the competitive acquisition strategy with the much more centralized and directed French weapons production system, which represents the opposite pole of types of defense industrial systems in the capitalist world. The French system tries to achieve efficiency by using a very professional, centralized bureaucracy (the DGA, Delegation General de Armaments) which closely controls the weapons planning and production process. The French strive for efficiency in military acquisition and production by training an elite managerial corps at the Ecole Polytechnique. The Americans strive for efficiency by trying to imitate the efficiency of the market system.

The main difference between the French and the American systems is that the French system can control defense industrial capital stock directly while the American system is designed to control the end products. In the words of Edward Kolodziej, a University of Illinois professor who has written extensively about French weapons acquisition, the French system gives priority to

> the contribution of the weapons program to the maintenance of a technologically advanced, financially solvent, and internationally competitive arms industry. The task of filling immediate military requirements has been in every case accompanied by the dominant objective of promoting an independent arms production capacity.[9]

Thus, it seems that a French-style system would be more appropriate in an era when preserving the defense industrial capital stock is a high priority and when procurement will be very low. However, there is a grave danger that a centralized acquisition system with monopoly companies could be both unresponsive to military needs and very inefficient.

A French-style system also goes against the grain of the American bureaucratic and legal system. The U.S. system is based on well-defined and explicit criteria. Any major weapons system in the United States must go through a series of "milestone" reviews and cannot proceed without fulfilling the well-specified criterion of each successive milestone. The French system is much more fluid and less legalistic.[10]

Even laying aside the broader question of planning industries that supply inputs for defense industries, deliberately planning even specialized defense-related industries is a very serious decision with many implications for the economy. A decision to "plan" an industry necessarily involves a decision to support some companies and not support others. This decision would be made on the basis of some criterion other than their ability to fulfill a near-term production contract. The favored companies would become de facto regulated monopolies. All the inefficiencies of such companies will appear. The competitive acquisition model that has driven U.S. acquisition strategy for at least twenty years would have to be fundamentally changed. Make no mistake that a decision to plan the defense industrial base is a decision to move toward a French-style acquisition system that includes de facto nationalized companies. It is not obvious that there is any viable intermediate position between the French system and the competitive American system.

The Bureaucratic Processes for Making Defense Budget and Acquisition Decisions

As mentioned earlier, the only way the DoD can affect the defense industrial base is through letting contracts. Thus, it is important to go into some detail about the two interlocking procedures that the DoD uses to decide which contracts will be let. These are the PPBS, which allocates money to the many possible DoD purposes, and the milestone acquisition process, which sets a series of intermediate goals that an individual weapons acquisition program has to meet.[11] The goal of the PPBS process is to prioritize the various military requirements so that the mix of weapons actually procured fulfills the national strategy and at the same time is affordable within the current and future years' budget constraints. The purpose of the milestone process is to procure as efficiently as possible a weapon system designed to fulfill a well-specified requirement of one of the military services.

In the milestone process, each new system has to pass through four well-defined steps before production can begin. Before going from one step to the next, the program has to be approved by a board that concludes that the criteria for passing the milestone have been fulfilled. The steps are as follows:[12]

> Milestone 0: Need Identification
> Milestone 1: Concept Exploration
> Milestone 2: Demonstration/Validation
> Milestone 3: Engineering and Manufacturing Development

It is useful to look at each of these milestones as a question that must be answered. A rough interpretation of these questions might be:

> Milestone 0: What is the military task that, if accomplished, would increase the capability of the operators?
> Milestone 1: What are all the possible ways to accomplish this task? What are the two or three most promising ways?
> Milestone 2: Can these two or three promising ways really do the job? Which of them is the best value for the money?
> Milestone 3: How will the device chosen at milestone 2 be manufactured?

The key point is that the exact way in which these questions are asked will determine which weapons are manufactured. Milestones 0 and 2 are particularly important in this regard because they determine which system will be procured. The whole process is geared to acquiring as effectively and cheaply as possible a particular weapons system (determined in milestone 2) that fulfills a particular military need (determined in milestone 0). The flyoff competitions, such as that between the F-22 and F-23, occur at milestone 2. For a competition to make sense, each company must believe that it can win the competition if it best fulfills the statement of need that was agreed upon in milestone 0.

At first glance, it might seem possible to write an "industrial base milestone" that would ask something like the following:

Milestone X (Industrial Base): Which company (or research team, or industrial capability) will be most effective at producing the weapons systems that will be needed ten or twenty years from today?

However, incorporating such a milestone into the acquisition process would be a fundamental repudiation of the competitive acquisition model and of the entire current acquisition process with its logical procession from question to question.

The problem is that the answer to milestone X might be different from the answer to the current milestone 2. Companies competing against each other would never know whether their task was to fulfill milestone 2 or milestone X. So it is unlikely that anyone would be willing to risk money in such a poorly defined competition.

Furthermore, the DoD itself would have two internally inconsistent criteria with, at best, an arbitrary and unpredictable means of deciding between them. The value of the current milestone process is that it sets up as logical a system as possible for the DoD bureaucracy to make the very complicated decisions about which weapons system to purchase.

Similarly, the PPBS is an attempt to impose logical criteria for making trade-offs among the various needs stated by the services and regional joint commands. Of course, the results of that system are far from perfect, but at least there is a strong effort to ensure that decisions are made on the basis of logical, explicitly reasoned criteria. It is hard to see how PPBS would deal with such ill-defined criteria as "preserving the long-term industrial base."

This is not to say that maintaining the industrial base is not now a de facto consideration in the process. DoD sometimes, and Congress often, allocates money with the primary purpose of keeping a company afloat. However, these ad hoc decisions are violations of the inherent logic of the current acquisition system.

If the DoD moved away from choosing which weapons to buy by asking which best fulfill a well-defined military need, the whole system would be opened up, to a greater extent than it already is, to abuse. A host of other criteria might emerge: Which decision does the most for a chairman of an important congressional committee? Which decision does the most to promote civilian technological competitiveness? Which decision does the most to ease the transition of former defense workers into new civilian jobs? None of these tasks is within the competence or the responsibility of the DoD. The danger is that if DoD moves away from its current criteria, it will be very difficult for it to argue logically against such demands.

In the twenty-two page DoD document that summarizes the acquisition process, the industrial base is mentioned only once. That reference is in a vague provision for doing a study that assesses "the potential outyear impact of the defense acquisition program on the U.S. technology and industrial base." [13] The problem is not that decision makers in the Pentagon do not understand the long-term importance of the defense industrial base. Of course they do. It's that any attempt to preserve the industrial base goes against goals of efficiency and competitiveness.

That said, the DoD should be giving serious consideration as soon as possible to the question of whether fundamental changes are required in the acquisition system. The United States is now entering an era very different from the 1980s. The defense cutbacks will destroy large parts of the defense industrial base and it may be that industrial base criteria are now more important than the goals of efficiency and competitiveness.

The Defense Department Reforms of the Late 1980s

In the last part of the Reagan administration and the first years of the Bush administration there were three simultaneous and mutually supporting efforts to reform the way the Defense Department plans and procures. [14] The Packard Commission, the Goldwater-Nichols legislation, and the Defense Management Review were so closely connected that it is difficult to sort out which reform is related to each, but the thrust can be summarized as:

1. Reduce the power of the services and increase the authority of the unified commanders-in-chief (known universally as the CinCs, pronounced "sinks"). Each CinC has responsibility for an area of the world; basically, he or she is a theater commander. [15] For example, Gen. Norman Schwarzkopf was the CinC in charge of the Middle East (Commander-in-Chief, Central Command.) The idea is that the CinCs have direct

warfighting responsibility and thus will have less parochial interest than the services.[16]

2. Make the defense procurement process more closely model the
competitive consumer durables market.[17]

These reforms made a lot of sense in a world where the United States
faced an immediate, well-defined threat and where long production runs
encouraged contractors to bear large risks. Both of these conditions held in
1985; neither does now.

In a world where the threat is immediate and clear, it is possible to plan
the industrial base simply by purchasing the weapons needed to counter that
threat. But in a very uncertain world, it is necessary to explore areas that may
pay off but where no immediate procurement is foreseen. Similarly, we may
want to have industrial capability to produce some types of weapons without
actually producing them. These concerns probably cannot be handled under
the present acquisition policy.

The Goldwater-Nichols provisions that give the CinCs more authority
may cause problems in an uncertain world. Naturally (and rightly), a CinC
will be most concerned with near-term capabilities in his or her area of
responsibility. Thus, the CinCs' contributions to the documents (called mission needs statements) that are used to determine the programs chosen in
Milestone 0 will overlook some long-term, global needs.

Another major goal of acquisition reform over the last twenty years has
been to eliminate any appearance of conflicts of interests, to ensure that the
good-old-boy network does not determine which weapons are built or which
companies get contracts. There are two practical effects of this goal: the DoD
must have no favored companies; and all decision-making criteria must be
explicitly tied to a well-defined goal. A DoD official who took long-term
industrial base considerations into account when deciding which proposal to
accept would be at risk of going to jail. Any attempt to choose which capital
to preserve will naturally lead to charges of special dealing.

Finally, as was discussed above, the competitive acquisition model
was a fundamental element of the Packard Commission and has been central to all the reforms that have occurred at least since David Packard
was deputy secretary of defense in the Nixon administration. Any attempt
to plan the defense industrial capital stock will involve a repudiation of
this model.

What Is to Be Done?

It is possible that the whole concern of this paper is much ado about
nothing. In fact, there have been a slew of recent reports that the Pentagon

has reached just that conclusion. For example, Gen. Colin Powell, chairman of the Joint Chiefs of Staff, told *Aviation Week* that

> the Pentagon is not worried about the difficulty of reconstituting weapon production capabilities it would lose during the drawdown, if necessary. The U.S. would have years of warning time if Russia or any potential enemy tries to build up its military power. This is much more time than the U.S. expected. Also the U.S. would be able to reconstitute its forces faster than any other country could build up. . . . The Soviets are losing their ability to reconstitute as their defense industries collapse before our eyes. It would be much more difficult for them to put Humpty Dumpty together again than it would be for us. The Pentagon will fund R&D as a basis for reconstitution if necessary and the U.S. industrial infrastructure, however depleted, will remain superior. The U.S. cannot support a weapon production base artificially, however. There's going to be a significant shakeout in the U.S. defense industry. . . . There's no way to protect industry from that shakeout.[18]

Similarly, Eleanor Spector, the Bush administration's director of defense procurement, stated that the DoD would not attempt to take the defense capital stock into account when making procurement decisions:

> The philosophy of the department is not to interfere with the operation of the free market. We will not attempt to determine the appropriate size of the defense market. You can expect, therefore, that the department will continue to award to the contractor who offers the best value for the procurement in question. Such decisions are already complex enough. We will not further complicate them by trying to factor in the consequences of the selection of a contractor for the overall health of the industry.[19]

However, in the same speech she stated:

> As the defense budget decreases and contract opportunities diminish with it, we in the Defense Department, particularly those of us in procurement, must do what we can to make sure that we still retain a healthy contractor base to accomplish the critical work that still needs to be done.[20]

The basic purpose of this study is to raise the question of whether these two statements are consistent.

Murray Weidenbaum reports that the investment by defense companies in plant and equipment is low compared to civilian counterpart industries. For U.S. manufacturing as a whole, the ratio of capital spending to value of goods shipped rose from 3.8 percent in 1980 to 4.3 percent in 1985. For defense supply firms, the ratio fell from 3.9 percent to 3.6 percent. Weidenbaum says that Grumman's F-14 production line consists of machinery over thirty years old. He describes it as involving much manual metal-bending and cutting, and a rejection rate of 70-80 percent.[21] Clearly, any production lines of this sort need not be protected during the downsizing.

They would be easy to reconstruct, if anyone should choose to do so, during a reconstitution period. Other defense factories, the jet engine producers, for example, are highly automated with the most modern machine tools. However, there is now no institutional mechanism for sorting out such easily reconstitutable capital from specialized, irreplaceable capital. And even if this information were available, there is no provision in the current acquisition process for preserving one and not the other.

The centerpiece of the current thinking among both Les Aspin's staff and other Pentagon officials appears to be a plan to take weapons systems through milestone 2 (demonstration/validation) and then put the system on the shelf until some indefinite point in the future when there is a need for it. This amounts to a decision to concentrate on R&D while ignoring production capital. This approach seems to make a lot of sense in a time when production runs will be very short and when the threat is ambiguous, but there are several possible problems.

One problem is that the demonstration/validation stage costs a lot of money. One of the major jet engine manufacturers estimates that 60 percent of its nonrecurring costs are expended before milestone 2.[22] The demonstration/validation stage for the competing YF-22 and YF-23 prototypes cost the Air Force more than $5.2 billion and cost each of the two contractor teams almost $1.5 billion each. The companies will not be willing to put up funds of such size when there is no promise of a long production run, and it is doubtful that the U.S. government will be willing to invest the money. There has been some discussion of ways to reduce these costs, but they necessarily involve moving away from production-oriented development toward more basic research.[23]

This raises another fundamental problem with stopping at milestone 2. The obvious question is: Do we know how to stop at the demonstration/validation phase and wait years to proceed to production? Is there any value to demonstration/validation that is ten or so years old?

It seems likely that any prototypes built today, or any engineering and manufacturing development done today, would be unacceptably obsolescent in ten or fifteen years. A serious danger is that any attempt to preserve production capabilities is likely to pickle them at a fixed point. They will not take advantage of rapid changes in either tools or processes. Also, of course, they will not be able to take advantage of the kind of continuous productivity improvements emphasized by advocates of total quality management. A plant that is preserved today might be best used as a museum after the year 2000.

So it seems to make sense to concentrate on more basic R&D. However, this will not keep the defense industrial base alive. In essence, a decision to stop development projects at milestone 2 is a decision that production capability can take care of itself. Do we know that worthwhile work can be done at these stages if the companies are not involved in production? Do we know that it will be possible to produce anything after much of the defense industrial capital stock is decimated in the next decade? The most worrisome aspect of the current defense industrial downsizing is that crucial decisions are being made without knowing the answers to these questions.

It may be possible to design military equipment so that it uses fewer components that are not available in the civilian sector. If the DoD adopts a strategy of stopping weapons programs at demonstration/validation, it will be important that thought be put into ways of using civilian production machinery and workers for military production. This will be difficult. Most defense equipment is now developed exclusively for the military and is useful only to the military. Murray Weidenbaum found that only about 10 percent of military equipment now is the product of standard peacetime production lines.[24] This compares to 50 percent during World War I. Furthermore, this equipment increasingly uses high technology in the sense that a large portion of the cost of obtaining it was spent on R&D.

There may be a way of partially circumventing the problem of defense-specific manufacturing capability. Though some equipment may need to be built to specialized military specifications, the nonstandard nature of other equipment is due to unnecessary DoD regulations and standards. For example, there is little reason most DoD electronics could not use standard civilian computer chips and programming techniques rather than the current DoD standards, which are technologically behind the civilian market place.[25] A minimum first step would be for the DoD to develop procedures to classify equipment into three categories: the civilian product can be used directly; the product must be specialized but civilian production lines can be used; and the product will require specialized production lines.

If some way is not found to reduce DoD reliance on specialized equipment and production facilities, it seems unlikely that the Defense Department will be able to reconstitute forces even with quite long lead times. It will be necessary to change and streamline many of the current procurement regulations that make it difficult and unrewarding for a predominantly civilian company to undertake a development contract for the DoD.

Further Research and the Need for Institutional Changes

All defense contractors' reports and many academic papers end with "suggestions for further research." Such research may really be crucial in this case but the world is changing so rapidly and the defense budget is falling so sharply that many decisions will have to be made with limited information.

This section maps out some research avenues. It is important to reiterate, however, that any conclusions must be integrated into the institutional structure of the DoD acquisition system if they are to have any effect. It is also important to close with a caveat acknowledging that many individuals and organizations can be cut safely from the defense budget without endangering national security. There is a danger that the argument that we need to preserve irreplaceable capabilities, like the defense arguments for trade protectionism, could be used to protect every inefficient or unnecessary claimant on the defense budget. On the other hand, there is some defense industrial plant that needs to be protected. The problem is that we now have little idea which is which. It is important, but both intellectually and politically difficult, to try to develop well-defined criteria for sorting out real strategic goals from self-serving canards. There are four main areas where further research would be useful.

The first is to categorize capabilities according to reconstitution time. It would be very useful to be able to prioritize defense capital stock (both human and physical) according to its effect on a reconstitution effort. The DoD should be able to sort out capabilities into three categories: those purchasable on the civilian market; those purchasable with less than two years' lead time; and those not purchasable without a long-term capital commitment. This research should explore the mobility of particular skills and equipment between civilian and military industry.

The second avenue of research is to explore institutional ways to tie decisions about defense industrial capital stock to long-term strategic needs. Answers to this question can be determined only as part of an ongoing DoD acquisition process. Furthermore, it is hard to see how the DoD would make use of this information without fundamental changes in the acquisition system. If the United States is serious about having reconstitution as a defense option, it must be prepared to make such changes.

The current acquisition system is designed to encourage companies to make large R&D investments with the hope of recovering them in the large-scale production phase. Since that hope will no longer be there, it is not plausible that companies will continue to make investments. During a time of low procurement, companies might liquidate plants and research facilities even though these assets would be needed should the United States find, at some time in the future, that it has to increase procurement. If we are to solve this problem, some fundamental changes in the competitive acquisition strategy and the laws and regulations that go with it will be necessary.

Furthermore, the PPBS system needs to be changed so that long-term defense industrial capital needs can be planned explicitly. This will have to be an integral part of the Pentagon's strategic planning process.

Academic researchers can make only a limited contribution to solving these fundamental institutional problems. A major in-house Pentagon review or an outside commission similar to the Packard Commission is called for.

The third of four proposed research efforts should examine the connection between research, development, and production. The proposed acquisition strategy of stopping development projects in the prototype stage (milestone 2) needs to be fleshed out. It seems likely that this makes sense for some types of technology and not for others. But what are the criteria for deciding which is which? It is important to realize that production capability is not just a technical question. Some detailed research on production engineering and on the institutions needed for production would be useful.

And lastly, opportunities should be explored to use ordinary civilian goods in weapons production. The research on the transition from development to production might give the DoD some ideas about how to redesign the procurement process so that it is easier to use standard civilian companies, manufacturing equipment, and components in weapons production.

The national interest is in protecting production assets, not companies per se. We need to examine the question of whether it is necessary to protect the entire company in order to protect the specific assets that the DoD wants to preserve. Again, it is important to realize that any attempt to do this will involve heavy direct government control of the defense industry.

Also, there is a lot of talk about military conversion, but most conversion destroys the military production capability of the factory or the team just as effectively as if the factory or team were dissolved. Discussion of conversion might be relevant for alleviating some of the negative social effects of the defense downsizing, but it probably is not relevant to preserving U.S. capability to reconstitute military forces.

The bottom line is that the U.S. defense acquisition system was designed for a different environment than that prevailing in the 1990s. The problems will have to be dealt with as part of a long-term plan of fundamental changes in the bureaucracies, regulations, and markets that make up the acquisition system.

Notes

1. George Bush, *National Security Strategy of the United States* (The White House, August 1991), 29. The term *reconstitution* strikes most military officers as a strange term to use for this concept. It was originally used to refer to taking a defeated or devastated military unit off the line and bringing it to the rear for reorganization and remanning. I want to thank Lt. Col. Russel Honore, USA, for pointing this out to me.
2. Ibid.
3. See, for example, Air Force Association, *Lifeline Adrift* (Arlington, Va.: Aerospace Education Foundation, September 1991); and John N. Ellison et al., *Mobilizing U.S. Industry: A Vanishing Option for National Security?* (Boulder, Colo.: Westview Press, 1988).
4. "Mr. Clinton's Tough Choice," *New York Times,* March 24, 1992, A12.
5. For a discussion of the fragility of specialized defense capabilities, see David Blair, "Criteria for Planning the Transition to Lower Defense Spending," *Annals of the*

American Academy of Political and Social Science (September 1991): 146-156.

6. A good discussion of this strategy is in J. Ronald Fox, *Arming America, How the U.S. Buys Weapons* (Boston: Harvard Graduate School of Business, 1974), 224ff.

7. Merton J. Peck and Frederic M. Scherer pointed out the problems with such an acquisition strategy more than thirty years ago in *The Weapons Acquisition Process: An Economic Analysis* (Cambridge: Harvard University Press, 1962).

8. Leading examples of the use of a flyoff are the F-16 versus F-17, the F-100 versus F-110 engine, and the F-22 versus F-23. The F-16 case is discussed in Roger Franklin, *The Defender: The Story of General Dynamics* (New York: Harper and Row, 1986), 234-261. On dual-sourcing, see Bill Drinnon and David Hodulich, "Production Competition Lessons Learned: Elements of a Business Deal," *Program Manager* (September-October 1989): 28-31. The F-100 versus F-110 case is discussed in Robert W. Drewes, *The Air Force and the Great Engine War* (Washington, D.C.: National Defense University, 1987).

9. Edward A. Kolodziej, *Making and Marketing Arms: The French Experience and Its Implications for the International System* (Princeton, N.J.: Princeton University Press, 1987), 152.

10. This is partly because of the short length of time that people spend in each job in the United States. When a person moves into an unfamiliar job which he or she is going to hold for only two or three years, the first thing that person will do is look up the legal requirements of that job. In fact, this is the wisest approach because one can get into serious trouble by violating any of the regulations in the very legalistic American system. It is very hard to imagine an American bureaucratic-industrial complex that relies upon an old-boy network to the extent the French system does. (One must acknowledge that the French do have some remarkably well-trained old boys.)

    An interesting example of the difference between the French and the American view of doing business is illustrated by the attempt by the Italian Agnelli family to take over Perrier:

    > The 'mistake' reports an official close to the Italians was to believe that Paris is an open market. "The Agnellis were thinking like Americans and not like Frenchmen," the official says. "They said, what does the book say we should do? Then they went by the book. They didn't consider the psychological reaction."

    Peter Gumbel and E.S. Browning, "The Agnellis of Italy Learn How Not to Do A Takeover in Paris," *Wall Street Journal*, March 4, 1992, A1.

11. The system is now called the Biennial PPBS, or BPPBS.

12. For an introduction to this process, see Maj. Charles R. Nelson, "Keeping the Edge: Understanding the Importance of Acquisition," *Program Manager* 20, no. 6, DSMC 105 (January-February 1992): 32-41.

13. Department of Defense Directive 5000.1, pp. 1-2.

14. The Defense Management Review is summarized in Dick Cheney, "A Plan to Improve the Defense Acquisition Process and Management of the Pentagon," *Defense 89*, 2-19. A good summary of the Packard Commission and other commission reports appears in David E. Lockwood, Andrew C. Mayer, and Cheryl A. Crow, "Summary of Principal Reports," in *Defense Acquisition: Major U.S. Commission Reports* (1949-1988) (November 1, 1988): 1-23, prepared for the Defense Policy Panel and Acquisition Policy Panel of the Committee on Armed Services, House of Representatives, 100th Congress, 2d session. The reports of the various commissions are reproduced in that volume.

15. This characterization of the CinCs is simplified. In addition to the unified commanders, who are responsible for an area of the world, there are also "specified

commanders" in charge of the strategic forces (STRATCOM), the Transportation Command (TRANSCOM), and the Special Operations Command (SOCOM). The entire CinC arrangement is being rearranged, but the CinCs will retain authority consistent with the Goldwater-Nichols legislation.

16. The idea of giving more authority to the local commanders goes back a long way. For example, Abba Lerner proposed in World War II that each theater commander be given a budget with which to purchase resources from the services. See Charles J. Hitch and Roland N. McKean, *The Economics of Defense in the Nuclear Age* (Cambridge: Harvard University Press, 1960), 220.

17. See the discussion of uncertainty in Merton J. Peck and Frederic M. Scherer, *The Weapons Acquisition Process: An Economic Analysis* (Cambridge: Harvard University Press, 1962), chap. 2. They argue forcefully that the weapons acquisition market cannot mimic the consumer durables market.

18. Quoted in David A. Bond, "Clouded Threats, Lost Urgency Blur Debate on Defense Cuts," *Aviation Week & Space Technology*, March 16, 1992, 27.

19. Quoted in Eleanor Spector, "Drawdown Focuses DoD Concerns on Healthy Contractor Base," *Defense Issues* 6, no. 47 (November 1991) from a speech given to the Association of Old Crows Annual Technical Symposium, Washington, D.C., October 10, 1991, p. 1.

20. Ibid., 2.

21. Murray Weidenbaum, *Small Wars, Big Defense* (New York: Oxford University Press, 1992), 146.

22. David Blair interview with executives of the Allison Gas Turbine Division of General Motors, December 1992.

23. David A. Bond, "Clouded Threats, Lost Urgency," 29.

24. Murray L. Weidenbaum, "The Transferability of Defense Industry to Civilian Uses," *Convertibility of Space and Defense Resources to Civilian Needs: A Search for New Employment Potentials* (Washington, D.C.: Government Printing Office, 1964), 848-855.

25. See John A. Alic et al., *Beyond Spinoff: Military and Commercial Technologies in a Changing World* (Boston: Harvard Business School Press, 1992). See also Gilbert R. Hawk, "Reconstituting the U.S. Defense Industry: The Software Side of the Equation," in David Blair, ed., *Milestone 2: The Transition from Development to Production*, 1993, forthcoming.

3

Congressional—DoD Relations After the Cold War: The Politics of Uncertainty

Kenneth R. Mayer

I n two years, from the fall of the Berlin Wall in November 1989 to the formal dissolution of the Soviet Union in December 1991, the foundation of postwar U.S. defense planning—the need to contain Soviet expansion—imploded. The consequences for defense policy in the United States, and the problems these pose for planners, can scarcely be overstated. Virtually every element of U.S. defense and foreign policy was driven, in some fashion, by the competition between the United States and the Soviet Union, which Zbigniew Brzezinski characterized in 1986 as "a two-nation contest for nothing less than global dominance." [1] Decisions about defense missions, force structure, and weapons research were driven by current or projected Soviet military capabilities, and what would otherwise have been marginal regional security problems became significant when viewed through the lens of the cold war.

The magnitude of the change was amplified by its suddenness and unpredictability. Though on several occasions in the postwar period policy makers envisioned a time when U.S.-Soviet relations might be transformed into a manageable and stable rivalry, nobody had seriously argued that the Soviet threat would simply disappear.[2] Historian John Lewis Gaddis calls this the dog-and-car syndrome, referring to "the fact that dogs spend a great deal of time chasing cars but very little time thinking about what they would actually *do* with a car if they were ever to catch one. Our leaders are not all that different: they pour their energy vigorously into the pursuit of victory, whether in politics or in war, but when victory actually arrives, they treat it as if it were an astonishing and wholly unforeseen development." [3] The debate over the future of U.S. military power reveals a paucity of long-range thought, and as a result the initial stages of the debate were dominated by reaction and continual revision. As late as January 1991, Secretary of De-

Kenneth R. Mayer is assistant professor of political science at the University of Wisconsin at Madison.

fense Dick Cheney cautioned that despite "significantly reduced East-West tensions . . . the Soviet military forces remain the largest of any country in Eurasia, and the Soviet Navy and Air Force continue to modernize and remain the largest in the world." [4] One year later, the former Soviet military was in crisis, and discussions over force projection were displaced by controversy over how forces should be apportioned to the various republics. The speed of the revolution took both policy makers and academics by surprise and stimulated a new look at the reasons why world politics is so erratic.[5] That unpredictability is also a source of uncertainty as to what the world will look like in the future; our capacity to forecast events fifteen years ahead is surely suspect, given our failure to predict the last three.

Though the Soviet threat loomed large, planners could take some comfort from the fact that the enemy was easily identifiable and well understood. Soviet capabilities and tactics were thoroughly scouted, and many U.S. systems were designed specifically to counter known or projected Soviet capabilities. More importantly, the threat of global nuclear war gave each side a measure of certainty that the other would avoid provocative moves. The probability of war was seen as inversely proportional to the level of destruction. Absent the perversely stabilizing effects of Mutual Assured Destruction, the possibility of conflict at lower levels of violence rises. Thus, defense policy must now focus on problems that for years had been overshadowed by the strategic nuclear threat: nuclear and chemical weapons proliferation and the spread of ballistic missile technology. Along with these problems exist others that were hard to foresee: assuring positive command and control of thousands of nuclear weapons in a disintegrated superpower, fostering economic stability and growth in countries making the difficult transition from centrally planned to capitalist economic systems, and shifting the strategy and planning apparatus away from thinking about a single, unifying threat, to analyzing a much wider array of lower-order security problems.

This centrality of the Soviet threat also conditioned debates over defense budgets and provided a measure of certainty to the political relationship between the Department of Defense (DoD) and Congress. Though Congress at times disagreed (often with exasperation) with DoD over funding levels and priorities, it rarely made deep cuts in budget requests or denied DoD the military equipment that it required. Some observers attributed this relative deference to the power of the "military-industrial complex," others to the risk presented by Soviet military capabilities, which tempered enthusiasm for radical change. The budgetary game was clearly established: DoD would ask for more than it thought it would get, and Congress would cut at the margins but would rarely cancel any programs outright. Though neither side really liked the arrangement, both learned to accept it.

Both Congress and DoD are having difficulty adjusting to the new circumstances. The collapse of the Soviet threat has changed the context of the defense debate by forcing a reassessment of U.S. policy along lines that have long been settled. The cold war engendered a large degree of consensus about what the U.S. role in the world should be and on the nature of the major threats to national security.[6] As Les Aspin (D-Wis.), then chairman of the House Armed Services Committee, put it in early 1992, "we are cut loose from a lot of our certainties, and we must ask ourselves first-principle questions which haven't been asked in 40 to 50 years."[7] Robert Jervis, a scholar who has studied this issue, notes that this debate will be complicated because of the unprecedented nature of a peaceful transformation of the world system. "World politics has rarely been reordered without a major war," he writes, and though the collapse of the Soviet Union is akin to a military defeat, "this is a war without another coalition or country that acts like a winner, ready to move into the power vacuum and structure a new set of rules to guide international behavior."[8]

Military strategy and defense postures are thus in constant flux and will become stable only when the political debate over the U.S. role in the world is settled; the only certainty is that future budgets and force structures will be much smaller than anyone envisioned before 1989. As a result, budget proposals and the congressional responses are less important as statements of policy than as indicators that there is still no consensus, either in government or in the public, about the threats facing the United States, its global position, or what the overall defense strategy should be. Confusion is not an indicator of analytical flaws or shortsightedness but is an inevitable and natural part of the process of rethinking defense issues and the struggle to achieve a new consensus.

The major difficulty facing Congress and DoD is that the debate over strategy is far from settled even as force structure and budget decisions are made today that will have implications far into the future. To give one example, we have only begun to consider seriously the implications of sharp, permanent reductions in defense spending on the industrial base and how best to manage economic conversion. The debate over the 1993 defense budget in particular took place without resolving any "first-principle" questions and was affected by short-term economic considerations and procedural factors that limited the initial eagerness for deeper cuts in the president's budget request.[9]

The congressional debate over the fiscal year 1993 defense budget and accompanying Future Years Defense Plan (FYDP) was unusual in two respects. First, the initial demands for cuts much deeper than President George Bush had proposed faded rapidly as members began to see the implications: massive regional economic dislocation and industrial base problems that no one had thought through. Even though the 1993 budget contained few substantive revisions from the previous year, many legislators found themselves in the unfamiliar position of opposing cuts they had once supported. While it is easy to attribute the quick conversion solely to pork barrel questions—and concern over disappearing jobs undeniably played a role—that interpretation fails to provide a complete explanation of a complicated phenomenon. Second, discussion of the 1993 budget was constrained by a powerful procedural impediment to deeper reductions: the 1990 budget agreement, which prohibited using money from defense cuts for domestic programs. Both the House and Senate failed to overturn the agreement, and without the ability to transfer funds members lost their zeal for pursuing the elusive peace dividend. Overall, the debate took place in an environment of great uncertainty, with regard to both the threats and the effects of reduced defense spending. Absent consensus about the nature of the U.S. role in the world, it is not surprising that congressional deliberations were dominated not by a coherent strategic rationale but by an attempt to grapple with serious short-term questions about what the transition to a noncold war footing meant. In part, Congress's incremental response reflects a standard reaction to conditions of uncertainty; congressional scholars have long noted the institution's tendency to avoid dramatic action and defer to the executive branch on controversial issues.[10] However, domestic pressures on the budget will intensify in the coming years, and fiscal 1994 is the likely setting for a critical evaluation of the U.S. defense posture because it offers Congress an opportunity to make direct trade-offs between defense and domestic spending.

Defense Strategy After the Cold War: The 1993 Defense Budget Request

It was in this muddied context that President Bush submitted his 1993 defense budget request. The 1993-1997 FYDP proposed $1.35 trillion in current dollar expenditures over five years, a reduction of $64 billion from the 1992 plan (Table 3-1). Defense budgets would decline in real terms by 3 percent annually for five years, reducing 1997 defense spending to $274.6 billion. Spending by title (Table 3-2) indicates that most of the near-term savings would come from reductions in procurement: planned 1993 budget authority for procurement is $54.5 billion, down 9.8 percent from 1992, and one-third below 1990 levels (in constant dollars). Spending for personnel and operations and maintenance is relatively flat, and research and development shows a modest 1.8 percent increase from 1992 to 1993.

The new national security strategy that President Bush offered in August 1990 placed less emphasis on the Soviet Union and more emphasis on a regional focus. With the Soviet conventional threat no longer the linchpin

Table 3-1   Department of Defense Proposed Budget Authority
(current $, billion)

	1992	1993	1994	1995	1996	1997	Total, 1992-1997
DoD FY 1992 proposal	278.3[a]	277.9	278.2	280.7	282.6	287.4	1,685.1
DoD FY 1993 proposal	270.9[b]	267.6	267.8	269.9	270.4	274.6	1,621.2
Reduction	7.4	10.3	10.4	10.8	12.2	12.8	63.9[c]

Source: Department of Defense.

Note: Excludes national security functions of the Department of Energy.

[a] Proposed; [b] Estimated; [c] Including inflation readjustments.

of defense planning, and with the strategic threat waning as a result of the potential for deep bilateral reductions, the planning focus has turned away from a threat-based force (one tailored to a specific enemy), to a "base force" designed to respond to unexpected regional conflicts and various proliferation threats. The new defense strategy calls for a flexible force capable of responding to regional conflicts throughout the world, especially in the Middle East, and to ethnic and civil war in Eastern Europe;[11] continued spending on antimissile defense systems to counter ballistic missile and nuclear weapons proliferation; a strong global presence that can deter attack on the United States and its allies; and attention to lower levels of conflict, such as counterterrorism and control of drugs.[12] The new strategic concept relies on a continued U.S. forward military presence in key regions, continued emphasis on strategic deterrence and defense, and the ability to reconstitute a large military force should the need arise. Such a strategy, DoD maintains, will provide insurance against potential threats that might be difficult to envision today.

The 1993 budget left unchanged the proposed base force, which was first announced in 1990; the base force was proposed after the collapse of the Warsaw Pact but before the Soviet Union's disintegration. The major elements of the structure are shown in Tables 3-3 and 3-4. The 1997 base force, which is approximately 25 percent smaller than 1989 force levels, represents an attempt to rely more on enhanced mobility and force projection than on forward presence, and will take advantage of U.S. technological superiority to counter opponents who may be sizable but who will probably lack the sophistication of Soviet forces. The number of active duty Army personnel will drop sharply, largely because units once dedicated to the defense of Western Europe will be disbanded as the overall U.S. presence there drops by 50 percent; the 1997 force will have one-third fewer active divisions than in 1989. The Air Force will shrink as well and will lose nearly

Table 3-2   DoD Budget Authority by Title (constant 1993 $, billions)

	1990	1991	1992	1993
Military Personnel	$ 88.3	$ 84.3	$ 81.8	$ 77.1
Operations and Maintenance	97.6	89.5	89.5	84.5
Procurement	89.7	70.9	60.4	54.5
RDT&E	40.3	38.5	38.1	38.8
Military Construction	5.6	5.6	5.1	6.2
Other	2.7	4.2	6.1	6.6
TOTAL	$324.2	$293.0	$281.0	$267.6

Source: Department of Defense.

Note: Figures converted to constant dollars using DoD deflators.

nine active wings (over 600 aircraft). The Navy fares the best: though it will lose 100 ships and 15 percent of its personnel, it retains the core of its surface warfare capability—the carrier battle groups. The Navy will commission several new supercarriers during the 1990s but will shrink to twelve groups from the present thirteen.

The 1993 budget incorporated few substantial revisions from the 1992 version, and the actual spending reduction from 1993 to 1997 was smaller than the total cuts announced. Of the $63.8 billion in savings over that period, $13.4 billion (over 20 percent) resulted from reduced inflation estimates and, hence, were not a function of any programmatic reduction. Actual program reductions accounted for $50.4 billion in spending cuts, but $7.7 billion of that came from rescissions, or reductions in prior year budget authority already granted. Roughly $1.1 billion of this amount was put back into the budget to pay for environmental restoration and cleanup. As a result, the actual spending reduction over the 1993-1997 period was $43.8 billion, a 2.6 percent cut from the 1992 FYDP.[13]

There were two major policy changes in the 1993 budget. The first was the termination of two major programs; the Pentagon proposed ending the B-2 program at twenty bombers instead of the seventy-five the Air Force had been requesting, and it terminated orders for two SSN-21 Seawolf attack submarines that had already been funded. The B-2 had been in trouble on Capitol Hill for some time, and the twenty bomber proposal was a realistic counter to a Congress that was unlikely to authorize more than that number under any circumstances. The SSN-21 is an advanced attack submarine designed specifically to counter expected advances in Soviet submarines; with the collapse of the Soviet Union, the Seawolf would have searched the oceans for an enemy that no longer existed.

The other change was a new acquisition policy that entailed slower development of the latest systems and a reduced pace of weapons modern-

Table 3-3   Projected Base Force Structure

	1990	1997
Army Divisions	18	12
Naval Forces		
Carrier Groups	13	12
Carrier Air Wings	13	11
Ships	547	435
Air Force Fighter Wings	24	15.5
Reserves		
National Guard Divisions	10	6
Naval Reserve Air Wings	2	2
Air Force Reserve Fighter Wings	12	11

Source: *Fiscal Implications of the Administration's Proposed Base Force,* Congressional Budget Office (December 1991), 3; Secretary of Defense, *Annual Report to the President and Congress,* February 1992.

ization. This represents a departure from the cold war experience, where strong emphasis was placed on moving new systems into the field as quickly as possible. Under the policy, the Pentagon will delay production of some systems, relying instead on extended development and prototype testing that will, in theory, allow the military to field new systems only when absolutely needed. The largest program so far affected is the Army's RAH-66 Comanche helicopter, the follow-on to the AH-64 Apache; deferring production indefinitely will save $3.4 billion through 1997.

The major actions in the 1993 FYDP and their budgetary effects are summarized in Table 3-5. Two-thirds of the money from program reductions comes from the B-2, SSN-21, and RAH-66 actions; most of the rest is from cuts in strategic programs that have been curtailed as the Soviet nuclear threat wanes.

The Congressional Response: Phase I

The initial congressional reaction to the 1993 FYDP was lukewarm, at best. Many legislators protested that the president's budget cuts did not take into account the collapse of the Soviet Union and criticized the general planning response to the end of the cold war. Democrats in particular scolded the president for not using defense cuts to pay for domestic programs. Despite DoD's argument that it took into account improved political and military relationships with the former Soviet Union in the 1992 budget, many observers were surprised by the lack of movement in DoD's planning assumptions.

Table 3-4   Military Personnel (thousands)

	1987	1995	1997	1987-1997 Reduction	Percent Reduction 1987-1997
Active Forces					
Army	781	536	536	245	31.4%
Navy	587	509	501	86	14.7%
Marine Corps	199	170	159	40	20.1%
Air Force	607	429	430	177	29.2%
Total Active	2,174	1,644	1,626	548	25.2%
Selected Reserves	1,151	922	920	231	20.1%
Civilians	1,133	912	904	229	20.2%
Total DOD Employment	4,458	3,478	3,450	1,008	22.6%

Source: Department of Defense.

The testiest exchanges between Congress and DoD revolved around the questions of whether the Pentagon had produced a budget that recognized the vastly changed security environment and whether the military had successfully devised a strategic rationale. Yet it became clear that even DoD had not completely worked out its fundamental strategy. That the U.S. military was seeking an analytic construct that would replace the cold war paradigm became clear when elements of the 1994-1999 Defense Planning Guidance were leaked to the press in mid-February 1992.[14] Unlike previous policy statements which did not point to specific threats as the basis for planning,[15] these documents identified seven "illustrative" contingencies that were to guide long-range military planning: a renewed Iraqi threat to the Persian Gulf in the late 1990s; a North Korean attack on South Korea; a simultaneous conflict arising in the Persian Gulf and the Korean peninsula; a Russian attack on the Baltic republics, after a coup that establishes an "expansionist authoritarian government" in Moscow; a coup in the Philippines which threatens Americans who remain after the American military bases there close; a narco-terrorist threat to the Panama Canal; and the emergence of a new expansionist superpower that would "adopt an adversarial security strategy and develop a military capability to threaten U.S. interests through global military competition."[16]

Predictably, criticism of the scenarios emerged immediately. A *New York Times* editorial called the effort an attempt to "pump up the threats facing America" and urged Congress to "greet these claims with healthy skepticism."[17] Even some staunch defenders of the Pentagon found fault; Sen. John Warner (R-Va.) argued that Congress had "a right to be critical of the plans."[18] Other senators warned that the plans themselves might under-

Table 3-5   Major Actions and Budgetary Effects ($, millions)

	Savings, 1993-1997
Terminate B-2 at 20 bombers	$14,500
Terminate SSN-21 Seawolf submarine	14,100
Delay production of RAH-66 Comanche	3,400
Terminate ADATS Air Defense System	1,700
Terminate Small ICBM (Midgetman)	1,472
Terminate SRAM II/T air-to-surface missile	1,659
Terminate Advanced Cruise Missile	1,300
Terminate KC-135 Re-engine program	1,128
Total	$39,259
Other savings from terminations and acquisition changes	$6,550
Total	$ 46,809

Source: Department of Defense.

Note: Totals do not include $3.6 billion in 1992 rescissions for the SSN-21 and Small ICBM programs.

mine Pentagon credibility and, hence, support for future budget requests because, as Sen. Carl Levin (D-Mich.) put it, "some of the scenarios are incredibly unlikely." [19] The Pentagon's politically defensive position was highlighted by the fact that it resisted providing details of the plans to Congress.

The reaction to these scenarios illustrates the dilemma faced by planners in the current environment. If they fail to identify specific threats, they are open to charges that the budget proposals are not grounded in any rational conception of what the military might be required to do. If planners try to postulate threats, they are accused of engaging in wild speculation. Even if the scenarios are considered realistic, opponents can attack budget requests indirectly by criticizing the planning assumptions. While such a debate is a welcome part of the process of defining policy goals, it requires that participants recognize that such assumptions are inherently uncertain. Forecasts necessarily traffic in probabilities. One ranking military officer summed up his frustration with the process this way:

> You're damned if you do and damned if you don't. . . . Everybody on the Hill is demanding that we do a threat based analysis of the force we need. But you immediately see the danger of being threat-based . . . everybody gets to be an instant expert if they like the threat or don't like the threat, and if they want to cut the budget they won't like the threat.[20]

Legislators also voiced objections when the geopolitical basis for the new defense strategy in the Defense Planning Guidance was leaked to the public.[21] At its root, the new defense strategy envisioned a world where the U.S. remains the only military superpower and called for a sustained global presence even though no worldwide conventional threat to U.S. and Western interests is foreseen "for many years to come." [22] The strategy explicitly provided for discouraging rivals, primarily by "convincing [them] that they need not aspire to a greater role or pursue a more aggressive posture to protect their legitimate interests." [23] Planners are clearly concerned that other nations may reject U.S. military leadership, and that a decline in influence is possible now in the absence of a unifying threat. Though officials quickly backed away from some aspects of the report, it showed that some in the planning community are having difficulty thinking about security in a multipolar international environment. Within two months the document had been substantially rewritten to retract the "one superpower" goal and place more emphasis on collective security arrangements; even so, there was no corresponding change in budget numbers.[24]

The base force concept is already coming under criticism, with congressional leaders charging that it is obsolete because DoD developed it in 1990, before the disintegration of the Soviet Union.[25] Shortly after DoD announced its 1993-1997 plan, in which it did not alter the base force concept or force structure, Senate Armed Services Committee chairman Sam Nunn argued that the plan was analytically unsound, and that the Pentagon's refusal to revise it was based more on political realities than defense needs:

> I don't think simply saying that "The base force is what we came up with two years ago and that is what we want now" is sufficient reason. It has to have a whole lot more analysis and logic behind it than that. ... What people are doing now—including, I'm afraid, the president so far—is just figuring out how much money they need for whatever their favorite domestic addition or tax cut is and saying that is the amount we need from defense.[26]

Aspin was more direct, calling the base force "out of date," [27] and many of his colleagues did not accept either Secretary of Defense Cheney's or Gen. Colin Powell's protests that planners had anticipated the breakup of the Soviet Union when devising the base force.[28]

Even some planners within the Pentagon considered the base force incomplete, because it ignored what they saw as the critical question of whether the traditional missions of the different services (such as the Air Force's control of the close air support mission) should be reorganized or consolidated. An editorial in the trade periodical *Aviation Week & Space Technology* noted that "several top military officials admit privately that the failure to address the [roles and missions] issue is a glaring deficiency in the Pentagon's Base Force concept. One senior Air Force official said a 'fundamental, far-reaching, no-holds barred' reassessment is essential." [29] Congress demanded as part of the 1993 budget that DoD submit such a study, with an emphasis on the role of combat aircraft missions.[30]

Nunn's and Aspin's charges that the base force has not been subjected to sufficient analysis underscore the difficulty of planning in a volatile environment. Some sort of baseline concept is necessary to begin the debate about what future force structures should look like. Yet it is unrealistic to expect an organization that has operated under a dominant paradigm, as DoD has for forty years, to conduct a fundamental reassessment of its function in the new environment within two years, and in addition get it right on the first pass. By offering detailed justification for the base force so long after the concept was first introduced, however, and by claiming that it is appropriate to both the pre- and post-Soviet Union defense environment, DoD leaves itself open to charges that it is simply backing into an established position. The base force concept, therefore, should be considered the opening move in a debate that will continue. During his tenure as chairman of the House Armed Services Committee, Les Aspin, for example, offered his own version of a base force, using what he calls the "Iraq Equivalent" standard, or the ability to respond to a conflict the size of the Persian Gulf War. Not surprisingly, the defense community is harshly critical of Aspin's analysis, a somewhat disingenuous position given the community's reaction to criticism of DoD's threat-based analysis.[31] The outcome will depend on the plausibility of the assumptions built into the concept, as well as public perceptions of the value of paying the "insurance costs" of defense.

The opinion voiced by many legislators, both hawks and doves, was that the 1993 budget and FYDP simply did not go far enough. Within a month of the president's budget submission, Aspin proposed four alternatives which incorporated up to $165 billion in additional cuts through 1997, and 350,000 fewer active duty personnel.[32] Senate Armed Services Committee member John McCain (R-Ariz.) wanted to cut $113.2 billion; House Budget Committee chairman Leon E. Panetta (D-Calif.) offered additional cuts of $158 billion.[33]

It appeared likely, then, that DoD would take a substantial hit in 1993, with more to follow. Apart from the disputes over whether the Pentagon had adequately responded to the end of the cold war, from the standpoint of competing with other programs for resources DoD's position could hardly have been worse. The defense budget is bracketed by two irresistible forces: on one side is the ballooning federal deficit, which will remain well above $300 billion for fiscal 1993 (the latest federal budget forecasts a national debt of nearly $6 trillion by 1997); on the other is increasing public pressure on the federal government to expand domestic programs for health insurance, the environment, crime, drugs, industrial and infrastructure investment, and education. Yet the size of the deficit left no room for additional spending anywhere, absent tax increases or corresponding cuts elsewhere in the budget. That made defense an attractive source of funds to pay for domestic programs, and congressional Democrats and Republicans lined up to propose what they intended to do with the money.

The Congressional Response: Phase II

Only three things stood in the way of those cuts: the procedural impediment of the 1990 budget accord, which made it more difficult for Congress to transfer money from defense to domestic programs; the opposition of influential members, especially Senate Armed Services Committee chairman Sam Nunn (D-Ga.); and the realization that rapid spending cuts lead to economic dislocation. Between January and April, what appeared to be a strong consensus in favor of deeper cuts faded as members realized the implications of what they wished to do.

The first obstacle was procedural. If Congress was to use defense cuts to pay for domestic programs, it had to break a key provision of the 1990 budget agreement, the "budget walls" that prohibited transfers among the three categories of spending—domestic discretionary, defense, and international. The spending limits over the life of the agreement are shown in Table 3-6. Budget totals *within* each category could not exceed specified limits, and any reductions would have to be used for either tax cuts or deficit reduction; savings from cuts in any one category could not be used to increase spending in any other category. Republicans had insisted on the budget walls specifically to limit the zeal with which Democrats could go after the defense budget; they had originally insisted on walls throughout the life of the agreement. Democrats resisted, and in a compromise the two sides agreed to adhere to budget ceilings by categories for the first three years of the agreement and total spending limits for the last two.

Revoking the budget walls required legislation passed by both chambers (over a likely presidential veto). House Democrats pressed their case for taking the walls down a year early, arguing that the world had changed substantially since October 1990, allowing for deeper reductions in defense spending, and that money was desperately needed for domestic purposes. They were opposed by a coalition of conservative Democrats and all Republicans, who were opposed to eliminating the walls because doing so would make it easier to reduce defense spending and because of concern that overall federal spending would rise. They were joined by a handful of liberal Democrats trying to protect some major programs from budget cuts. Ultimately, the legislation failed in both the House and Senate, and the budget walls remained intact.[34]

Even before the defeat of that legislation diminished support for further cuts, many members had become apprehensive about the economic implica-

Table 3-6   1990 Budget Agreement Spending Limits (budget
              authority, current $, billions)

	1991	1992	1993	1994	1995
Domestic Discretionary	$182.9	$202.7	$206.1	—	—
International	21.2	34.5	22.8	—	—
Defense	332.9	301.7	289.0	—	—
Total	$537.1	$538.9	$517.9	$512.3	$522.0

Source: *Budget of the United States Government, Fiscal Year 1993*, Appendix Two, 6-7.

Note: Only total spending is specified for 1994 and 1995, with transfers among categories permitted; Defense category is budget Category 050, which includes national security functions of the Department of Energy.

tions of the defense drawdown. Though the macroeconomic consequences of cutting the defense budget will be relatively mild, since defense spending is only a small part of national economic activity, contract cancellations, base closures, and other reductions can cause substantial regional and sectoral dislocations.[35] In part, the early enthusiasm for more rapid and deeper cuts faded as members came to the uneasy realization that those cuts would mean job losses and the end of many programs on which members have come to depend. For example, the existing base force proposal will result in the loss of nearly one million DoD jobs by 1997. Approximately 550,000 active duty personnel, 230,000 civilian employees, and 229,000 part-time reservists will lose their positions. The Congressional Budget Office estimated that the cuts proposed in the FY 1992 budget would result in a total of 600,000 direct and indirect job losses in the defense industry by 1995, though many jobs were already being phased out as a result of cuts made before 1992.[36] Additional defense spending cuts of 6 percent per year through 1995 would result in another 300,000 job losses.[37] So, the lower limit of full-time job losses resulting from defense budget cutbacks is approximately 1.3 million, and plausible additional reductions could drive the total much higher; some estimates place the upper limit at 2 to 2.5 million displaced workers through 2001.[38] The regional effects are stark: the California Economic Development Administration estimates that as many as 580,000 jobs may be lost in Los Angeles County alone by 1996 (or nearly one-seventh of the entire labor force).[39] Closing Fort Ord, a large Army base in northern California, will lower total personal income in the surrounding county by one-third, according to Congressional Budget Office estimates.[40]

Faced with such data, many members lost their taste for making more cuts, especially in the midst of a sputtering recovery from the 1990 recession. Critics were quick to ascribe "pork barrel" motives to the growing reluctance to reduce spending, and in particular to attempts to protect a few large systems.

The attempt in Congress to reverse Bush's termination of the Seawolf nuclear attack submarine program is a useful metaphor for the congressional change of heart. The decision to cancel the Seawolf generated a storm in Congress, particularly among the Connecticut and Rhode Island delegations, who represented states where the work would be done. Though nobody questioned the wisdom of stopping the program, the 1993 budget request entailed canceling contracts for two submarines that had already been awarded (the second and third ships), which in turn required Congress to rescind money it had appropriated in earlier years. The affected members quickly mounted a campaign to stop the rescission, arguing that canceling the existing contracts would force General Dynamics' Electric Boat division, one of two shipyards able to build nuclear submarines, out of business; the contractor would complete in 1996 the one Seawolf already under construction and would have no other submarine business until the *next* attack submarine program, the Centurion, started around the year 2000.[41] The legislators were also concerned about job losses in a state whose economy was already reeling from other defense cutbacks: Electric Boat had already announced plans to lay off 50 percent of its work force by 1997 (more than 11,000 jobs), and the state's other major defense contractor, United Technologies, planned to cut its work force by 6,400 by 1995.[42]

The program's defenders were given virtually no chance of success. Though the money for the submarines had already been appropriated, if Congress refused to terminate the contracts it would have to come up with the money for the ships elsewhere in the defense budget to meet the expenditure goals in the 1993 FYDP.[43] The Seawolf's high cost presented a problem, as Sen. Joseph Lieberman (D-Conn.) noted early in the debate: "Those of us who think we need Seawolf have to come up with about $2 billion [each]. In the current environment, that isn't going to be easy." [44] Finding the money put Seawolf defenders in direct competition with other legislators worried about their own programs; in the Senate, Trent Lott (R-Miss.) complained that money devoted to Seawolf would drain resources from other shipbuilding programs, particularly those at Ingalls Shipbuilding, a major shipyard in his home state.[45]

Seawolf defenders focused on two arguments. First, the government would have to pay substantial termination costs if it canceled the contracts. The second Seawolf was estimated to cost $2.9 billion; canceling the contracts for the second and third ships would still leave the government with $1.8 billion in liabilities but with no submarine to show for the money.[46] Navy officials capitalized on this, and "in an unusual break with President Bush and Mr. Cheney over the submarine's future, Adm. Bruce DeMars, the Navy's director of nuclear propulsion, said at House and Senate hearings ... that it would make more financial sense to build the next two Seawolf submarines and then end the program." [47] Even in the midst of its effort to cancel the subs, the Pentagon was pressing ahead with work on some components of the second and third ships because they were either needed as spare parts for the first submarine or, according to spokesman Pete Williams, because they were "so close to completion that it was uneconomical to cancel them." [48] Second, Navy officials maintained that, as Sen. Christopher Dodd (D-Conn.) put it in a January 8 letter to Cheney, "terminating the contract would do 'incalculable' damage to the nation's ability to design and build submarines." [49] On this point, the Pentagon was on the defensive, as Cheney admitted that he did not know what impact the cancellation would have on the industrial base; before the Senate in March 1992 he testified that the Pentagon was studying the implications but that the results would not be available for six months. "That's about when Electric Boat's steel rolling plants at Quonset Point, R.I., would be running out of work," Senator Dodd responded. [50]

Eventually, neither chamber acceded completely to the rescission request; the House voted in April 1992 to preserve one Seawolf, and the Senate both, and in conference the two chambers agreed to continue funding 1.5 submarines; Cheney commented that "it's a package we can live with." [51] Though critics claimed the vote was a pure pork barrel grab, even some normally critical observers of the congressional defense process noted that the industrial base arguments (normally the last refuge of members who know they cannot win on the merits), were "not irrelevant." [52] Members may have been especially sensitive to the perception that DoD had taken action on Seawolf before it knew what the consequences would be; they were likely trying to establish a precedent that DoD should think through the implications for the industrial base before canceling any more programs. Ultimately, what the Seawolf story indicates is the difficulty of taking decisive action in the face of uncertainty and economic hardship, as well as the complications involved in taking into account both short-term (jobs) and long-term (industrial base) factors in deciding the fate of large programs

A third impediment to deeper cuts was Sen. Sam Nunn's (D-Ga.) announcement in March that he opposed any reduction to the president's budget request. Though Nunn argued that the FYDP total could be reduced by an additional $30 to $35 billion, he argued that cuts in 1993 could exacerbate economic difficulties. Nunn's opposition made it much harder for proponents of more cuts to press their case. [53] Aspin played a role in this as well, since his moderate spending proposals stemmed, in part, from concern among the party leadership that a bidding war over defense cuts among liberal Democrats would tie the party to an antidefense position—something they wanted to avoid in an election year. With the major defense players steering a middle course, those who wanted more cuts faced the weight of the experts' opposition.

At the end of the fiscal 1993 budget cycle, Congress had largely deferred the most difficult questions about the defense budget, choosing to make only marginal changes to the president's request. Congress revised a number of tactical aircraft programs, making funding for the F-22 contingent on the DoD roles and missions study, accelerating the A-X program and instituting a competitive prototype phase, reducing funding for the F/A-18 and C-17 aircraft, and requiring DoD to do an affordability study of combat aircraft modernization plans. It made deep cuts in SDI funding, reducing the request by over $1 billion. It reduced reserve strength by 40,000, refusing to agree to the administration's request of a cut of over 100,000. It provided $1.5 billion for defense conversion and aid to workers and communities hurt by the drawdown. None of these actions was especially unusual, however, and neither the House nor Senate versions of the defense budget made substantive changes in defense strategy. The final appropriations bills, sent to the president in early October, made only marginal changes in major programs and authorized $274 billion, or roughly $7 billion less than the president requested.[54]

Observations On the First Post-Cold War Budget Process

What can be learned from the first round of budget wrangling after the collapse of the Soviet Union? The process thus far has provided ample material for those who think that Congress and the Pentagon are moving too slowly on defense reductions, and also for those who think that Congress has jeopardized a smooth transition to a smaller defense footing by cutting too much (and by being preoccupied with pork). However, one must exercise caution when applying standards of strict rationality to what is, at root, a political process; it is unrealistic to expect conclusive action in a single iteration of the budget cycle. More generally, we can make the following observations about the 1993 budget.

It is abundantly clear that neither Congress nor the Pentagon has sorted through the immensely complicated strategic issues posed by the end of the cold war. The major problem is that the pace of international change has overwhelmed the capacity of either Congress or the defense planning community to absorb it. As a result, U.S. defense policy and spending plans have been thrown into disequilibrium and have undergone continuous change since 1989. The defense planning process has been characterized, even during more predictable times, as "so complicated, bureaucratized, unwieldy, and snail-paced ... that the output is usually obsolete by the time the Pentagon presents it to Congress." [55] With startling international events occurring every few months, planners barely have time to assess the latest development before something else comes along that renders the whole effort irrelevant.

Given that the defense budget process involves at least two years of preparation prior to final budget enactment, it is not surprising that plans were overtaken by events. In early 1991, for example, Cheney testified to the House Armed Services Committee that the Strategic Arms Reduction Treaty had still not been completed, and that Soviet actions in the wake of the Conventional Forces in Europe Treaty had "raised serious doubts on our part about submitting that treaty for ratification." [56] That same year, the Joint Chiefs of Staff Net Assessment cautioned that "Soviet military power, though at long last being reduced and changed in form and purpose, is hardly becoming irrelevant. Whatever the future Soviet state may look like, it will still have millions of well-armed men in uniform and will remain, by far, the strongest military force on the Eurasian landmass." [57] One year later those pessimistic evaluations became largely obsolete, but incorporating the constantly shifting threat assessments into the budget process has proven nearly impossible.

Even President Bush's dramatic announcement in September 1991 of unilateral reductions in U.S. tactical nuclear arsenals was eclipsed by cuts in strategic programs announced only four months later. DoD was revising the 1993 budget at the last minute because of changes President Bush wished to announce during his 1992 State of the Union message; line-item detail was not available for a month after the overall federal budget was released. Such rapid reworking of budgets in response to political pressures and international change inevitably leads to ad hoc solutions that will nearly always require considerable revision. In this regard, it is perhaps unfair to criticize DoD for failing to respond more quickly.

One reason for this failure to resolve conclusively budgetary issues is that there is still no public consensus on such basic questions as what role military force should play in the new international environment or which countries the public feels pose the greatest threat to national security. Public opinion data show a high degree of confusion: in February 1992, 31 percent of the public identified Japan as posing the greatest danger to the United States, followed by China (13 percent), the Commonwealth of Independent States (13 percent), and Germany (12 percent). Iraq was a distant sixth at 3 percent. At the same time, political leaders are also grappling with a growing isolationist sentiment; in March 1992, 68 percent of the public said they would be more likely to vote for political candidates who advocated less foreign aid and international involvement.[58] This confusion is reflected in DoD discussions of post-cold war strategy, which have served to polarize public debate rather than to move forward the process of finding a new consensus. At best, the new planning assumptions underscore the difficulty of constructing strategy and aligning it with force structures in an uncertain environment. At worst, they show that the Pentagon is resisting any change in the cold war assumption that U.S. global dominance must be preserved, and that doing so is overwhelmingly a function of military power. The initial policy pronouncements were insufficiently precise to provide much guidance about what force structures would be necessary, and the incremental details released since have given DoD's opponents specifics to attack. While criticism of defense policy and budgets is nothing new, the current debate has no fixed reference point on which most participants can agree, except that "everything has changed."

In such an environment it is hardly surprising that the congressional budget process—incremental and diffuse under the best of circumstances—was dominated by short-term considerations. This would be true even if the powerful procedural obstacles to further defense spending cuts were not present. Members, acting in their capacity as representatives of local constituencies, worried about the impact defense spending cuts have on voters, and sought ways to ease the transition. Uncertainty typically leads the institution to put off decisions and defer to the executive branch, as does confusion among the electorate.[59]

The conventional wisdom holds that Congress resisted cutting the budget solely to preserve pork barrel contracts. "Pork-filled sugar plums dance sprightly in Democratic heads," announced *Aviation Week & Space Technology* in an editorial, finding that Senate Democrats had "unveiled election-year delicacies to assuage the pangs of a leaner defense diet." [60] Congress has been criticized for refusing to agree to Seawolf termination, agreeing to buy the last four B-2 bombers requested by the Pentagon, and interfering with efforts to reduce National Guard and reserve forces: While there is some truth to the charge that Congress was concerned about jobs, it is easy to overestimate the influence of pork-barrel concerns. One overriding factor that will tend to limit the influence of parochial concerns is that the affected projects are competing head-to-head because the overall defense pie is shrinking: money to preserve the much-maligned Seawolf came, in part, from reductions to B-2 and SDI accounts, and anything Congress adds to the budget (or refuses to cancel) must be paid for from cuts elsewhere in the budget. This was clear from the final rescission package to which Congress agreed, which included $7.1 billion in budget authority rescissions from defense ($92 million more than President Bush requested), even as some projects, like Seawolf, were protected.[61] DoD complaints of congressional parochialism are, further, at least partially disingenuous, because the military has rarely failed to take advantage of the congressional reluctance to cancel big projects when doing so suits *its* interests.[62] In sum, while parochial considerations no doubt played a role in shaping congressional preferences on the defense budget, it is a mistake to focus on the desire to protect local interests as the only important dynamic. In any case, pork-barrel pressures will likely be overwhelmed in the 1994 cycle, because the budget walls come down. As a result, members will be free to propose direct trade-offs between defense and domestic spending. The 1994 budget cycle will also be very different because the initial request will be made by President Clinton, who called for deeper defense cuts in the election campaign; Clinton's victory had little impact on the 1993 request, as Congress completed major action in the spring and summer of 1992, well before anyone believed he had a chance to win.

Ultimately, both Congress and DoD resisted large-scale change in defense policy in 1993 because they were on unfamiliar territory; having grown accustomed to a stable threat and relatively consistent defense strategies, neither institution has been able to quickly respond to what is rightly called a revolutionary change in the international environment. To that change add uncertainty, an election-year dose of domestic politics, and procedural obstacles that no one could have predicted would be so effective a deterrent to deep defense cuts, and the result is incrementalism. Muddling through is, after all, what democratic institutions do best. Though "wait 'til next year" is a less than completely satisfying lesson to draw, the 1993 defense budget process was only the opening move in what will be a long, tumultuous transition to a much altered defense strategy and force structure.

Notes

1. Zbigniew Brzezinski, *Game Plan: How to Conduct the U.S. Soviet Contest* (New York: Atlantic Monthly Press, 1986), 8.
2. See, for example, Graham T. Allison and William L. Ury, eds., *Windows of Opportunity: From Cold War to Peaceful Competition in U.S.-Soviet Relations* (Cambridge: Ballinger Publishing, 1989). There was, however, an active critical literature suggesting that the magnitude of the Soviet military threat was vastly overstated; see Tom Gervasi, *The Myth of Soviet Military Supremacy* (New York: Harper and Row, 1986); and Andrew Cockburn, *The Threat: Inside the Soviet Military Machine* (New York: Random House, 1983).
3. John Lewis Gaddis, "Coping with Victory," in *Fundamentals of Force Planning, Volume I: Concepts*, ed. Naval War College Force Planning Faculty (Newport, R.I.: Naval War College Press, 1990), 55.
4. *Annual Report to the President and the Congress*, January 1991, 2.
5. See, for example, Robert Jervis, "The Future of World Politics: Will It Resemble the Past?" *International Security* 16, no. 3 (Winter 1991-1992).
6. There was, to be sure, less agreement on the details of the policy, or how it should apply in every circumstance. Even in the face of post-Vietnam doubts about the benefits of an interventionist foreign and military policy, there was still broad agreement that the U.S. had to sustain a global presence and a strong military capability. See Richard A. Melenson, *Reconstructing Consensus: American Foreign Policy Since the Vietnam War* (New York: St. Martin's Press, 1991), 16-17.
7. Quoted in Patrick E. Tyler, "As Fear of Big War Fades, Military Plans for Little Ones," *New York Times*, February 3, 1992, A6.
8. Jervis, "The Future of World Politics," 41.
9. Unless otherwise indicated, dates that reference budgets are fiscal years.
10. See, for example, Matthew D. McCubbins and Talbot Page, "A Theory of Congressional Delegation," in *Congress: Structure and Policy*, ed. Matthew D. McCubbins and

Terry Sullivan (New York: Cambridge University Press, 1987).

11. See, for example, John J. Mearsheimer, "Back to the Future: Instability in Europe After the Cold War," *International Security* 15, no. 1 (Summer 1990).

12. See *1991 Joint Military Net Assessment*, 2-1 to 2-5.

13. David C. Morrison, "Pentagon on a Downward Glide Path," *National Journal*, February 1, 1992, 279.

14. Patrick E. Tyler, "Pentagon Imagines New Enemies To Fight in a Post-Cold-War Era," *New York Times*, February 17, 1992, A1.

15. One exception to this generalization was the 1991 Joint Military Net Assessment, which identified five regional scenarios that might require a U.S. military response. See *1991 JNMA*, 9-1 and 9-2.

16. Patrick E. Tyler, "7 Hypothetical Conflicts Foreseen by the Pentagon," *New York Times*, February 17, 1992, A5.

17. "War Games, Money Games," *New York Times*, February 19, 1992, A10.

18. Quoted in Eric Schmitt, "Some Senators Say Military Exaggerates Threats of War," *New York Times*, February 21, 1992, A7.

19. Ibid. See also Patrick E. Tyler, "War in the 1990's? Doubt on Hill. Pentagon Plans Evoke Skepticism in Congress," *New York Times*, February 18, 1992, A1.

20. Quoted in Barton Gellman, "Debate Over the Military's Future Escalates Into a War of Scenarios," *Washington Post*, February 26, 1992, A20.

21. Patrick E. Tyler, "U.S. Strategy Plan Calls for Insuring No Rivals Develop," *New York Times*, March 8, 1992, 1.

22. "Excerpts From Pentagon's Plan: 'Prevent the Emergence of a New Rival,' " *New York Times*, March 8, 1992, 4.

23. Ibid.

24. Patrick E. Tyler, "Pentagon Drops Goal of Blocking New Superpowers," *New York Times*, May 24, 1992, A1.

25. William W. Kaufmann and John D. Steinbruner argue that DoD backed into the strategic concept after the initial decisions about force structure were made: "It is probable, and indeed more comprehensible, that the reduced force structure emerged before the strategic concept." Kaufmann and Steinbruner, *Decisions for Defense* (Washington, D.C.: Brookings Institution, 1991), 28.

26. Quoted in John Lancaster, "White House Outlines Vision of New Military," *Washington Post*, January 30, 1992, A10.

27. Ibid.

28. Eric Schmitt, "Powell Criticizes Further Military Cuts," *New York Times*, March 21, 1992, 7.

29. "Time to Reassess Roles and Missions," *Aviation Week & Space Technology*, March 30, 1992, 7.

30. Pat Towell, "Spending Bill Trims Some Now, Sets Bigger Cuts in Motion," *Congressional Quarterly Weekly Report*, October 10, 1992, 3187.

31. See, for example, Schmitt, "Powell Criticizes Further Military Cuts," 7; Thomas Duffy and Tom Breen, "Another Top Navy Official Questions Merit of Aspin's Base-Force Concept," *Inside the Navy*, March 30, 1992, 1.

32. Patrick E. Tyler, "Top Congressman Seeks Deeper Cuts in Military Budget," *New York Times*, February 23, 1992.

33. Morrison, "Pentagon's on a Downward Glide Path," 279.

34. See George Hager, "Rejection of Walls Bill Spells Spending Squeeze at Home," *Congressional Quarterly Weekly Report*, April 4, 1992; George Hager, "Democrats Falter in Drive to Claim Peace Dividend," *Congressional Quarterly Weekly Report*, February 28, 1992.

35. DoD outlays will make up only 4.5 percent of GNP in fiscal 1993, and by 1997 will comprise only 3.4 percent. This compares to peaks of 11.9 percent in 1953, 9.1

percent during the Vietnam War, and a Reagan-era high of 6.3 percent in 1985.

36. Congressional Budget Office, *The Economic Effects of Reduced Defense Spending*, February 1992, 22.

37. Ibid., 26.

38. The 2 million figure is from Pamela Fessler, "Economic Reality May Limit Hill's Urge to Outcut Bush," *Congressional Quarterly Weekly Report*, February 1, 1992, 253; the 2.5 million estimate is from the Office of Technology Assessment, *After the Cold War* (Washington, D.C.: GPO, February 1992), 18.

39. Robert Reinhold, "Industry Gets Help in Effort to Shift Gears," *New York Times*, March 3, 1992, A10. See also Ralph Vartabedian, "Aerospace Cuts to Devastate Area, County Study Says," *Los Angeles Times*, March 17, 1992, 1.

40. Congressional Budget Office, *The Economic Effects of Reduced Defense Spending*, 35.

41. David C. Morrison, "Sinking Sub Making Big Waves," *National Journal*, January 25, 1992, 219.

42. Pamela Fessler, "Members Lobby Hard to Protect Endangered Submarine Project," *Congressional Quarterly Weekly Report*, January 25, 1992, 177.

43. Pat Towell, "Bush Attacks Defense 'Pork,' Wants Add-Ons Removed," *Congressional Quarterly Weekly Report*, March 21, 1992, 736.

44. Fessler, "Members Lobby Hard to Protect Endangered Submarine Project," 177.

45. Ibid., 179.

46. "Second Seawolf Would Cost $2.9 Billion to Complete—Pentagon," *Defense Daily*, April 3, 1992, 17.

47. Eric Schmitt, "Congress Getting Cold Feet About Cutting Weapons Programs," *New York Times*, April 10, 1992, 25.

48. Quoted in Barton Gellman, "Navy Orders More Parts for Seawolf," *Washington Post*, April 3, 1992, 4.

49. Quoted in Pat Towell, "As Bush Budget Nears Release, Lawmakers Dig In for Fight," *Congressional Quarterly Weekly Report*, January 11, 1992, 56.

50. Quoted in David C. Morrison, "Changing Speed," *National Journal*, March 7, 1992, 555. Opponents of defense cuts have long warned of industrial base catastrophes that would surely result from even minor reductions. The volume of such warnings increased dramatically during the 1980s, and it became difficult to sort out the validity of the claims (or what could be done about them, short of doubling the budget). The Center for Strategic and International Studies concluded in 1989 that the defense industrial base shrank by *two-thirds* between 1982 and 1987 (at a time when defense outlays rose by over 27 percent in real terms); see Center for Strategic and International Studies, *Deterrence in Decay: The Future of the U.S. Defense Industrial Base* (Washington, D.C.: CSIS, 1989), 1. A consulting group at Harvard Business School suggested that acquisition policies had rendered defense contracting an unprofitable line of business, and that companies would soon abandon the field altogether; see The MAC Group, *The Impact on Defense Industrial Capability of Changes in Procurement and Tax Policy* (February 1988). More measured assessments can be found in the *1988 Defense Science Board Summer Study on the Defense Industrial and Technology Base* (October 1988), and Office of Technology Assessment, *Redesigning Defense: Planning the Transition to the Future U.S. Defense Industrial Base*, OTA-ISC-500 (Washington, D.C.: GPO, July 1991).

51. Quoted in *Aviation Week and Space Technology*, May 25, 1992, 17.

52. Morrison, "Changing Speed," 555.

53. Pat Towell, "Nunn Breaks From Democrats in Backing Bush's Request," *Congressional Quarterly Weekly Report*, March 28, 1992, 815.

54. Towell, "Spending Bill Trims Some Now, Sets Bigger Cuts in Motion."

55. Kaufmann and Steinbruner, *Decisions for Defense*, 25.

56. U.S. Congress, House Committee on Armed Services, *Hearings on National Defense*

Authorization Act for Fiscal Years 1992 and 1993, Authorization and Oversight, 8.

57. *Joint Military Net Assessment,* 1-3.
58. These data are from Times-Mirror polls, taken from *National Journal,* April 4, 1992, 836.
59. See, for example, Matthew D. McCubbins and Talbot Page, "A Theory of Congressional Delegation," in *Congress: Structure and Policy,* ed. Matthew D. McCubbins and Terry Sullivan (New York: Cambridge University Press, 1987).
60. May 25, 1992, 19.
61. George Hager, "Rescissions Top Bush's Target, Change What Will Get Cut," *Congressional Quarterly Weekly Report,* May 23, 1992, 1433-1434.
62. One famous case occurred in 1987, when Congress was considering legislation to cancel two nuclear aircraft carriers. The Navy, in concert with the prime contractor, prepared and distributed a list of the dollar value of carrier subcontracts broken down by congressional district. The legislation was soundly defeated. See Kenneth R. Mayer, *The Political Economy of Defense Contracting* (New Haven: Yale University Press, 1991), 104-107; and George C. Wilson, "Navy Lobbies to Add Two Carriers," *Washington Post,* March 29, 1987, A5.

4

Déjà Vu: Political Struggles over American Defense Policy

Peter Trubowitz

There is widespread agreement today that America's defense needs are changing.[1] The breakup of the Soviet Union and the opening of the borders in central Europe mean that the United States will be able to spend less on national security than it did during the cold war. Just how rapidly and deeply the defense budget should be cut is, however, a matter of considerable controversy. So are questions about how the "peace dividend" should be allocated and the role that the federal government should play in helping affected people, communities, and companies adjust to military cutbacks. For every analyst who believes the end of the cold war offers opportunities for America to solve domestic economic and social problems, there is another who warns against excessive optimism about the future of international politics and the dangers of rapid military demobilization. At a time when American leaders need to make wise choices about the future, there is little consensus over how to proceed.

This volume is primarily concerned with policy. A number of the chapters explore various options for restructuring the nation's military forces and managing the transition to a smaller military establishment. In the final analysis, however, the choices that the nation makes will be shaped less by the abstract merits of competing proposals for downsizing defense than by the power of those who back these proposals in the political arena. Like the debates over defense policy at other turning points in American history, the stakes in the current policy debate are high. Choices politicians face over the defense budget are not only choices about where to cut and by how much, but also about the nation's priorities. Those choices carry with them different visions of how the taxing, spending, and investment powers of the government should be used. They raise fundamental questions about the distribution of national resources, the locus of political

Peter Trubowitz is assistant professor of political science at the University of Texas at Austin.

power at the federal level, and last but not least, who will benefit and who will not.

The political dimensions of this debate over America's budgetary priorities are important. The conflict over national security policy can best be understood in regional terms, and its regional nature can be analyzed through roll-call voting in the House of Representatives. This study treats Congress as a proxy for the national polity and reconstructs patterns of political alignment over defense policy from "key" legislative votes on military spending. Three conclusions emerge from this analysis: first, the political fault line underlying the current debate over America's defense needs is regional in nature; second, this conflict pits states from the Northeast against states from the South; and third, the conflict over military spending is part of a larger political struggle over national priorities.[2] The conflicts over the Pentagon's budget are grounded in deeper, long-standing divisions over America's needs and how federal resources should be allocated.

Regional Politics and Defense Policy

Regionally based political competition is one of the most distinctive features of American politics. Ever since the historian Frederick Jackson Turner first identified the significance of regionalism in the United States in the 1920s, a large literature has developed on the sources of regional strife over national political decisions.[3] A common theme in this literature is that regional political competition is rooted in geographically uneven economic growth and development.[4] In other industrialized countries, where political systems are also based on spatial representation, regional economic differentiation is often coterminous with ethnic or religious difference. While ethnic and religious difference is also an important feature of American politics, it is most conspicuous at the neighborhood and city level. At the regional level, the absence of the kinds of cultural cleavages present in other nations has meant that regionalism is usually grounded in conflicts of economic interest.

Geographers identify a number of factors that lead to uneven regional growth. Some emphasize geographic differences in resources, markets, or the costs of factors of production.[5] Others focus on regional variation in technological innovation or on the organization of labor and production.[6] Factors internal to regions are stressed by some scholars, while others concentrate on the interaction between intra- and extra-regional factors and on the ways that larger international processes shape regional economic development.[7] Still others stress the role that the federal government plays in shaping patterns of private investment and spending in the national economy and, thus, the possibilities for regional growth and development.[8] The national government has rarely adopted policies that are avowedly regional in purpose and designed to influence the spatial distribution of economic activity. Many of its actions, however, have significant economic consequences at the regional level.

This has become increasingly evident as the power of the American government and the resources available to it have expanded. Given its enormous share of the federal budget, no issue has generated as much attention and controversy in recent decades as defense spending. In the 1960s a number of scholars began to examine the regional consequences of defense spending, but it was not until the 1970s that the issue sparked public debate.[9] In the 1970s politicians from the Northeast voiced concern about imbalances between the taxes collected to provide defense as a "public good" and the uneven allocation of federal defense expenditures across the country. In the 1980s the controversy grew even sharper as it became evident that states that reaped a net gain in federal defense funds, mostly located in the South and West, also experienced accelerated growth rates. What some viewed as an unintended consequence of the Reagan military buildup, others saw as a regional development policy veiled in the garb of national security.

Current conflicts over defense spending are a prolongation of the regionally based struggles of the 1970s. Like today's debates, the fights that erupted in the Nixon, Ford, and Carter years occurred in the context of broader regional conflicts over the fiscal priorities of the federal government. During the 1970s the most sectionally divisive policies were those that contributed to the shift in population and economic activity from the Manufacturing Belt to the Sun Belt.[10] Activists from older industrial states argued that federal fiscal and regulatory policies were regionally biased and that they contributed to the erosion of the Manufacturing Belt's economic base. This concern was quickly transformed into action. Politicians from the Northeast united to press Congress and the White House for a greater share of federal funds. Politicians from the Sun Belt, for their part, argued that despite economic gains in the previous decade, their states remained relatively poor and should continue to benefit disproportionately from federal spending.

The debate over federal funds grew even more intense once the popular press joined the fray and began to evaluate national economic trends in the context of regional disparities in growth. In February 1976 the *New York Times* ran a front-page series arguing that the South was the largest and fastest growing region in the country and that much of the region's growth was a result of a favorable balance of payments with the federal government.[11] The controversy sparked by this series was exacerbated by a cover story appearing in *Business Week* a few months later on increasing migration from the Northeast to the South and West.[12] This migration was attributed to lower wages, lower utility costs, and lower state and local taxes in the growing regions as well as to regional biases in federal flow-of-funds accounts. This was followed by a highly publicized article appearing in *National Journal,* arguing that states from the Sun Belt were receiving far more from Washington in grants and spending than they paid in federal taxes.[13] The implication was that such inequities were at least partly responsible for regional disparities in growth.

Federal military outlays provoked the most controversy and criticism. In the 1970s the defense portion of the federal budget alone accounted for an estimated net "loss" of over $25 billion in revenues for the Northeast.[14] Without the "inequitable burden" of defense spending, the Northeast would have held its own in the federal budget. Some charged that the shift in the regional allocation of defense spending was politically motivated and traced it to the Nixon administration's desire to create political patronage in the South and West—the electoral base of the Republican party.[15] Yet this tilt toward the Sun Belt continued during the Carter years, and counter-pressures to redirect federal spending toward the Manufacturing Belt intensified. Elected officials from the Northeast, most of them Democrats, pursued a two-pronged strategy. They combined attempts to cut the Pentagon budget with various proposals to reformulate and liberalize criteria for allocating or targeting federal funds for such programs as revenue sharing, highway construction, and unemployment compensation.

The national parties served as the institutional vehicles for expressing and advancing the regionally based conflicts of interest of the 1970s. As liberal Democrats gained greater control over their party's national agenda, they pressed for an end to the Vietnam War, cuts in the military budget, and greater federal funding for domestic programs. Such initiatives exacerbated existing tensions between the northern and southern wings of the party over civil rights. One consequence was that the center of the Democratic party began to shift into the Northeast.[16] Just as the center of gravity in the Democratic party shifted, so did the center of the Republican party. Starting in the 1960s the electoral base of the Republican party began to move from the East to the West.[17] At the same time, the Republicans started to penetrate the once solid Democratic South by embracing a platform that rejected the welfare state and stressed its commitment to laissez-faire economics, law and order, and a strong national defense. This coincidence of a party-regional division has become a defining and persistent feature of contemporary American politics in general and defense politics in particular.

In the 1970s, as during other periods of the nation's history, politicians viewed the issue of defense spending against a larger political canvas. Elected officials tried to protect and promote the interests of the districts and states that they represented. The ways in which political representatives understood local interests, however, was more subtle and nuanced than most analysts of defense policy assumed. The traditional approach was to examine the politics of defense spending within the framework of the "pork barrel," or "distributive politics" model, searching for a connection between congressional votes on defense spending and the geographic distribution of military contracts, bases, and payrolls.[18] Finding no direct or enduring connection, many concluded that politicians' views on matters of national defense had very little to do with whether (or how much) their constituents benefited from military spending. Such conclusions were not unique to the 1970s. Similar judgments were reached by analysts studying the politics of defense spending during the Reagan build-up of the 1980s.[19]

Upon further inspection, the conventional approach to thinking about the relationship between local interests and defense policy turns out to be far too crude. Who supports and who opposes military spending depends on more than how military goods are allocated. It depends on politicians' judgments about the net benefits of those budgetary allocations for their constituencies. For politicians, the real issue is how decisions over the nation's spending priorities are likely to affect the economic fortunes of the districts and states they represent. When thinking about defense policy, politicians face difficult political trade-offs. They weigh the economic benefits of federal military spending against opportunity costs.[20] In the 1970s and 1980s those trade-offs were defined in terms of "guns versus butter." The choices of elected representatives were shaped by regional variations in the sensitivity of local labor markets to military spending, the degree to which their localities depended on federally funded social services, and the extent to which sustaining economic growth hinged on maintaining international economic competitiveness. These factors determined what, and how much, their states stood to gain or lose from military spending. This is the political/economic context within which electorally oriented politicians weigh the benefits and costs of defense policies.

Similar calculations will shape the debate over defense cuts in the 1990s. The collapse of communism and the end of the cold war mean that the defense budget will be reduced over the next five years. This much is certain. What is less clear is how deep and rapid those cutbacks will be, and how the savings will be allocated. The situation is complicated by the 1990 Budget Act, which prevents members of Congress from using money cut from the Pentagon's budget to fund various domestic programs.[21] The budget act has thus far prevented such transfers in federal budgetary resources. But it has not stopped legislators from targeting the defense budget for further reductions or from seeking ways to provide more funds for domestic programs.[22] The pressure will intensify in 1993 when the 1990 budget agreement expires. If the past is any guide to the future, regional considerations will loom large in debates over the defense budget.

The Debate over the Peace Dividend

An examination of roll-call voting in the House of Representatives demonstrates the importance of regional considerations. Figure 4-1 is based on voting behavior in the 101st Congress (1989-1991). The figure was derived using multidimensional scaling. This method has proven to be particularly useful in analyzing legislative voting patterns.[23] This, the simplest nonmetric version of the scaling technique, provides a spatial display of the voting alignments among congressional delegations. The goal of this technique is to describe the empirical relationships between some set of objects (here, congressional delegations). The states (that is, congressional delegations) are represented as points, and the distance between points is an analog for the voting similarity among pairs of state delegations. Those House delegations that agree most often in voting on national security issues are closest to each other in the figure. Those that disagree most often are farthest apart in the figure.

The analysis is based on roll-call votes that were defined as "key" votes by organizations that monitor political activity in Congress on a regular basis. These organizations include Americans for Democratic Action, American Conservative Union, and *National Journal.* Each group publishes annually a list of congressional votes on important national issues, foreign as well as domestic. These votes constitute a test of legislators' policy preferences, and the political significance of "key" votes is unlikely to be lost on elected officials. Only those votes concerning military procurement and construction, defense research and development, and military operations and maintenance were selected for this analysis.[24]

The votes were used to construct a measure of voting similarity among congressional delegations. Each state delegation's position on a vote was based on how a majority of the delegation's members voted on the issue.[25] The voting similarity score measures the percentage of agreement (or disagreement) between each pair of state delegations over all of the key defense policy votes during the 101st Congress. The score is one hundred when there is agreement on all key votes between the majority position of two state delegations; it is zero if there is disagreement on all key votes. Following convention, paired votes and announced positions were treated as formal votes.

The voting similarity scores of congressional delegations were then submitted to the multidimensional scaling program ALSCAL. In ALSCAL the quality of a solution is defined by R^2, which measures the degree to which the configuration reproduces accurately the empirical relationships present in the data. In principle, a scaling solution can be derived in any number of dimensions, and R^2 will be higher as the number of dimensions increases. Since this technique works in a space of fixed dimensions, it is necessary to determine the most appropriate number of dimensions, recognizing that

Figure 4-1   Spatial Analysis of Defense Votes

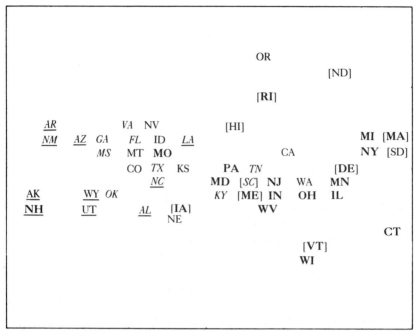

Source: Based on roll-call votes in U.S. Congress.
Notes: States in the Northeast are bold, states in the South are italic, and those in the West are in regular typeface. Underlined states strongly supported SDI. Bracketed states strongly opposed SDI.

there is a trade-off between the quality of the fit (high R^2) and parsimony (a small number of dimensions). ALSCAL also produces an alternative "bad-ness of fit" function, known as STRESS, which is presented below along with R^2.

The results of the scaling analysis are summarized in Table 4-1. Con-figurations were generated in one, two, and three dimensions. The two-dimensional configuration was selected as the best representation of the voting alignment over defense policy. It accounts for 97 percent of the vari-ance in the roll-call data. Adding a third dimension improves the quality of the fit by only 1 percent. The one-dimensional configuration would be ade-quate on the basis of R^2, but there is no particular advantage in restricting the figure to a single dimension. For these reasons, and because voting alignments are easier to visualize and interpret in a plane, the two-dimen-sional solution is presented in Figure 4-1.

An examination of the voting pattern in Figure 4-1 reveals two things. First, a large proportion of the state delegations cluster at opposite ends of the horizontal axis. Again, those state delegations that agree most often in

Table 4-1   Summary of Multidimensional Scaling Solutions

Dimensions	R²	STRESS
1	.909	.175
2	.959	.105
3	.972	.081

voting on defense spending are closest together in the figure. Second, it is apparent that the pattern of interstate alignment is regional in nature. States from the Northeast tend to cluster on the right side of the voting space; most of those from the South align on the left side of the configuration. By contrast, the pattern of voting among states from the West is more mixed. Some align with the Northeast, others with the South.

A number of methods may be used to assess the policy orientation of these two voting blocs. For present purposes, an index measuring each state delegation's support for the Strategic Defense Initiative (SDI) in the 101st Congress was computed.[26] A vote on SDI funding was used to determine how strongly a state delegation supports or opposes defense spending. The ten delegations that offered the strongest support for SDI are underlined in Figure 4-1. The ten that most strongly opposed the high-tech initiative are in brackets. It is evident that support for defense spending is stronger in the South than it is in the Northeast.

The analysis confirms that there is little consensus over American defense policy. At the same time, the scaling analysis raises questions about the underlying sources of conflict. At one level, the current debate may be seen as a debate over military priorities: nuclear versus conventional forces, weapons versus personnel, research and development versus operations and maintenance. It is true that the strategic situation facing the country today is dramatically different than it was only a few years ago, and there is a considerable uncertainty about what type of threat to plan against in the future. The alignment pattern in the 101st Congress, however, suggests that representatives from the Northeast tend to resolve this uncertainty in ways that differ systematically from the choices of their colleagues in the South. To explain why this is so, it is necessary to understand the current debate over America's defense needs as part of a wider debate over the nation's priorities in the post-cold-war world. The conflicts over funding levels for specific programs (such as the MX missile, the Strategic Defense Initiative, and the B-2 bomber) are part of a larger political struggle over how America should spend its money in a changed world.

The fault lines of this political debate—both in policy terms and in terms of regional competition—are already evident. Politicians on both sides of the debate (and on both sides of the regional divide) justify their positions in domestic, economic terms. At the heart of this debate is how the peace dividend should be used to promote economic growth: Should the peace dividend be channeled into public investment, or should it be used to spur private consumption?[27] On one side are politicians from the Northeast, mostly Democrats, who favor large-scale reductions in the Pentagon's budget and using the savings to revitalize the nation's industrial base and urban infrastructure.[28] They define the primary threat to America in economic, as opposed to military, terms and emphasize the need to restore American competitiveness in the world economy. Leaders of the Democratic party argue that federal spending on social services, job retraining, urban infrastructure, and the like will increase productivity in the private sector, producing higher levels of economic growth and larger federal revenues that could be used to reduce the federal budget deficit over the longer haul.

On the other side are those from the South who favor a more gradual, limited, and planned reduction of American military power, one that will not eviscerate the nation's military-industrial base and jeopardize its long-term ability to mobilize quickly and project military power abroad. Whatever savings the nation might derive from cutting the defense budget should, they argue, be used to reduce the federal deficit or cut personal income taxes, rather than to fund domestic programs. The members of this coalition are mostly Republican. In contrast to their Democratic colleagues, they argue that cutting the budget deficit or personal taxes is the most efficient and direct route to higher rates of economic productivity. Immediate deficit reduction, it is argued, will increase national savings, mobilizing capital which is then available for private investment in productive assets, rather than public investment in essentially redistributive programs (health care, housing, job retraining) and in public goods like roads, bridges, and railroads. Meanwhile, cuts in the marginal tax rate could enhance incentives for work, saving, and entrepreneurship.

These issues are not new. They map onto deep divisions that separate the Rust Belt and Sun Belt. Since the 1970s politicians from the nation's older industrial and urban centers in the Northeast have attempted repeatedly to reduce the competitive advantages that many parts of the South and West have enjoyed (including lower state and local taxes, cheaper real estate, and lower wage rates). There has been no shortage of attempts by politicians and interest groups from the Northeast to use the federal government to retard the shift of population and economic activity to areas outside the Manufacturing Belt. Strategies employed range from proposals to reduce disparities in energy costs that worked to the disadvantage of states in the Northeast, to efforts to end right-to-work laws that allegedly contributed to economic decline in the Manufacturing Belt, to efforts to reduce the defense budget and increase federal spending for the nation's oldest cities.[29] Political opposition to such policy initiatives has been strongest in the South and, in the case of energy, the West.

The fate of the peace dividend will be determined in this political context. Debates over the taxing, spending, and investment powers of the federal government are highly partisan, but as Figure 4-2 suggests, they are shaped by conflicting regional imperatives. The figure presents a scatterplot of the relationship between House voting on defense policy issues and domestic economic policy issues (for example, deficit reduction, minimum wage laws, taxes on capital gains, and social welfare spending) in the 101st Congress (1989-1991). The same method that was used to select votes and construct a measure of voting similarity among state delegations on the nation's defense needs was used to produce a measure of voting similarity on domestic economic priorities.[30]

Each point in the figure represents the position of a given state delegation in these two scalings. For most of the state delegations there is a strong linear relationship between their positions on defense and economic policy. States (that is, congressional delegations) that favor reductions in defense spending also support greater domestic spending.[31] Put another way, political support for "reorienting" federal spending away from the Pentagon to domestic programs is strongest in the Northeast. It is weakest in the South. The same regional cleavage underlying the debate over America's defense needs surfaces when legislators vote on important domestic economic issues. The political imperatives shaping the debate over the requirements of national defense are also driving conflicts over how to promote economic productivity and restore American competitiveness in the international economy.

Conclusion

The end of the cold war has raised difficult questions about America's priorities at home and abroad. There is little consensus over how to "reduce" the nation's military establishment. A major reason for this is that different parts of the country have different stakes in how the savings should be allocated. In the short term, the debate is likely to focus largely on which areas of the defense budget are most expendable and how to cushion the blow that many localities and companies will experience. There is no shortage of calls for federal assistance in promoting "military conversion," and as last year's debate over the Seawolf submarine suggests, the politics of the conversion debate are fluid and cross regional and party lines. The debate is likely to broaden and intensify as it becomes possible to transfer funds from the defense budget directly to domestic programs and as President Clinton confronts the task of making good on his campaign pledge to "invest" in the American economy.

Figure 4-2   Domestic Economic Policy Alignment Versus National
              Security Policy Alignment

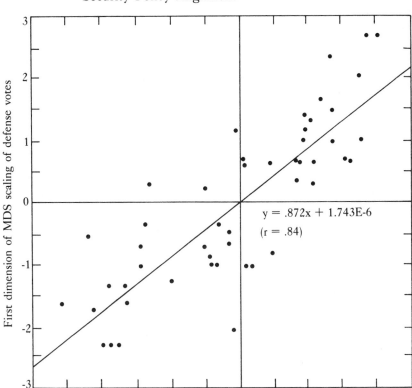

$$y = .872x + 1.743E\text{-}6$$
$$(r = .84)$$

First dimension of MDS scaling of domestic votes

The political cleavages already present are likely to deepen during the
Clinton years. Politicians from the Northeast will lead the way in efforts to cut
the defense budget and reorient federal spending toward domestic programs.
Opposition will be stiffest in the South. The recent attempt by the former
chairman of the House Armed Services Committee, Les Aspin, to shift Pentagon funds to aid American cities in the wake of the Los Angeles riots probably
is a harbinger of things to come.[32] Like the debate over the military buildup in
the 1980s, the debate over the military cutbacks in the 1990s will be framed
in "guns versus butter" terms. The debates over the cutbacks will be shaped
less by the abstract merits of various proposals for downsizing and diversifying
the country's military-industrial base than by political competition for regional
and partisan advantage, just as they were in the past. It's déjà vu.
    Proposals to slash the Pentagon's budget are part and parcel of a longer-
term political strategy to redefine the nation's priorities and to redistribute

federal revenues and income. This is what the commotion over the peace dividend is all about. The outcome is likely to turn on a larger set of issues concerning the national economy and how to restore economic productivity and competitiveness. There is more than one way to address these issues, and the political stakes are high. As always, politicians from regions of the country with different economic bases, different markets, and differing claims on the federal budget will find themselves on opposing sides of the debate.

Notes

1. I wish to thank Catherine Boone, Aaron Friedberg, Timothy McKeown, and Joseph Nye for their comments and suggestions. This study was completed while I was a research fellow at the Center for International Studies at Princeton University. The roll-call data were provided by the Inter-University Consortium for Political and Social Research. An earlier version of this chapter was presented at the 1992 annual meeting of the American Political Science Association, Chicago, Illinois, September 3-6.
2. Northeast refers to states in New England, the Middle Atlantic, and the Midwest: Connecticut, Delaware, Illinois, Indiana, Iowa, Maine, Maryland, Massachusetts, Michigan, Minnesota, Missouri, New Hampshire, New Jersey, New York, Ohio, Pennsylvania, Rhode Island, Vermont, West Virginia, and Wisconsin. The South includes states from the Southeast and Southwest: Alabama, Arizona, Arkansas, Florida, Georgia, Kentucky, Louisiana, Mississippi, New Mexico, North Carolina, Oklahoma, South Carolina, Tennessee, Texas, and Virginia. The West refers to states from the Great Plains, Mountain West, and Pacific Coast: Alaska, California, Colorado, Hawaii, Idaho, Kansas, Montana, Oregon, Nebraska, Nevada, North Dakota, South Dakota, Utah, Washington, and Wyoming.
3. Frederick Jackson Turner, "Section and Nation," *Yale Review* 12 (October 1922): 1-21.
4. See John Agnew, *The United States in the World-Economy: A Regional Geography* (Cambridge: Cambridge University Press, 1987); Ann Markusen, *Regions: The Economics and Politics of Territory* (Totowa, N.J.: Rowman and Littlefield, 1987); Richard Bensel, *Sectionalism and American Political Development, 1880-1980* (Madison, Wis.: University of Wisconsin Press, 1984); J. Clark Archer and Peter J. Taylor, *Section and Party: A Political Geography of American Presidential Elections* (New York: John Wiley and Sons, 1981).
5. See, for example, Michael J. Healey and Brian W. Ilbery, *Location and Change: Perspectives on Economic Geography* (Oxford: Oxford University Press, 1990), 45-68. The classic application of this approach to the United States is Douglas C. North, *The Economic Growth of the United States, 1790-1860* (Englewood Cliffs, N.J.: Prentice-Hall, 1961).
6. On the regional consequences of technological innovation see Michael Storper and Richard Walker, *The Capitalist Imperative: Territory, Technology, and Industrial Growth* (Oxford: Basil Blackwell, 1989); and John Rees and Howard Stafford, "Theories of Regional Growth and Industrial Location: Their Relevance for Understanding High-Technology Complexes," in *Technology, Regions and Policy*, ed. J. Rees and H. Stafford (Totowa, N.J.: Rowan and Littlefield, 1986), 23-50. On the role of labor markets see Doreen Massey, *Spatial Divisions of Labor: Social Production and the Geography of Production* (New York: Methuen, 1984).
7. There is a growing body of work on the international sources of regional growth and decline. A review of the issues and literature can be found in Iain Wallace, *The Global Economic System* (London: Unwin Hyman, 1990). For a recent application of this

approach to the United States, see John Agnew, *The United States in the World-Economy.*

8. On the importance of the state in analyzing regional development see, for example, Robert J. Johnston, "The State, Political Geography, and Geography," in *New Models in Geography,* Vol. 1, ed. R. Peet and N. Thrift (London: Unwin Hyman, 1989), 292-309; and Robert Sack, "Territorial Bases of Power," in *Political Studies for Spatial Perspectives,* ed. A. Burnett and P. Taylor (New York: John Wiley and Sons, 1981). For a discussion of the role of the state in the American context, see Ann Markusen, *Regions,* 32-39, and Norman J. Glickman, *The Urban Impacts of Federal Policies* (Baltimore: Johns Hopkins University Press, 1980).

9. Three examples include Wassily Leontieff, Alison Morgan, Karen Polenske, David Simpson, and Edward Tower, "The Economic Impact—Industrial and Regional—of an Arms Cut," *Review of Economics and Statistics* 47 (1965): 217-241; Murray L. Weidenbaum, *The Economics of Peacetime Defense* (New York: Praeger, 1974); Roger Bolton, *Defense Purchases and Regional Growth* (Washington, D.C.: Brookings Institution, 1966). For more recent studies on this subject see Ann Markusen, Peter Hall, Scott Campbell, and Sabina Deitrick, *The Rise of the Gunbelt: The Military Remapping of Industrial America* (New York: Oxford University Press, 1991); Edward J. Malecki and Lois M. Stark, "Regional and Industrial Variation in Defense Spending: Some American Evidence," in *Defense Expenditure and Regional Development,* ed M. Breheny (New York: Mansell Publishing Ltd., 1988), 67-101; Breandan O'hUallachain, "Regional and Technological Implications of the Recent Buildup in American Defense Spending," *Annals of the Association of American Geographers* 77 (1987): 208-223; and John Rees, "The Impact of Defense Spending on Regional Industrial Change in the United States," in *Federalism and Regional Development,* ed. G. Hoffman (Austin, Texas: University of Texas Press, 1981).

10. See Richard Bensel, *Sectionalism and American Political Development,* 256-316; *Regional Growth: Historic Perspective* (Washington D.C.: Advisory Commission on Intergovernmental Relations, 1980), 1-8; Robert Dilger, *The Sunbelt/Snowbelt Controversy: The War Over Federal Funds* (New York: New York University Press, 1982); and Ann Markusen, *Regions,* 158-192.

11. Robert Reinhold, "Sunbelt Region Leads Nation in Growth of Population: Section's Cities Top Urban Expansion," *New York Times,* February 8, 1976, 1, 42; Wayne King, "Federal Funds Pour Into Sunbelt States," *New York Times,* February 9, 1976, 24; Roy Reed, "Sunbelt Still Stronghold of Conservatism in U.S.," *New York Times,* February 11, 1976, 1, 11; B. Drummond Ayres, Jr., "Developing Sunbelt Hopes to Avoid North's Mistakes," *New York Times,* February 12, 1976, 1, 24.

12. "The Second War Between the States," *Business Week,* May 17, 1976, 92-113.

13. Joel Havemann, Rochelle Stanfield, and Neil Pierce, "Federal Spending: The Northeast's Loss is the Sunbelt's Gain," *National Journal,* June 26, 1976, 878-891.

14. James R. Anderson, "The State and Regional Impact of the Military Budget," printed in the *Congressional Record,* 94th Cong., 2d sess., July 28, 1976, 24274. Not surprisingly, these estimates were quite controversial. Some members charged that the estimates were based on spurious assumptions about the impact of federal spending. Most members from the Northeast and Midwest believed that the regional imbalances were actually starker than this study indicated. See Bensel, *Sectionalism and American Political Development,* 467, note 30.

15. Asked about a particular case of regional bias in defense spending, the Speaker of the House of Representatives, Thomas "Tip" O'Neill of Massachusetts, claimed that it was "a political vendetta by the Nixon Administration, no question about it. We lost all these shipyards because Nixon hated the Northeast, he hated Massachusetts. There's no question about that." Quoted in Martin Nolan, "The Northeast—Our New Appalachia?" *Boston Globe,* July 11, 1976.

16. On the regional divisions within the Democratic party see James L. Sundquist, *Dynamics of the Party System: Alignment and Realignment of Political Parties in the United States* (Washington, D.C.: Brookings Institution, 1983); and Earle and Merle Black, *Politics and Society in the South* (Cambridge, Mass.: Harvard University Press, 1987). The impact of liberal Democrats on the party's national agenda is examined in Steven M. Gillon, *Politics and Vision: The ADA and American Liberalism 1947-1985* (Oxford: Oxford University Press, 1987).

17. For accounts about the changing regional composition of the Republican party see Jerome L. Himmelstein, *To the Right: The Transformation of American Conservatism* (Berkeley: University of California Press, 1990); Nicol C. Rae, *The Decline of the Liberal Republicans from 1952 to the Present* (Oxford: Oxford University Press, 1989); David W. Reinhard, *The Republican Right Since 1945* (Lexington, Ky.: University Press of Kentucky, 1983).

18. There is a large literature on this subject. Several studies carried out during the 1970s include Robert A. Bernstein and William A. Anthony, "The ABM Issue in the Senate, 1968-1970: The Importance of Ideology," *American Political Science Review* 68 (1974): 1198-1206; James Clotfelter, "Senate Voting and Constituency Stake in Defense Spending," *Journal of Politics* 32 (1970): 979-983; Wayne Moyer, "House Voting on Defense: An Ideological Explanation," in *Armed Forces in American Society*, ed. B. Russett and A. Stepan (New York: Harper and Row, 1973), 106-141; Bruce Russett, *What Price Vigilance?* (New Haven: Yale University Press, 1970); and Barry S. Rundquist, "On Testing a Military Industrial Complex Theory," *American Politics Quarterly* 6 (1978): 29-53.

19. See, for example, James M. Lindsay, "Parochialism, Policy, and Constituency Constraints: Congressional Voting on Strategic Weapons Systems," *American Journal of Political Science* 34 (1990): 936-960; Ralph G. Carter, "Senate Defense Budgeting, 1981-1988: The Impacts of Ideology, Party, and Constituency Benefit on the Decision to Support the President," *American Politics Quarterly* 17 (1989): 332-347; and Richard Fleisher, "Economic Benefit, Ideology, and Senate Voting on the B-1 Bomber," *American Politics Quarterly* 13 (1985): 200-211.

20. For a more detailed discussion of these political trade-offs and their impact on congressional voting on defense policy, see Peter Trubowitz and Brian E. Roberts, "Regional Interests and the Reagan Military Buildup," *Regional Studies* 26 (1992): 555-567.

21. The Omnibus Budget Reconciliation Act of 1990 set caps on discretionary spending for defense, foreign aid, and domestic programs. Under the Budget Enforcement Act, a key provision of the budget agreement, money cut from defense can go to deficit reduction but cannot be shifted to foreign aid or domestic programs because those categories would then exceed their caps. Although the Budget Enforcement Act contains overall deficit targets that extend through 1995, these targets are adjustable after 1993 and can be met, at least in theory, without allocating specific portions of those totals for national defense, foreign assistance, and domestic programs.

22. A recent example was Sen. Tom Harkin's (D-Iowa) amendment to the fiscal 1992 Labor-HHS-Education appropriations bill (HR 2707). The Harkin amendment would have shifted $3.15 billion from the Pentagon's budget to ten popular programs, such as Pell grants and Head Start, funded by the departments of Labor and Health and Human Services. The amendment failed by a 28-69 vote on the Senate floor. See Pat Towell and George Hager, "Soviet Union's Disintegration Spurs Call for Defense Cuts," *Congressional Quarterly Weekly Report*, September 14, 1991, 2631-2634.

23. See, for example, Douglas V. Easterling, "Political Science: Using the General Euclidean Model to Study Ideological Shifts in the U.S. Senate," in *Multidimensional Scaling: History, Theory, and Applications*, ed. F. Young and R. Hamer (London: Law-

rence Erlbaum Associates, 1987), 221-526; James F. Hoadley, "The Emergence of Political Parties in Congress, 1789-1803," *American Political Science Review* 74 (1980): 757-779; George B. Rabinowitz, "An Introduction to Nonmetric Multidimensional Scaling," *American Journal of Political Science* 19 (1975): 343-390.

24. Following are the key national security votes in the House of Representatives, 101st Congress.

Date	Subject
7/25/89	Kyl (R-Ariz.) amendment to increase funds for SDI program
7/25/89	Dellums (D-Calif.) amendment to cut funds for SDI program
7/25/89	Bennett (D-Fla.) amendment to cut funds for SDI program
7/25/89	Dellums (D-Calif.) amendment to delete funds for Lance missile
7/25/89	Dickinson (R-Ala.) amendment to restore Bush defense budget
7/26/89	Kasich (R-Ohio) amendment to delay production of B-2 bombers
7/26/89	Synar (D-Okla.) amendment to cut funds for B-2 bomber
7/26/89	Hertel (D-Mich.) amendment barring funds for MX rail-garrison
7/26/89	Spratt (D-S.C.) amendment to cut funds for MX missile
7/27/89	Owens (D-Utah) amendment to delete funds for binary weapons
9/18/90	Dornan (R-Calif.) amendment to increase funds for SDI program
9/18/90	Dellums (D-Calif.) amendment limiting SDI funds to research
9/18/90	Kyl (R-Ariz.) amendment to increase funds for SDI program
9/18/90	Bennett (D-Fla.) amendment to cut funds for SDI program
9/18/90	Frank (D-Mass.) amendment to cut funds for mobile missile

25. The vertical and horizontal dimensions in Figure 4-1 are not labeled and are not interpreted here in terms of two linear dimensions. While dimensional structure is often emphasized, it is equally valid to focus on the clustering pattern in the figure.

26. The state scores are based on the Bennett (D-Fla.) amendment of July 25, 1989, to reduce spending for the Strategic Defense Initiative.

27. For a general discussion of these competing approaches see the recent study by the Congressional Budget Office, *The Economic Effects of Reduced Defense Spending*, February 1992, 5-20.

28. A number of journalists have summarized the broad outlines of this debate. See, for example, Gerald F. Seib, "Conservatives Argue over Best Ways to Spend a Peace Dividend, and Whether There is One," *Wall Street Journal,* January 31, 1990, 18; David C. Morrison, "Sizing Up That 'Peace Dividend,' " *National Journal,* January 1, 1990, 24-26; David E. Rosenbaum, "Two Senators Say Peace Bonus Should Pay for Social Needs," *New York Times,* April 14, 1990, 8; David E. Rosenbaum, "Pentagon Savings Unlikely to Be Spent Elsewhere," *New York Times,* November 22, 1989, 14. The debate over the defense budget during the 101st Congress is also discussed in Daniel Wirls, *Buildup: The Politics of Defense in the Reagan Era* (Ithaca, N.Y.: Cornell University Press, 1992), 212-223.

29. For an excellent analysis of these strategies see Richard Bensel, *Sectionalism and American Political Development*, 256-316.

30. Following are the key domestic economic votes in the House of Representatives, 101st Congress.

Date	Subject
3/23/89	Goodling (R-Pa.) amendment to revise minimum wage bill
5/04/89	Kasich (R-Ohio) amendment to freeze discretionary spending
5/24/89	To approve supplemental appropriations for fiscal 1989
6/14/89	To pass minimum wage increase over president's veto
7/20/89	Bartlett (R-Texas) amendment to transfer HUD funds

7/27/89	Murphy (D-Pa.) amendment to revise Davis-Bacon Act ceiling
9/28/89	Rostenkowski (D-Ill.) amendment to delete capital gains cut
10/05/89	Edwards (R-Okla.) amendment to delete child care program
10/05/89	Stenholm (D-Texas) amendment to strike child care program
3/29/90	Stenholm (D-Texas) amendment to cut funds for child care plan
4/26/90	Kasich (R-Ohio) amendment to freeze federal spending
5/01/90	Dellums (D-Calif.) amendment to approve Black Caucus budget
6/07/90	To override president's veto of an Amtrak subsidy bill
7/17/90	To pass constitutional amendment requiring balanced budget
10/05/90	To adopt conference report on federal budget for 1991-1995
10/07/90	Michel (R-Ill.) amendment for an across-the-board budget cut
10/16/90	Rostenkowski (D-Ill.) amendment to increase taxes on wealthy
10/26/90	To approve the Omnibus Budget Reconciliation Act of 1990

31. Figure 4-3, below, was derived using "key" roll-call votes on domestic economic policy. The votes included in the analysis are listed in note 30. State delegations from the Northeast are in bold typeface. States from the South are in italics. States from the West are in regular typeface. To provide a substantive measure of policy orientation of the state delegations, the ten delegations that offered the strongest support for

Figure 4-3   Spatial Analysis of Domestic Votes

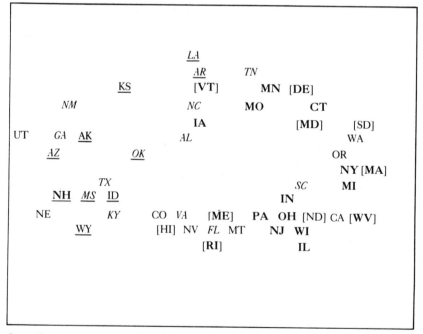

Source: Based on roll-call votes in U.S. Congress.

cuts in Head Start in the 101st Congress are underlined. The ten delegations that most strongly opposed such cuts are in brackets. These designations are based on the October 5, 1989, Stenholm (D-Texas) amendment to the Budget Reconciliation Act.

32. See Pat Towell, "Aspin Urges Shifting $7 Billion from Pentagon to Cities," *Congressional Quarterly Weekly Report,* May 16, 1992, 1361-1364.

5

Regional Effects of Defense Cutbacks

John E. Lynch and Billy R. Dickens

Today's declining defense spending involves a potentially divisive debate over its regional impact. In part, this regional debate is exacerbated by the uncertainty of the current national recession. More importantly, there is a general lack of public awareness as to which military bases and which weapons procurement programs are likely to be affected as the defense budget is reduced.

Any analysis of the regional impact of reduced defense spending must be tempered by the realization that "meaningful statistical data on the defense industry and its products are virtually impossible to secure"— especially on the DoD subcontractor and interindustry-supplier networks.[1]

In contrast to earlier periods of defense cutbacks, however, there is far greater public information available today on the internal DoD basing structure and DoD procurement programs. These additional public data also identify the likely incremental effects of reduced defense spending on specific regions and communities across the nation. The purpose of this chapter is to identify the potential regional effects of the announced reductions in defense programs and force structure through 1997.

Defense cutbacks do not occur evenly or proportionately throughout the economy. In this regard, a region's defense dependency is an early warning sign but not a certain indicator of future defense reductions.

Though the expected steady decline in defense spending should not be harmful in macroeconomic terms, it can be devastating locally. The policy problem, then, lies in not overreacting at the federal level, but nonetheless in finding the set of job-creation policies and regional development mechanisms that can help hard-hit communities deal with the defense downturn.

John E. Lynch serves as vice chairman of the Fairfax County (Virginia) Economic Development Authority; formerly, he was associate director of economic adjustment with the Office of the Secretary of Defense. Billy R. Dickens is visiting professor of economics at Bowie State College.

To clarify the debate over the effect of reduced defense spending from the late-1980s through the 1997 planning levels, it is important to review the economy's adjustments to previous defense cutbacks.

Experience from World War II to the Vietnam War

The World War II reconversion process saw the demobilization of more than 9.8 million men and women from the armed forces by 1946-1947. GNP declined only slightly in 1946 before resuming its strong growth in 1947 and 1948. Unemployment rose from 1.2 percent in 1944 to 3.9 percent in 1947, which was well below the prewar experience for the economy.

Early transition planning began with the enactment in 1944 of the War Mobilization and Reconversion Act and the Servicemen's Readjustment Act (better known as the GI Bill). Some individual industries—such as aircraft and shipbuilding—experienced difficult transition periods, but the economy did not revert to its prewar slump. Pent-up personal and corporate savings— together with low interest rates—encouraged consumer confidence and new plant expansions. Many older workers and women left the work force. Further, by 1947, more than 1,120,000 veterans had enrolled in college.[2]

During the Korean War buildup, defense spending rose from $14.1 billion in 1950 to $48.7 billion in 1953. Unlike World War II, defense spending declined only modestly after the war; it declined to $38 billion by 1956 and then remained relatively stable in real terms until the Vietnam War. The Eisenhower administration initiated no new fiscal or monetary transition programs, but the unemployment rate reached only 5.4 percent during the brief recessionary period in 1954. The post-Korean War reductions might have been more severe had several major aircraft and electronics firms not diversified into such civilian markets as commercial aircraft, industrial controls, small gas turbines, and heavy construction vehicles.[3]

The Vietnam War was one of the few conflicts in which an adjustment plan was available at the beginning of the conflict, in 1965, and during its latter stages in 1969, but these plans were largely ignored.[4] The Vietnam cutbacks from 1968 to 1972 were fairly gradual in dollar terms, from $77 billion to $73 billion. When adjusted for the average 7.4 percent inflation rate, however, they were significant—especially in the procurement of conventional equipment (aircraft engines, tank-automotive equipment, weapons, ammunition, and other conventional armaments). The impact on the nation's Industrial Belt, from the Eastern Seaboard to the Midwest, could have been anticipated, but the Nixon administration did not adopt any offsetting macroeconomic stimulus program. The administration, however, did create the interagency Economic Adjustment Committee for addressing the specific adjustment needs of communities and workers.

After Vietnam, nearly 1.3 million defense-related industrial jobs were lost, with a particularly heavy concentration in Connecticut, Massachusetts, New Jersey, New York, Pennsylvania, Ohio, and Missouri as well as in the aerospace industry in southern California, Seattle, and Florida. Job expansions and subsequent contractions were found to be especially acute in the cities of Cleveland, Chicago, Minneapolis, and in the Dallas-Fort Worth area.[5]

The Vietnam War cutbacks coincided with the 1970-1971 reduction in the NASA Apollo program, the cancellation of the Supersonic Transport Program, and a sharp decline in the civilian aerospace market. The small business community experienced particularly severe shocks; its share of defense prime and subcontract awards declined from 33 percent in 1967 to 24.1 percent by 1972. This effect on secondary and tertiary subcontractors was especially evident in Bridgeport, Seattle, and Wichita. As a result of the defense reductions and the soft overall economy, unemployment rose from 3.5 percent in 1968 to 5.9 percent by 1971.

The reduction in defense spending in real terms amounted to less than 1.6 percent of GNP. But without any special monetary or fiscal programs to offset the cuts in military spending, the resulting loss in potential GNP was far more serious than the World War II or the Korean War adjustment experiences.[6] The expected Vietnam War "peace dividend" failed to materialize, and there were limited budget resources available for civilian needs.

Current Defense Cutbacks

As highlighted in Table 5-1, defense budget authority in current dollars has remained fairly constant since 1987-1990, but in real terms (constant FY93 dollars) there has already been an overall downward trend in defense resources and personnel staffing levels, which will continue through 1997.

The FY93 DoD budget was the first submitted following the abrupt collapse of the Soviet threat and coincided with continued realignment in Eastern Europe. The reductions proposed by then secretary of defense Dick Cheney through 1995 were substantial: a one-third cut in Army divisions, from 18 to 12; the downsizing of the Air Force from 36 fighter wing equivalents to 26; and a reduction in active Navy ships from 546 to 451.

Secretary Cheney also announced cancellation of over one hundred weapon programs, including the Apache helicopter; the M-1 tank; the Trident submarine; the F-14D and F-15 fighters; the F-16 aircraft; the Naval Advanced Tactical Fighter; the A-12 (previously curtailed) and the Air Force Advanced Tactical Aircraft; and the Peacekeeper missile. The new DoD budget also reflected President Bush's nuclear initiative of September 27, 1991, with the cancellation of the Midgetman ICBM program,

Table 5-1   National Defense Budgets and Personnel Levels

	1987	1990	1993[a]	1997
National defense (current $, billion)	287.4	301.3	275.0	290.6
National defense (cons. FY93 $, billion)	369.0	335.6	275.0	251.3
Outlays as percent of GNP (%)	6.4	5.5	4.5	3.4
Military personnel (millions)	2.174	2.070	1.767	1.626
Civilian personnel (millions)	1.133	1.101	.958	.904
Defense industry employment (millions)	3.365	3.150	2.645	2.290
Total defense employment (millions)	6.672	6.321	5.144	4.810

Source: DoD Press Release No. 26-92, "DoD to Slow Pace of Modernization, Cut Strategic Nuclear Arsenal While Maintaining Essential Forces," January 29, 1992; Steven Kosiak and Paul Taibl, *Analysis of the FY93 Defense Budget Request* (Washington, D.C.: Defense Budget Project, March 1992).

[a] Figures for 1993 reflect the 1993 appropriation process.

the proposed elimination of 50 multiple-warhead Peacekeeper missiles, and the "deMIRVing" of 500 Minuteman ICBMs to a single warhead configuration.[7]

The secretary also enunciated new "acquisition approaches" for ten major weapons systems, including a twenty-aircraft limitation on the B-2 bomber program and the curtailment of the Seawolf submarine program after completion of the one boat already under construction. (See Table 5-2.) These cutbacks involved $8 billion in current savings and a cumulative savings of $42 billion, but they set off a strong political debate in Congress. The acquisition deferrals, like the Comanche helicopter, will reduce future jobs. Seventeen other programs were to be terminated at a total savings of $7.3 billion.[8] These reductions are summarized in Table 5-3.

The reductions in weapon systems (such as aircraft, missiles, and ships) offered by the secretary are going to have significant effects upon specific communities with major assembly facilities. In contrast, the regional impacts following the Korean and Vietnam wars were heavily influenced by cutbacks in procurement of armaments, equipment, and munitions.

The 1990 budget agreement, which set separate budget guidelines for defense and domestic programs, has tended to cushion the pressure for cutbacks in select weapon systems. In many instances, such as the case of the Seawolf submarine, which is produced in Connecticut, the fear of job losses is cooling the "ardor to trim the defense budget."[9]

The secretary's 1993 budget was built around a baseline force of approximately 1.6 million active duty military personnel.[10] However, Les Aspin, chairman of the House Armed Services Committee and more recently secretary of defense, suggested an alternative baseline force of 1.4 million military personnel, which was the force level accepted by the Clinton-Gore campaign. During the summer of 1992, budget analysts in the National

Table 5-2   Impact of New Acquisition Approach ($, billions)

	Prior Years	FY1993	Cumulative through 1997
B-2 bomber		−0.6	−14.5
SSN-21 submarine	−3.4	−2.5	−17.5
Comanche helicopter		−0.1	−3.4
SICBM improved guidance	−0.2	−0.6	−1.0
ADATS air defense system		−0.2	−1.7
ACM cruise missile		−0.4	−1,3
FDS mobile sonar			−0.7
AAAM missile		−0.1	−0.6
Block III tank			−0.4
LOSAT missile			−0.9
Total adjustments	−3.6	−4.4	−42.1

Note: Totals may not add due to rounding.

Security Division of the Office of Management and Budget indicated that the 1.4 million force level might be a more realistic baseline force.

Defense spending did not become a major issue in the 1992 campaign. The Clinton-Gore campaign urged a further reduction of $100 billion in defense spending through 1997—involving 75,000 to 100,000 U.S. troops in Europe rather than the 150,000 troops proposed by the Bush administration.[11] Following the election, president-elect Clinton met with Gen. Colin Powell, who accepted the 1.4 million base force level but expressed concern on the rate of personnel reductions.[12]

Regional Analyses of Defense Cutbacks

The track record of regional impact models in assessing reductions in defense spending has been mixed—often because the models confuse regional defense dependency with vulnerability. As a case in point, in 1968 the U.S. Arms Control and Disarmament Agency commissioned an interindustry input-output model to assess the expected regional impact from the Vietnam War cutbacks.[13] Of the ten communities forecasted to receive the most cutbacks, with unemployment above 8.7 percent, only three cities experienced actual unemployment rates higher than the national unemployment rate of 5.9 percent in 1971. The study forecast only nominal job losses for those communities across the Industrial Belt with large armaments and weapons production contracts, but they actually bore the brunt of the Vietnam cutbacks.

One major failing of regional input-output tables is the presumption that all regions will decline in proportion to nationwide procurement cut-

Table 5-3   Program Terminations in FY1993 Budget ($, millions)

	Reductions to FY1992 Budget Level	
	FY1993	FY1993-1997
TOW sight improvement program	−58	−255
LAMP-H landing raft	−11	−98
HARM missile	−71	−511
Supersonic low altitude target	−279	−302
ADCAP propulsion system	−35	−127
SQY-I ASW combat system	−211	−893
MK-50 vertical launch ASROC	−37	−91
SH-2 SLEP	−73	−147
ARS class salvage ship		−334
E-2C early warning aircraft	−444	−444
LSD-41 amphibious ship	−251	−251
Peacekeeper rail garrison[a]	−100	−202
SRAM II strategic missile[a]	−259	−1,218
SRAM-T tactical missile	−107	−441
Mobile small ICBM[a]	−291	−672
Space-based wide area surveillance	−29	−195
KC-135 reengining	−92	−1,128
Total adjustments	−2,348	−7,309

Source: Department of Defense, "Program Acquisition Cost by Weapon System," accompanying the Fiscal Year 1993 Department of Defense budget, January 29, 1992.

[a] Component of the president's nuclear initiative of September 27, 1991.

backs or DoD staffing cutbacks. Another severe handicap is the assumption of stable expenditure patterns over time. Instead, defense cutbacks affect specific procurement programs, selective weapon systems, and individual military bases near specific communities.

By contrast, regional models work fairly well in measuring expansions. The Defense Economic Impact Modeling System (DEIMS) provided a reasonable gauge of the expected industrial and regional allocation of the Reagan defense expansion.[14] The DEIMS model factors the DoD budget by procurement category and allocates growth or reductions across each of the Standard Industrial Classifications according to the national input-output table. The model then distributes the industrial growth by locale proportionate for that specific industry. A similar regional input-output model was used to assess the regional effect from the expansion of the Reagan defense budget in relation to the pending cutbacks in domestic federal programs.[15]

A variety of regional input-output models have been structured for individual communities, beginning with Philadelphia in 1977.[16] The departments of Commerce and Defense have cooperated over the past ten-to-twelve years to adapt the Bureau of Economic Analysis regional models to accommodate the specialized effects of defense budget spending.[17]

Two well-documented analyses of the potential regional impact of the current defense cutback have been prepared by the Office of Economic Adjustment within the Office of the Secretary of Defense and by the Defense Budget Project.[18] At a 4 percent rate of reduction in real defense spending, the DoD study—as summarized in Table 5-4—anticipates job losses averaging 126,000 annually, with major losses in California, Connecticut, Florida, Maryland, Massachusetts, Missouri, New York, Ohio, Texas, and Virginia.

A parallel Defense Budget Project analysis, the results of which are shown in Table 5-5, anticipates an average annual loss of 151,000 defense contractor jobs through 1997.

The Defense Budget Project analysis allocates the employment losses first by type of appropriation, so that states with proportionately higher research and development (Colorado, for instance) experience fewer job losses overall. This analysis includes many of the same states identified in the DoD study as being unusually sensitive to future cutbacks in the defense industry, but also includes Indiana, Arizona, Utah, Rhode Island, and Maine.

Selected Regional Effects

The potential impact of defense reductions is difficult to evaluate. First, the "lack of comprehensive data on subcontracting is [a] major handicap in analyzing the industrial and geographic distribution of DoD and NASA spending." [19] Second, even when the analysis indicates that a specific weapons system production line will be closed, it is difficult to assess the actual economic impact without on-scene investigation, for a variety of reasons:

- The regional economy may be experiencing robust growth, and the defense cutback may be nominal in terms of overall regional job growth. For instance, the current closure of Fort Benjamin Harrison in Indianapolis may have only a nominal effect in relation to the decision of United Airlines to locate its new aircraft overhaul and maintenance facility there as well as the recent decision by the Postal Service to locate its air freight hub at the Indianapolis airport.
- The affected prime contractor may already have other civilian production within the same plant or may have prospects for foreign military sales. For instance, the sale of F-15Es to Saudi Arabia and other potential customers could keep the McDonnell Douglas F-15 production line in St. Louis open beyond September 1993.

Table 5-4   Decreases in Defense-Related Civilian Employment
(thousands)

State	1990 State Employment	Annual Impact of Cutback	
		3% Rate	4% Rate
Alabama	1,778,500	1,474	1,965
Alaska	241,100	342	457
Arizona	1,670,200	2,685	3,580
Arkansas	1,062,900	2 12	282
California	13,827,700	17,604	23,472
Colorado	1,682,300	2,594	3,459
Connecticut	1,696,100	3,353	4,470
Delaware	344,900	65	87
District of Columbia	274,700	1,306	1,742
Florida	6,075,500	3,818	5,090
Georgia	3,056,300	1,411	1,882
Hawaii	525,500	404	538
Idaho	464,700	28	37
Illinois	5,698,800	994	1,325
Indiana	2,678,700	1,338	1,784
Iowa	1,443,300	383	511
Kansas	1,247,400	723	964
Kentucky	1,680,900	323	431
Louisiana	1,780,400	1,125	1,501
Maine	600,500	667	889
Maryland	2,415,900	3,404	4,538
Massachusetts	2,929,800	6,448	8,597
Michigan	4,236,100	1,066	1,422
Minnesota	2,357,800	1,355	1,807
Mississippi	1,092,000	1,071	1,428
Missouri	2,476,400	4,758	6,345
Montana	368,600	51	68
Nebraska	819,400	188	251

- The nominal prime contractor "place of performance" may not be the scene of the actual impact. The end of B-1B bomber production in 1988-1989 and the overall loss of 28,000 B-1B jobs in the Los Angeles basin did not concern North American Rockwell at all because of other aerospace industry growth. However, the company did request assistance in placing the 6,500 affected workers at its Palmdale Plant 42. An intensive worker out-placement program was organized by the Antelope Valley Board of Trade, the State of California, and DoD.[20]
- There are wide variations in the proportion of any weapon system allocated to subcontractors. For some systems, DoD provides the components from a broad range of prime contractors. For instance, in 1988, there were over 300 prime contractors located in thirty-five states for the M-1 tank.

Table 5-4   Continued

| State | 1990 State Employment | Annual Impact of Cutback | |
		3% Rate	4% Rate
Nevada	603,500	143	191
New Hampshire	595,700	302	403
New Jersey	3,847,500	2,826	3,769
New Mexico	661,200	525	700
New York	8,160,900	5,386	7,181
North Carolina	3,232,100	939	1,253
North Dakota	314,700	74	99
Ohio	5,186,700	3,452	4,603
Oklahoma	1,470,000	475	633
Oregon	1,439,300	223	297
Pennsylvania	5,550,500	2,165	2,887
Rhode Island	487,500	438	584
South Carolina	1,640,200	509	679
South Dakota	348,500	26	34
Tennessee	2,289,600	915	1,220
Texas	7,961,100	7,109	9,478
Utah	781,200	722	963
Vermont	293,900	59	78
Virginia	3,103,900	6,223	8,297
Washington	2,350,600	1,890	2,520
West Virginia	703,900	123	164
Wisconsin	2,517,500	734	979
Wyoming	231.900	50	66
TOTAL	118,298,300	94,500	126,000

Source: Joseph V. Cartwright, "Potential Defense Work Force Dislocation and U.S. Defense Budget Cuts: An Illustration" (Washington, D.C.: Department of Defense, March 1991).

- The expected mergers and new partnerships within the defense industry (such as the November 1992 Martin-Marietta purchase of GE Aerospace or General Dynamics' proposed sale of its tank production and advanced fighter activities) will result in corporate restructurings that cannot be anticipated in advance.

In contrast with previous defense cutbacks, however, there is a great deal of public information available on the current long-term reductions. The defense budget for FY93 and its accompanying weapon system annex identify the likely effects, disaggregated by location, on weapon system prime contractors.[21] Additional information is available from *DMS Market Intelligence Reports*, which identify by geographic location the plants of major subcontractors most likely to be affected.

Table 5-5   Employment Effects of the FY93 DoD Budget: FY91 to FY97

State	Base Year 1991	Defense Industry Employment (fiscal years)						
		Impact 1992	Impact 1993	1993 Impact as % of 1991 Employment	Impact 1994	Impact 1995	Impact 1996	Impact 1997	Total Impact 1991 to 1997
District of Columbia	17,817	(284)	(2,357)	−0.93%	(1,253)	(396)	(337)	(313)	(4,940)
Connecticut	99,419	(9,395)	(10,786)	−0.65%	(7,517)	(3,268)	(2,371)	(1,728)	(35,065)
Virginia	155,270	(8,125)	(18,568)	−0.59%	(11,239)	(4,354)	(3,343)	(2,713)	(48,340)
Maryland	87,608	(4,687)	(9,481)	−0.40%	(6,118)	(2,472)	(2,077)	(1,756)	(26,592)
Utah	23,106	(1,069)	(2,920)	−0.38%	(1,690)	(626)	467	(378)	(7,151)
Massachusetts	140,352	(9,392)	(10,832)	−0.37%	(9,041)	(4,762)	(4,170)	(3,448)	(41,646)
Missouri	86,991	(7,732)	(8,831)	−0.35%	(6,360)	(2,658)	(2,190)	(1,752)	(29,522)
Rhode Island	12,859	(823)	(1,521)	−0.32%	(948)	(377)	(281)	(219)	(4,169)
Arizona	54,436	(4,237)	(5,002)	−0.31%	(3,773)	(1,662)	(1,468)	(1,227)	(17,368)
Indiana	68,406	(5,540)	(7,412)	−0.29%	(5,040)	(2,125)	(1,629)	(1,258)	(23,005)
Maine	15,460	(1,070)	(1,701)	−0.29%	(1,118)	(399)	363	(317)	(4,969)
California	569,523	(25,930)	(38,333)	−0.28%	(33,652)	(18,034)	(17,942)	(16,040)	(149,931)
Oklahoma	28,365	(513)	(3,799)	−0.27%	(2,011)	(546)	(529)	(525)	(7,922)
Delaware	7,091	(180)	(914)	−0.27%	(502)	(154)	(139)	(131)	(2,020)
Texas	202,676	(12,392)	(20,785)	−0.26%	(14,086)	(5,598)	(5,035)	(4,368)	(62,264)
Mississippi	33,188	(1,755)	(2,728)	−0.26%	(2,096)	(524)	(954)	(1,055)	(9,113)
Ohio	132,442	(9,099)	(13,032)	−0.26%	(9,218)	(3,949)	(3,399)	(2,840)	(41,537)
New Jersey	93,841	(5,700)	(9,390)	−0.25%	(6,468)	(2,806)	(2,375)	(1,981)	(28,719)
New Hampshire	16,306	(1,329)	(1,422)	−0.25%	(1,120)	(506)	(455)	(381)	(5,213)
New Mexico	17,161	(340)	(1,517)	−0.22%	(1,035)	(361)	(470)	(486)	(4,209)
Kansas	25,759	(1,332)	(2,823)	−0.22%	(1,800)	(695)	(604)	(523)	(7,777)
New York	185,532	(14,108)	(17,416)	−0.22%	(12,911)	(5,965)	(4,929)	(3,962)	(59,291)

Georgia	65,935	(3,187)	(6,685)	−0.22%	(4,435)	(1,340)	(1,651)	(1,667)	(18,964)
Pennsylvania	123,108	(7,919)	(12,154)	−0.22%	(8,511)	(3,855)	(3,148)	(2,553)	(38,140)
Alabama	44,192	(1,252)	(3,799)	−0.22%	(2,699)	(1,197)	(1,231)	(1,152)	(11,330)
Alaska	7,304	162	(486)	−0.21%	(355)	(26)	(230)	(329)	(1,213)
Washington	79,158	(2,422)	(4,899)	−0.21%	(4,408)	(2,299)	(2,571)	(2,438)	(19,037)
Louisiana	40,973	(2,234)	(3,327)	−0.18%	(2,587)	(654)	(1,186)	(1,308)	(11,297)
Hawaii	11,284	136	(1,002)	−0.18%	(627)	(61)	(307)	(403)	(2,264)
Florida	119,406	(7,384)	(10,718)	−0.18%	(7,954)	(3,574)	(3,259)	(2,806)	(35,693)
Wyoming	3,573	(25)	(398)	−0.18%	(228)	(48)	(82)	(95)	(875)
Vermont	6,353	(523)	(517)	−0.18%	(429)	(216)	(184)	(148)	(2,018)
Wisconsin	39,139	(3,969)	(4,237)	−0.17%	(2,993)	(1,257)	(937)	(693)	(14,085)
South Carolina	26,766	(292)	(2,689)	−0.17%	(1,651)	(316)	(671)	(798)	(6,417)
Colorado	53,184	(1,053)	(2,774)	−0.17%	(2,762)	(1,617)	(1,823)	(1,733)	(11,763)
Minnesota	47,557	(3,429)	(3,445)	−0.15%	(3,042)	(1,574)	(1,458)	(1,236)	(14,185)
Illinois	87,217	(4,872)	(8,011)	−0.15%	(5,768)	(2,149)	(2,345)	(2,222)	(25,366)
Kentucky	22,318	(837)	(2,292)	−0.14%	(1,473)	(378)	(552)	(595)	(6,126)
Michigan	70,869	(4,501)	(5,857)	−0.14%	(4,615)	(2,079)	(2,031)	(1,801)	(20,884)
Nebraska	9,512	(242)	(1,087)	−0.13%	(640)	(192)	(213)	(215)	(2,589)
Arkansas	18,091	(834)	(1,372)	−0.13%	(1,097)	(239)	(542)	(625)	(4,709)
West Virginia	11,339	(481)	(882)	−0.13%	(688)	(172)	(335)	(377)	(2,935)
Tennessee	34,374	(1,847)	(2,780)	−0.12%	(2,172)	(816)	(996)	(979)	(9,591)
North Dakota	3,510	(9)	(330)	−0.11%	(207)	(29)	(92)	(116)	(782)
North Carolina	48,065	(995)	(3,362)	−0.10%	(2,692)	(982)	(1,486)	(1,583)	(11,101)
Nevada	6,037	(91)	(641)	−0.10%	(385)	(90)	(145)	(163)	(1,515)
Iowa	20,129	(1,264)	(1,426)	−0.10%	(1,252)	(606)	(622)	(560)	(5,731)
Oregon	15,625	(957)	(1,345)	−0.10%	(1,021)	(323)	(438)	(446)	(4,531)
Montana	3,670	(14)	(311)	−0.08%	(208)	(20)	(103)	(134)	(790)
Idaho	4,450	44	(306)	−0.06%	(227)	0	(138)	(191)	(817)
South Dakota	3,253	25	(186)	−0.05%	(158)	6	(108)	(151)	(572)
USA	3,100,000	(175,297)	(278,888)	−0.24%	(204,278)	(88,288)	(84,411)	(74,920)	(906,082)

Source: Conrad Peter Schmidt and Steven Kosiak, Defense Budget Project, Washington, D.C., March 1992. Reprinted by permission.

In the case of military base closures, Congress authorized a cumbersome but thorough public evaluation process for handling this politically sensitive issue. The president and Congress have put in place an all-or-nothing decision process that requires an up-or-down vote on an entire closure package offered by independent base closure commissions.

In December 1988 the secretary of defense's Commission on Base Realignments and Closures recommended the closure of eighty-six facilities and the realignment of forty-five other installations.[22] The commission's closure package was eventually accepted by the secretary and Congress. Several states, such as California and Illinois, shouldered a major share of the 1988 closures.

In enacting the 1990 Defense Authorization Act, Congress continued the same general process, but with DoD making the initial closure recommendations to an independent commission.[23] The recommendations were based on published selection criteria, primarily involving military value but also including return on investment as well as local economic-environmental impacts. This new statutory base closure process was completed for 1991, and further base closure rounds are called for in 1993 and 1995. The president and Congress are required by statute to accept the commission-validated base closure packages in total or not at all.

The 1991 Base Closure Commission recommended that thirty-four bases be closed and forty-eight bases be realigned, and the commission closure recommendations were accepted by the president and Congress.[24] The 1991 closures had a major impact in Philadelphia, with the closure of the naval station and the Navy shipyard as well as a major realignment at the nearby Warminster Air Development Center. Texas also experienced several major closures, at Bergstrom Air Force Base (AFB) in Austin; at Carswell AFB in Fort Worth; and at Chase Field Naval Air Station in the small community of Beeville. California suffered the closure of Fort Ord on the Monterey Peninsula; Moffett Field in Sunnyvale; Long Beach Naval Station; and Castle AFB near Merced.

During 1993 and 1995 another 470 major bases across the nation will be subject to careful evaluation for closure.[25] A further round of military base closures may also be called for in 1997.

The detailed analyses of each base prepared by the military departments for the 1991 commission on the basis of comparative military value, return on investment, and the expected local economic and environmental impact provide a wealth of public information on which to judge the more likely candidates for closure in 1993 or 1995.

Even with this logical process, the DoD base structure will be subject to further turbulence, such as the creation of the Air Force Combat Command and the new Mobility Command as well as the new "composite wings." The base structure will also be influenced by other outside political factors, such as Sen. Strom Thurmond (R-S.C.) reassuming the position of ranking minority member on the Senate Armed Services Committee, where he may influence decisions regarding the Charleston Navy complex.

The weapon system cutbacks identified in the DoD budget and the military base closures in the 1988 and 1991 closure rounds will not result in immediate job losses, but rather in the gradual completion of production and the orderly closure of the bases, which may take four-to-five years. For instance, there has been only one major base closed to date from the 1988 and 1991 closure rounds—Pease Air Force Base in New Hampshire.

These select weapon system cutbacks and likely military base closures through 1997 are heavily concentrated, as expected, in New England, Philadelphia, St. Louis, Fort Worth, southern California, Arizona, and the San Francisco Bay area. (See appendix at the end of this chapter.)

In contrast with previous defense budget cutbacks, however, the summary of affected regions for 1993 to 1997 also includes Tidewater Virginia (Norfolk-Newport News); Charleston, South Carolina; and Jacksonville, Florida.

The affected areas also include a number of small communities, such as Adak, Alaska; Blytheville, Ark.; Marysville, Calif.; Rantoul, Ill.; Bath, Maine; Oscoda, Mich.; Lima, Ohio; and Magna, Utah, where defense spending has been the mainstay for the local economy.

Closing military bases during the 1993 and 1995 closure rounds will be especially demanding. The 478 major DoD bases currently in the United States far exceed the basing structure needed for a baseline force of 1.6 million military personnel, let alone 1.4 million. These military base reductions will have to consider:

- The further merger of many military department agencies into single tri-service or DoD entities.
- Some rationalization of the DoD laboratory structure.
- Joint service use of a single military base, such as relocating Army headquarters offices from an outmoded facility to a nearby Air Force base.
- A major reduction in the number of command levels within each of the military departments. (For instance, the Army Materiel Command's "Vision 2000" considers merging many of its eight commodity commands.)
- Further efforts to consolidate military hospital care.
- Greater efforts to co-locate combined arms units that require joint training.

National and Regional Adjustments to Defense Cutbacks

For all the significant impact that these changes in defense spending will have on specific communities and individual workers, it is important to realize that their effect on the economy is relatively modest in relation to the recession of 1981-1982 or even the more recent recession of 1991-1992. These defense cutbacks (identified in the appendix) are also fairly nominal in relation to other adjustments in the economy due to corporate downsizing; the banking and savings and loan crisis; foreign trade imbalances; and dislocations in the mining, timber, and power industries caused by environmental concerns—among other major dislocations of the past decade.

The nation is constantly responding to technological and economic forces that continuously reshape its industrial fabric. The adjustments needed in responding to both civilian and defense dislocations depend on a strong, growing national economy, a fact that was best described as far back as the mid-1960s by the Committee on the Economic Impact of Defense and Disarmament:

> The adjustments required by defense shifts are not different in kind—or perhaps degree—from the adjustments that are required and that occur each year from causes unrelated to defense. . . .
>   Readjustments are most successful when the economy is expanding vigorously and when employers and workers have strong incentives to make the shifts that are required.[26]

In perspective, all the weapon system and military base cutbacks cited above, as well as all the expected FY93-97 defense budget reductions, will amount to less than 1 percent of GNP in any one year, which should permit the Federal Reserve to respond with the proper offsetting macroeconomic stimulus.[27]

It is also important to understand the job-creation process in a market economy. Economic development in response to civilian plant closures occurs in a highly decentralized manner. The fifty states have active statewide economic development programs—with promotional budgets ranging in 1988 from $1.2 million to upwards of $246 million annually—for attracting new industrial growth.

There are over ten thousand other community groups with active local economic development programs seeking new plant investment by expanding firms and new jobs based on the distinctive competitive advantages offered by their communities.[28] These communities and states have a large number of allies, such as utilities and railroads, helping to attract new plant investments.

Within this state- and local-oriented economic development context, the federal government provides a reasonable level of worker retraining and placement resources (about $577 million annually) under Title III of the Jobs Training Partnership Act (JTPA) to help alleviate major job dislocations. However, the federal government provides wholly inadequate community assistance resources, amounting to only $23 million annually for all plant closures nationwide under Title IX of the Economic Development Authority program.

Aside from the new sixty-day advance worker notice requirements mandated by the 1988 Worker Adjustment and Retraining Notification Act, the federal government functions almost entirely on a *laissez faire* mentality with regard to normal civilian plant closures. In fact, the only type of dislocation where the federal government offers a coordinated interagency response in cooperation with state and local governments is for defense cutbacks, under the auspices of the Economic Adjustment Committee.

The market economy and the decentralized economic development process created about 3 million net new jobs annually between 1983 and 1990. These jobs were created almost entirely by small, expanding firms and were fueled in part by the 620,000 to 675,000 new firms that were created annually since the mid-1980s. During this period, the economy created some 17 million jobs, but the *Fortune 500* firms eliminated 3,650,000 jobs.[29]

In one study of twenty-eight community responses to plant closures there was little or no difference found between the community response to major defense cutbacks and private sector plant closures.[30] The one possible difference found was in the civilian reuse of former military bases, where the base assets provided an attractive tool for new industry and for a trained work force. In one hundred community base-reuse efforts assisted by the Economic Adjustment Committee and the DoD Office of Economic Adjustment from 1961 to 1986, the communities in total replaced the loss of 93,400 DoD civilian jobs with 138,100 new civilian jobs on the former bases. In addition, 53,700 students were attending full-time college or vocational-technical training at 33 former bases.[31]

In summary, job creation in a market economy experiencing plant closures "can be eased by enlightened government policy. In such an environment, defense conversion largely 'happens' rather than being directed." [32]

Policy Implications

There have been two conflicting approaches in responding at the national level to defense cutbacks. First, the prestigious Committee for Economic Development has recommended against the creation of special programs to handle the current defense dislocations and has recommended that the defense budget savings be used to reduce the federal deficit, thereby lowering pressure on interest rates.[33]

A similar view has been expressed by Murray Weidenbaum, whereby America should be "anxious to see the civilian sector productively use the valuable resources released by the military, but [with] a minimum role for government in the process." [34]

There is an alternative school of thought which urges the nation to commit itself to a "demand-pull" program of federal spending on energy-saving, environmentally friendly technologies that in turn would propel the economy further into the future.[35] This second school of thought is built around the "economic conversion" movement that Richard Minnich discusses in his chapter on defense industry conversion, where government spending on new technology and advanced planning at the plant level can lead to a prompt recovery. In summary, there is little evidence that a government-led "conversion" has ever worked in a market economy.[36]

The final House-Senate Conference Committee on the FY93 Defense Authorization Bill adopted a third approach by authorizing $694 million in dual use civilian-military technology programs. Congress also appropriated $79 million for community planning and operating costs of the DoD Office of Economic Adjustment, with $50 million earmarked for economic adjustment projects at the Philadelphia Naval Shipyard. An additional $80 million was funded in DoD transfers to the Economic Development Administration for public infrastructure improvements at the affected communities, similar to Part D of the FY91 Defense Authorization Act. These several new dual-use technology initiatives and economic adjustment authorities will work within the normal state-local economic development process.

At the time of this writing, the specific goals of the Clinton administration toward converting defense industries, as outlined in *Putting People First*, appear ill-defined and uncertain.[37] Nevertheless, from the viewpoint of economic development practitioners, there are several policy implications from these pending defense cutbacks for the new administration to consider:

- The creation of strong aggregate national demand and a prosperous national economy will remain the most important elements in helping individual communities and displaced defense workers recover promptly.
- Placing the defense-related workers in new jobs as soon as possible should be the most important objective of the local and state adjustment efforts. The JTPA program has been improved in recent years but more responsive approaches to local needs are still needed.
- The nature of the recovery effort will vary from region to region and community to community. Federal adjustment programs should con-

tinue to act in partnership with the on-going state and local economic development programs.

- It is important to recognize that the federal capacity to respond to major plant closings and mass layoffs is deficient in the area of community infrastructure needs, such as new utility lines and roads to support civilian reuse of a former military base.

- DoD Community Planning Assistance, authorized by 10 USC 2391, should be increased from the annual range of $4 to $5 million in FY92 to at least $25 to $30 million for FY93 to FY97, including predevelopment planning.

- DoD supplemental assistance through Title IX of the Economic Development Authority Program should be authorized in the range of $80 to $100 million annually through FY97 to meet the needs for community infrastructure redevelopment to support civilian reuse.

- New attention should be given to entrepreneurship training for the small portion (maybe 2-to-3 percent) of the displaced defense work force who wish to enter business for themselves.

- The Small Business Innovative Research Program has provided an invaluable tool for small business diversification and should be expanded.

- Some mechanism must be found to expedite the interim use of DoD base facilities. The interim use process now takes up to 190 days, including approval by the deputy secretary of defense, for communities to secure new civilian jobs pending transfer of the property. The Bush administration virtually blocked implementation of the new environmental indemnification provisions for base closure facilities enacted by the 102nd Congress.

- Finally, some sales financing mechanism should be found that would permit community borrowing at low interest rates when a local government purchases portions of a former military base. The Federal Finance Bank at the U.S. Treasury is an excellent tool for such credit sales, but flexibility will be needed in "scoring" (calculating budget authority for) the loan amounts in the federal budget.

In conclusion, the expected community and worker dislocations caused by defense cutbacks are well within the capacity of our economy to respond to effectively. It is important that federal adjustment mechanisms support on-going state and local economic development initiatives. Finally, the federal government must not overreact to the problem of defense adjustment but must find that set of incentives and regional development mechanisms that can help seriously affected communities respond and create new jobs at the local level.

Appendix: Summary of Expected Community and Regional Defense Cutbacks

In summarizing the potential community and regional effects from the pending defense spending cutbacks through 1997, it is important to recognize that defense weapon system cutbacks and base closures do not occur in proportion to an overall defense budget cutback. Instead, selective reductions occur in specific communities with individual procurement contracts and individual military bases subject to closure.[38]

It is difficult for a layman to receive a good picture of the defense basing structure and the DoD weapon systems and production facilities.[39]

The impact of cutbacks in weapon systems can best be identified from the DoD budget submission data. The military bases include those selected by the 1988 Base Closure Commission (denoted "++" in the text) and those accepted by the 1991 Base Closure Commission (denoted "+++"). Only those closure actions that result in significant regional job losses are included.

Other bases identified below are those that were among the middle or lower rankings in military department analyses. The number of military personnel and DoD civilians working at the base are also given. The state and metro area are given for each base and major weapon system, and the communities' vulnerability to cutback or closure in the 1992-1997 time-frame is evaluated.

Alabama:

- *Anniston:* Fort McClellan and the Army Chemical Training Center were saved from closure by the 1991 Base Closure Commission; there are 3,960 military and 1,310 civilian personnel assigned to the fort, which is likely to be a candidate for future closure.
- *Huntsville:* This city and Redstone Arsenal may be two of the few "winners" from the Army's long-rumored "Vision 2000" plan to consolidate commodity activities of the Army Materiel Command.

Alaska:

- *Adak:* During the 1991 closure deliberations the Navy indicated that it would look again at the closure of Adak NAS, involving 1,830 military and 200 civilian jobs.
- *Anchorage:* Fort Richardson ranked near the bottom of the Army Fighting Installations in a 1991 analysis, and there could be major cutbacks in the 4,480 military and 1,040 civilian personnel associated with the light infantry division.

- *Fairbanks:* Fort Wainwright also ranked near the bottom of the Army Fighting Installations, and there could be major cutbacks in the 4,870 military and 660 civilian personnel associated with the light infantry division who are assigned there.

Arizona:

- Phoenix *(Mesa):* The FY93 DoD budget calls for terminating the AH-64 Apache helicopter, built by McDonnell Douglas at its Mesa plant.
- Phoenix *(Mesa):* Pilot training activities at Williams AFB $(+++)$ are scheduled to be eliminated by late 1993, with the loss of 1,570 military and 280 civilian jobs.
- *Tucson:* The Hughes Aircraft plant was previously affected by the completion of the Maverick and Phoenix missiles. The TOW missile Sight Improvement Program, with Hughes Aircraft as the prime contractor, was terminated in the FY93 budget.
- *Tucson:* Davis Monthan AFB did not rate highly in the 1991 Air Force tactical base analysis. The 625 civilian jobs at the Air Force "bone yard" for older aircraft are likely to remain, but the remaining 4,620 military and 770 civilian jobs are vulnerable.

Arkansas:

- *Blytheville:* Eaker AFB $(+++)$ closed in December 1992 with the loss of 2,710 military and 790 civilian personnel.
- *Fort Smith:* The transfer of the Army Joint Readiness Training Center from Fort Chaffee $(+++)$ in 1993 will involve the loss of 2,620 military and 790 civilian jobs.

California:

- Los Angeles-Long Beach *(Anaheim):* The cancellation of the MX, or Peacekeeper, missile will affect Rockwell International activities in Anaheim, Hawthorne, and Canoga Park.
- *Los Angeles:* Hughes Aircraft produces the avionics for the B-2 bomber, which will be limited to twenty aircraft.
- Los Angeles-Long Beach *(Palmdale):* The curtailment of B-2 production at twenty aircraft will affect the Northrop final assembly facility at Plant 42.
- Los Angeles-Long Beach *(Pico Rivera)*: The curtailment of B-2 production at twenty aircraft will affect the major B-2 Northrop production facility.

- Los Angeles-Long Beach *(Pomona):* Stinger air defense missile production at the General Dynamics plant will be reduced.
- Los Angeles-Long Beach *(Long Beach):* The Long Beach Naval Station and the Navy hospital (+ + +) will close with the loss of 9,530 military and 830 civilian positions.
- Los Angeles-Long Beach *(Long Beach):* The Long Beach Naval Shipyard—with 5,110 civilian jobs—was a candidate for closure in 1991 and may be a future candidate for closure.
- Los Angeles-Long Beach *(Tustin):* The MCAS Tustin (+ + +) will be closed and redeveloped but without any real impact (due to its potential for civilian reuse) from the loss of the 4,100 military and 350 civilian positions.
- *Merced:* The closure of Castle AFB (+ + +) in 1995 will involve the loss of 5,240 military and 1,160 civilian jobs.
- Los Angeles-Long Beach *(El Toro):* MCAS El Toro received cautious ratings in the 1991 Navy base analysis on current land and facilities. The land is very valuable, and there are also serious problems with community encroachment in the airfield flight patterns. The airfield now employs 5,840 military and 990 civilian personnel.
- *Marysville:* Beale AFB, a SAC base with 3,690 military and 320 civilian jobs, could be a candidate for closure in 1993-1995.
- Monterey *(Seaside-Marina):* The transfer of the 7th Division from Fort Ord (+ + +) to Fort Lewis during 1992-1993 will result in the loss of 13,620 military and 2,830 civilian positions.
- *Riverside:* March AFB was not ranked highly among SAC bases in the 1991 base analysis. It is now a multimission base, but its 3,670 military and 1,810 civilian jobs are vulnerable.
- *Sacramento:* Mather AFB (+ +) will be closed in late 1993 with the loss of 1,990 military and 1,010 civilian jobs.
- *Sacramento:* The Sacramento Army Depot (+ + +) will close in 1992-1993 with the loss of 3,500 civilian jobs.
- *Sacramento:* It will be costly to close any of the five Air Force air logistics centers. McClellan AFB with 3,150 military and 13,000 civilian jobs is an older and a more vulnerable base.
- *Sacramento:* The Aerojet General plant has produced subsystems for the MX missile and had planned future work on the Small ICBM program, which was canceled.
- *San Bernardino:* The closure of Norton AFB (+ +) in mid-1994 will result in the loss of 4,520 military and 2,130 civilian positions.
- *San Diego:* Production of the Tomahawk cruise missile and the Advanced Cruise Missile at the General Dynamics plant will be cut back.

- *San Diego:* No new orders will be placed at the NAACO shipyard for the AOE-6 Fast Combat Support Ship.
- *San Diego:* At some point, reductions in Navy and Marine Corps staffing may result in pressures to close the Navy Training Center and the Marine Recruit Depot.
- *San Francisco:* The Presidio (++) will be closed and transferred to the National Park Service in early 1995, affecting 2,140 military and 3,150 civilian positions.
- *San Francisco:* The Hunters Point Annex (++) closed in 1992.
- San Francisco-Oakland *(Alameda):* Alameda NAS and the aviation depot were previous candidates for closure, and these proposals could be raised again. These activities employ 11,400 military personnel and 5,400 civilians.
- San Francisco-Oakland *(Oakland):* The Oakland Naval Hospital and the Naval Supply Center were previously candidates for closure, and these proposals are likely to be offered again in 1993 and 1995. There are 2,960 military and 3,300 civilian positions at these two facilities.
- San Francisco *(San Bruno):* The closure of the Public Works Center with 30 military and 490 civilian jobs is likely.
- *San Jose:* The FMC Corp. production line for the Bradley fighting vehicle will be closed.
- *Sunnyvale:* The cutback in Trident II missile production will affect the Lockheed plant.
- *Sunnyvale:* Moffet Field NAS (+++) will be transferred to NASA management, involving the transfer of 3,340 military and 630 civilian positions.
- *Vallejo:* Mare Island Naval Shipyard, with 1,360 military and 6,700 civilian jobs, may be a future candidate for closure.
- *Victorville:* The closure of George AFB (++) in 1993 will result in the loss of 4,850 military and 510 civilian jobs.

Colorado:

- *Denver:* The closure of Air Force training activities at Lowry AFB (+++) by mid-1994 will involve the loss of 4,050 military and 2,290 civilian positions.
- *Denver:* Fitzsimmons Army Hospital would be a prime closure candidate with 1,890 military and 1,630 civilian jobs.

Connecticut:

- *Groton:* The completion of Trident submarine production and the proposed curtailment of the Seawolf nuclear attack submarine could affect 8,600 jobs at Electric Boat Co. For FY93 the House and Senate had agreed to retain spending for two follow-on boats.

- *Hartford:* United Technologies' Norden Systems has announced a 2,400-job layoff in its radar assembly unit.
- Hartford *(East Hartford):* The completion of the F-15E and the F-16 will affect engine production at the Pratt & Whitney plant.
- *Stratford:* There have been job cutbacks at Sikorsky Helicopter even though production of the UH-60L Black Hawk and the CH-53 Super Stallion helicopters remain stable in the budget. The decision to defer production of the Comanche helicopter will also affect employment at the Sikorsky plant.
- *Stratford:* Textron-Lycoming has experienced engine and subcontract cutbacks.

Florida:

- Miami *(Homestead):* Homestead AFB was not included in the 1991 closure competition among tactical bases, but the declining threat from Cuba may permit its closure involving 3,730 military and 1,020 civilian positions.
- *Jacksonville:* The 1991 Navy base analysis indicated that Cecil Field, with 3,270 military and 580 civilian jobs, had significant facility deficiencies.
- *Jacksonville:* The Mayport base, with 2,950 military and 900 civilian jobs, received cautious 1991 ratings for mission suitability and community encroachment.
- *Key West:* The naval air station, with 1,460 military and 420 civilian personnel, received cautious ratings in the 1991 Navy base closure analysis.
- *Pensacola:* The naval aviation depot, with 3,400 civilian jobs, may contribute to excess depot capacity for Navy aircraft.
- Pensacola *(Milton):* Base closure pressures are likely to reopen the proposal for combining Navy helicopter pilot training at Whiting Field—involving 1,650 military and 220 civilian jobs—with the Army at Fort Rucker.
- *Orlando:* The LOS-F-H air defense system built by Martin Marietta was terminated in the FY93 budget.
- *Orlando:* It is likely that the Navy will close its training center in 1993 or 1995—involving about 13,600 military and 2,140 civilian positions.
- *Titusville:* The reductions in the Advanced Cruise Missile program will be felt at the McDonnell Douglas plant.
- *Tampa:* The elimination of airfield and air mission activities at

MacDill AFB (+ + +) by early 1994 will result in the loss of 2,770 military and 230 civilian positions. MacDill AFB juts into Tampa Bay and is very valuable property. A likely scenario would be the transfer of Central Command activities currently at MacDill to another base, with subsequent closure of the facility.

Georgia:

- Atlanta *(Forest Park)*: Reductions in the overall Army staff levels are likely to call for the closure of Fort Gillem, with its 800 civilian jobs.
- *Valdosta*: Moody AFB was a candidate for closure in 1991 but escaped the final closure decision. This F-16 tactical fighter base with 3,160 military personnel and 480 civilians would be a strong candidate for future closure. There currently are offsetting proposals to locate a "composite wing" at Moody AFB.

Hawaii:

- *Honolulu*: During the 1991 closure analysis, the Navy indicated that it would look again at Barbers Point NAS, with its 1,220 military and 330 civilian positions.
- *Honolulu*: Fort Shafter—with 1,270 military and 1,903 civilian positions—received poor ratings in the 1991 Army base analysis for "Fighting and Maneuver Installations."

Illinois:

- Chicago *(Highland Park)*: The closure of Fort Sheridan (+ +) in mid-1994 will affect 1,320 military and 1,680 civilian positions.
- *Rantoul*: Air Force training activities at Chanute AFB (+ +) will be concluded by late 1993 and the base will be closed with the loss of 2,100 military and 1,030 civilian jobs.
- *Savanna*: The Savanna Army Depot employs 500 civilians and was rated second to last in 1991 among Army depots.

Indiana:

- *Indianapolis*: The end of production of the E-2C Hawkeye and the possible cancellation of the V-22 Osprey might affect engine production of the GM Allison plant.
- *Indianapolis*: The pending closure of Fort Benjamin Harrison (+ + +) will result in the loss of 3,440 military and 1,100 civilian personnel, assuming that DoD will retain its accounting and finance functions in the city.

- *Madison:* The closure of Jefferson Proving Ground (+ +) in 1995 will affect 400 civilian jobs in this rural town.
- *Peru:* The transfer of Grissom AFB (+ + +) in mid-1994 to the Air Force Reserve will result in the loss of 2,500 military and 810 civilian jobs.

Kansas:

- *Wichita:* The KC-135 re-engining/modernization program at the Boeing plant was terminated in the DoD budget.

Kentucky:

- *Lexington:* Closure of the Army's Lexington Depot (+ +) in late 1995 will result in the loss of 1,130 civilian jobs.
- *Louisville:* The reduction in munitions requirements may permit the closure of the naval ordnance station, with 230 military and 2,640 civilian jobs.

Louisiana:

- *Alexandria:* The 1992 closure of England AFB (+ + +) resulted in the loss of 3,040 military and 700 civilian positions.
- *New Orleans:* The production of the Land Craft-Air Cushioned at Bell Aerospace will be completed without the Navy placing orders for any new ships.
- *New Orleans:* The last of four Landing Dock Ships has been ordered at the Avondale Shipyard.

Maine:

- *Bath:* The Bath Iron Works received the contract for the lead DDG-51 but the follow-on ships were awarded to Ingalls Shipbuilding. Bath Iron Works anticipates 2,300 job losses over the next year.
- *Limestone:* Loring AFB (+ + +) will close in mid-1994 with the loss of 3,590 military and 500 civilian jobs.
- *Brunswick:* Of the three Navy bases in the maritime patrol role, Brunswick NAS rated the lowest in the 1991 analysis; the field has 1,150 military and 400 civilian jobs.

Maryland:

- *Adelphi:* The Harry Diamond Lab—with 1,360 civilian employees—was rated low in Army military value levels.

Massachusetts:

- Boston *(Ayer):* The closure of Fort Devens (+ + +) will result in the loss of 1,660 military and 2,180 civilian jobs.
- Boston *(Lynn):* Engine production for the F-14, B-2, the Apache helicopter, and other aircraft will be reduced at General Electric.
- Boston *(Natick):* Among the commodity-oriented commands, the Natick Lab. was ranked well below the Army norm; the facility has 160 military and 1,340 civilian positions.
- Boston *(South Weymouth):* The Naval Air Station has been a candidate in the past and is a likely candidate for future closure, with its 270 military and 230 civilian positions.
- Boston *(West Andover):* Production of the Patriot and Stinger missiles will be completed at the Raytheon plant. Raytheon has reduced its staffing by 5,200 jobs, or 6.9 percent, over the past year.

Michigan:

- Detroit *(Warren):* The M-1 tank production line at the General Dynamics plant will be terminated.
- *Marquette:* As a SAC base, K.I. Sawyer AFB did not rank high during the 1991 base analysis and it could be a candidate for closure, with 3,600 military and 600 civilian jobs.
- *Oscoda:* Wurtsmith AFB (+ + +) will close in late 1993 with the loss of 2,900 military and 700 civilian jobs.

Mississippi:

- *Columbus:* Flying training operations at Columbus AFB—with 1,880 military and 530 civilian positions—will be vulnerable to closure during the 1993-1995 rounds.
- *Gulfport:* Production of the Landing Craft-Air Cushioned will be completed at the Avondale Shipyard.
- *Meridian:* The Navy may have surplus pilot training capacity, which would permit closure of the naval air station by 1995-1997, with the loss of 2,000 military and 660 civilian jobs.
- *Pascagoula:* The last of four LHD-1 amphibious assault ships will be completed at Ingalls Shipbuilding.

Missouri:

- *St. Louis:* The production line for the F-15E is scheduled to close in September 1993; purchases of the AV-8B Harrier aircraft will also be phased down at McDonnell Douglas. The company also makes the

Harpoon and the Tomahawk, which will likewise be phased down. The 1991 cancellation of the A-12 advanced naval fighter affected McDonnell-Douglas and the St. Louis economy. There have been 10,000 aerospace job losses to date at McDonnell Douglas in St. Louis.

- *St. Louis:* In the category industrial-commodity-oriented activities, the St. Louis Federal Center (involving merger of the Aviation Systems Command and the Troop Support Command) was rated last in 1991 in military value. The possible transfer of these functions to other Army agencies would involve 370 military and 5,730 civilian jobs.

Montana:

- *Great Falls:* The SAC mission at Malmstrom AFB could be affected by the retirement of the 450 Minuteman II missiles in the region, with 3,840 military and 600 civilian jobs.

New Hampshire:

- *Portsmouth:* The only actual closure to date among the 1988 or 1991 announcements has been Pease AFB (+ +), in 1991, with the loss of 3,610 military and 650 civilian positions. The Pease Development Authority accepted title to the airfield in April 1992, and the authority has attracted an aircraft overhaul facility, the State Department visa processing center, and the Air National Guard—with over 2,000 new civilian jobs to date.
- *Portsmouth:* The Portsmouth Naval Shipyard (located in Kittery, Maine) received a low rating in the 1991 Navy closure analysis; the shipyard has 7,160 civilian positions.

New Jersey:

- Trenton *(Burlington County):* Fort Dix (+ +) was designated for semiactive status with the phase down in Army basic training by 1993 and the loss of 3,140 military and 1,510 civilian personnel.
- Trenton *(Burlington and Ocean Counties):* Military Airlift Command activities at McGuire AFB—with 10,140 military and 720 civilian jobs—could be a candidate for closure during the 1993-1995 rounds.

New Mexico:

- *Clovis:* Cannon AFB, with 4,270 military and 520 civilian jobs, rated in the mid-range for Air Force tactical (F-111) bases in the 1991 review.

New York:

- New York City *(Bethpage)*: The Navy F-14D Tomcat fighter production line and the E-2C Hawkeye early warning aircraft line at the Grumman plant will be terminated.
- *New York City:* In light of local cost factors, the Navy homeporting facility on Staten Island would be a strong candidate for closure, involving 1,200 military and 260 civilian jobs.
- *New York City:* Fort Totten and Fort Hamilton would be likely candidates for closure in 1993 or 1995, with 420 military and 360 civilian positions.
- *Plattsburgh:* As a SAC base, Plattsburgh AFB escaped closure in 1991 but it would be a prime candidate in 1993-1995 rounds, involving 3,770 military and 490 civilian jobs.
- *Romulus:* The Seneca Army Depot, with 640 military and 960 civilian jobs, has been threatened with further cutbacks.
- Utica-Rome *(Rome)*: Griffiss AFB did not rate highly among SAC bases in the 1991 Air Force analysis. The Rome Air Development Center could also be at risk with a total of 4,820 military and 2,800 civilian positions.
- *Watertown:* Fort Drum—the home of the 10th Mountain (light infantry) Division with 10,730 military and 2,070 civilian personnel—was rated last in the 1991 Army base analysis for "Fighting and Maneuver" bases.

North Dakota:

- *Minot:* Minot AFB, with 5,000 military and 590 civilian jobs, received mediocre marks in the 1991 Air Force analysis and will be looked at closely again in 1993 and 1995.

Ohio:

- Cincinnati *(Evendale)*: Reduction in engine needs for the F-16, the KC-135, and the B-2 will affect the General Electric Evendale engine plant.
- *Lima:* The M-1 tank production line will close at the General Dynamics plant.

Pennsylvania:

- *Philadelphia:* The Boeing Vertol CH-47 helicopter modernization and the controversial V-22 vertical takeoff aircraft are both subject to phase out over the long term.

- *Philadelphia:* The Philadelphia Shipyard and the naval station (+++) will close in late 1992 with the loss of 2,140 military and 8,940 civilian jobs.
- Philadelphia *(Warminster):* The Naval Air Development Center (+++) is being realigned, with the loss of 230 military and 2,030 civilian jobs.
- *York:* Cutbacks in the M109 modification program for the self-propelled howitzer will affect employment at the BMY plant.

Rhode Island:

- *Quonset Point:* Production of Trident submarine components will be eliminated at the Electric Boat Company plant.

South Carolina:

- *Charleston:* During the 1991 review, the Navy identified quality-of-life problems at Charleston Naval Station, with a current staffing of 6,700 military personnel. The Navy also indicated that it would look again at the entire Charleston complex in 1993.
- *Myrtle Beach:* Myrtle Beach AFB (+++) will close in early 1993, displacing 3,190 military and 800 civilian jobs.
- *Sumter:* Shaw AFB was not ranked high as an F-16 tactical base in the 1991 Air Force closure analysis; the base has 5,520 military and 1,610 civilian positions.

Tennessee:

- Memphis *(Millington):* Memphis NAS received a cautious rating in 1991 on the availability of facilities. The NAS employs 7,610 military personnel and 1,050 civilians.

Texas:

- *Amarillo:* The termination of the Trident II warhead will affect the Pantex plant.
- *Austin:* Bergstrom AFB (+++) is slated for closure in mid-1993, with the loss of 3,940 military and 940 civilian positions.
- *Beeville:* Over 730 military and 910 civilian jobs will be affected by the closure of Chase Field NAS (+++) in 1993, but the community has already attracted new industrial clients and a new state prison administrative-medical complex. The Beeville recovery prospects are promising.
- Corpus Christi *(Ingleside):* It is likely that the Navy will be forced to

reconsider the new homeporting base.

- *Dallas:* No new orders will be placed for the HARM antiradiation missile produced by Texas Instruments.
- *Dallas:* The reduction in the B-2 bomber program to twenty aircraft will affect the composite materials and airframe manufacturing at the LTV plant. The LOSAT program at LTV will also be deferred.
- *Fort Worth:* The V-22 Osprey vertical take-off aircraft program at Bell Helicopter could be curtailed.
- *Fort Worth:* Production of the F-16 at the General Dynamics plant will be cut back after FY93 and the production line will be closed.
- *Fort Worth:* Carswell AFB (+++) will close in mid-1993, with the loss of 4,660 military and 880 civilian positions.
- *Lubbock:* Reese AFB flight training activities—with 1,670 military and 590 civilian jobs—will be vulnerable to closure.
- *San Angelo:* Air Force training activities at Goodfellow AFB have been threatened with closure in the past and the base is likely to be on the 1993-1995 closure lists, affecting 1,960 military and 620 civilian positions.
- *San Antonio:* There are currently five major bases in San Antonio. The most vulnerable is Brooks AFB, with 1,590 military and 1,250 civilian positions.

Utah:

- *Brigham City:* The cancellation of the Peacekeeper missile will affect the Thiokol plant operations.
- *Magna:* The termination of the Peacekeeper and other missiles will affect the Hercules Corp. propellant plant.
- *Tooele:* Excess Army equipment overhaul capacity may affect the future of Tooele Army Depot, with 3,500 civilian jobs.

Virginia:

- *Lynchburg:* Serious cutbacks have been announced at the Babcock & Wilcox plant, which makes marine reactors.
- Norfolk-Newport News *(Hampton):* Fort Monroe has been offered as a candidate for closure in the past—with the possible relocation of the 930 military personnel and 1,780 civilians assigned to the Army Training and Doctrine Command to modern office facilities nearby.
- Norfolk-Newport News *(Hampton):* Fort Eustis—with 6,130 military personnel and 3,030 civilians—and nearby Fort Story received middle ratings in the 1991 Army training base analysis. (Fort Eustis has good transportation assets, however.)

- Norfolk-Newport News *(Newport News):* Three Nimitz class carriers are under construction. Advanced procurement is in the FY93 budget for a fourth replacement carrier in the FY94 budget, which could be in jeopardy for future budget cuts. Finally, the Navy may be forced to curtail submarine building to just one shipyard, thereby further threatening Newport News.
- *Norfolk:* Cutbacks can be anticipated in the 1993 and 1995 closure rounds at the Norfolk Naval Station and other related activities such as Little Creek.
- Richmond *(Petersburg):* Fort Lee was rated second from last among the Army training bases in 1991; there are 4,590 military personnel and 3,230 civilians at the fort.
- *Warrenton:* Vint Hill Farms Station, with 980 civilian jobs and other contractor jobs, could be a logical candidate for future closure.

Washington:

- *Seattle:* The cancellation of the SRAM air-to-ground missile will affect Boeing Aerospace. Boeing also manufactures composite materials and components for the B-2 Stealth bomber, which will be limited to twenty aircraft.
- *Spokane:* Fairchild AFB, a SAC base with 4,360 military and 960 civilian jobs, did not rank high during the 1991 base analysis and could be a candidate for closure.

Notes

1. U.S. Arms Control and Disarmament Agency, *Report to the Congress on Defense Industry Conversion* (Washington, D.C.: Government Printing Office, August 1990), Appendix C. See also Charles M. Tiebout, "The Regional Impact of Defense Expenditure: Its Measure and Problems of Adjustment," in *Defense and Disarmament,* ed. Roger E. Bolton (Englewood Cliffs: Prentice Hall, 1966), 125. This problem of tracking defense subcontracts and interindustry-supplier inputs is also highlighted in the recent studies on declining defense spending by the Congressional Budget Office and the Office of Technology Assessment: U.S. Congressional Budget Office, *Summary of the Economic Effects of Reduced Defense Spending* (Washington, D.C.: Government Printing Office, 1990); U.S. Office of Technology Assessment, *Redesigning Defense* (Washington, D.C.: U.S. Government Printing Office, 1991).
2. Hugh G. Mosley, *The Arms Race: Economic and Social Consequences* (Lexington, Mass.: D.C. Heath and Company, 1985), 167-175; John E. Lynch, ed., *Economic Adjustment and Conversion of Defense Industries* (Boulder, Colo.: Westview Press, 1987), 13-16.
3. Murray L. Weidenbaum, "Problems of Adjustment in Defense Industries," in *Disarmament and the Economy,* ed. Emile Benoit and Kenneth Boulding (Westport, Conn.: Greenwood Press, 1963), 82-83.
4. Executive Office of the President, Council of Economic Advisors, Garner Ackley, chairman, *Report of the Committee on the Economic Impact of Defense and Disarmament*

(Washington, D.C.: Government Printing Office, 1965). Executive Office of the President, "Report from the Cabinet Coordinating Committee on Economic Planning for the End of Vietnam Hostilities," *Economic Report of the President* (Washington, D.C.: January 1969), 187-211. (The latter report was a legacy of the departing Johnson administration, and it was largely ignored by the incoming Nixon administration.)

5. John E. Lynch, "Regional Impact of the Vietnam War," *Quarterly Review of Economics & Business* (Summer 1976): 37-50. Defense prime, subcontract, and supplier inputs were easier to track by state and metropolitan area in the 1960s and 1970s through the U.S. Bureau of the Census annual MA-175 Report on Shipments to Defense-Oriented Industries, an adjunct to the *Survey of Manufactures*. The MA-175 report has since been canceled by the Bureau of the Census.

6. Emile Benoit, "Cutting Back Military Spending: The Vietnam War and the Recession," *Annals of the American Academy of Political and Social Science* 406 (March 1973): 76.

7. The elimination of the MX missile and the downloading of the Minuteman III were presidential proposals that depended on mutual cutbacks by President Yeltsin; the proposals have not yet been fully agreed to. The termination of the MX missile program did not have a significant effect on spending beyond spares and test missiles.

8. Statement of Secretary of Defense Dick Cheney before the House Armed Services Committee in connection with the FY93 budget for the Department of Defense, February 6, 1992.

9. Jackie Calmes, "Guns For Butter, Ardor to Trim Defense Hits Political Obstacle: The Fear of Job Losses—Connecticut Liberals Strive to Keep Money Flowing for Nuclear Submarine," *Wall Street Journal*, May 7, 1992, 1.

10. Statement of Secretary of Defense Cheney, February 6, 1992, 19.

11. Bill Clinton and Al Gore, *Putting People First* (New York: Times Books, 1992), 133-134.

12. John Lancaster, "Powell Relents on Defense Cut, But Not on Gays," *Washington Post*, November 19, 1992, A16.

13. John H. Cumberland, "Dimensions of the Impact of Reduced Military Expenditures on Industries, Regions, and Communities," in *Adjustment of the U.S. Economy to Reductions in Military Spending*, ed. Bernard Udis (Washington, D.C.: Arms Control and Disarmament Agency, 1970), 121-231.

14. George F. Brown, "The Economic Impact of Alternative Defense Strategies," *Data Resources Review* (December 1981): 30-38.

15. Thomas L. Muller, "Regional Impacts," in *The Reagan Experiment*, ed. John L. Palmer and Isabel V. Sawhill (Washington, D.C.: Urban Institute Press, 1982), 441-457.

16. Norman J. Glickman, *Econometric Analysis of Regional Systems: Explorations in Model Building and Policy Analysis* (New York: Academic Press, 1977).

17. Joseph B. Cartwright and Richard M. Beemiller, *The Regional Economic Impact of Military Base Spending* (Washington, D.C.: Department of Commerce, 1980); *Modeling the Regional Economic Impacts of Major New Military Bases* (Washington, D.C.: Office of the Secretary of Defense, 1983).

18. Joseph V. Cartwright, "Potential Defense Work Force Dislocations and U.S. Defense Budget Cuts: An Illustration" (Washington, D.C.: Department of Defense Office of Economic Adjustment, March 1991); Conrad Peter Schmidt and Steven Kosiak, "Potential Impact of Defense Spending Reductions on the Defense Labor Force by State" (Washington, D.C.: Defense Budget Project, August 1991).

19. Murray L. Weidenbaum, "Shifting the Composition of Government Spending: Implications for the Regional Distribution of Income," *Peace Research Society Papers*, Vol. 5 (1966), 15.

20. Fred Trueblood, Phillip D. Wyman, Vern Lawson, and Pete Eskis, "Organizing Industry Manpower Programs: Lancaster and Palmdale, California," in *Plant Closures & Community Recovery*, ed. John E. Lynch (Washington, D.C.: National Council for Urban Economic Development, 1990), 33-35.
21. Department of Defense FY93 Budget, "Program Acquisition Cost by Weapon System" (Washington, D.C.: January 29, 1992).
22. Secretary's Commission on Base Realignments and Closure, *Base Realignments and Closures* (Washington, D.C.: December 28, 1988).
23. Public Law 101-510, Title XXIX.
24. Defense Base Closure and Realignment Commission, *Report to the President, 1991* (Washington, D.C.: July 1, 1991).
25. "Department of Defense Base Structure Report for FY1993," Office of the Assistant Secretary of Defense for Production and Logistics, February 1992.
26. Executive Office of the President, Council of Economic Advisors, Garner Ackley, chairman, *Report of the Committee on the Economic Impact of Defense and Disarmament* (Washington, D.C.: Government Printing Office, 1965), 17-18.
27. Murray Weidenbaum, *Small Wars, Big Defense* (New York: Oxford University Press, 1992), 202.
28. Alan S. Gregerman, "Competitive Advantage: Framing a Strategy to Support High Growth Firms," *Economic Development Commentary* (Summer 1984): 18-23.
29. Glenn Yago, "The Regulatory Reign of Terror," *Wall Street Journal,* March 4, 1992.
30. John E. Lynch, ed., *Plant Closures & Community Recovery* (Washington, D.C.: National Council for Urban Economic Development, 1990).
31. Department of Defense, "Twenty-five Years of Civilian Reuse: Summary of Completed Military Base Economic Adjustment Projects" (Washington, D.C.: 1986).
32. Kenneth L. Adelman and Norman R. Augustine, "Defense Conversion," *Foreign Affairs* (Spring 1992): 42.
33. Committee for Economic Development, *The Economy and National Defense: Adjusting to Military Cutbacks in the Post-Cold War Era* (New York: 1991).
34. Weidenbaum, *Small Wars, Big Defense,* preface.
35. Ann Markusen and Joel Yudken, *Dismantling the Cold War Economy* (New York: Basic Books, 1992).
36. Department of Defense, *Economic Adjustment/Conversion* (Washington, D.C.: Office of the Secretary of Defense, July 1985); later reissued as John E. Lynch, ed., *Economic Adjustment & Conversion of Defense Industries* (Boulder, Colo.: Westview Press, 1987). Arms Control and Disarmament Agency, *Report to the Congress on Defense Industry Conversion* (Washington, D.C.: ACDA, August 1990). For a good summary of the various conversion bills before the Congress up to 1992, see Weidenbaum, *Small Wars, Big Defense,* 61-71.
37. Bill Clinton and Al Gore, *Putting People First,* 134-135; and Thomas R. Ricks, "Some Defense-Spending Funds Go Elsewhere, But Clinton's Comments Leave Goals Ill-Defined," *Wall Street Journal,* November 16, 1992, A12.
38. Abbreviations used in this summary of base closures are as follows: AFB = Air Force Base; MCAS = Marine Corps Air Station; NAS = Naval Air Station; NS = Naval Station.
39. The best sources are *DoD Atlas/Data Abstract for the U.S. and Selected Areas* and *DoD Distribution of Personnel by State and by Selected Locations,* issued annually by the Directorate of Information, Washington Headquarters Service. Another good source is Betty G. Lall and John Tepper Marlin, *Building a Peace Economy* (Boulder, Colo.: Westview Press, 1992). Superb analyses are provided annually on the distribution of defense weapon systems by the Defense Budget Project in Washington, D.C.

6

Defense Downsizing and Economic Conversion: An Industry Perspective

Richard T. Minnich

Defense firms *can* transform themselves into competitive industries, given time, management persistence, and realistic expectations. Plant-level conversion, however, is unlikely. Further, the implications for national security strategy of closing plants should not be minimized. Defense plants cannot be "reconstituted," and once current defense production lines have been shut down, the time, political cost, and difficulties of restarting them will prove overwhelming.

The Problem

In a 1992 speech, then-representative Les Aspin, chairman of the House Armed Services Committee, stated bluntly the situation confronting the United States and the firms that supply defense materiel:

> Even as we watch developments in the former Soviet Union, we should be preparing for a third revolution, a revolution in the way we go about the business of providing for our defense. It isn't really a matter of choice. . . . With old world defense budgets, we had to figure out how to apportion the increases. Now we have to figure out who gets the cuts—real cuts. [1]

In fact, "real cuts" in defense budgets have been occurring since 1986,[2] but the point is still well taken: the chaotic situation in the former Soviet Union and Warsaw Pact nations has clearly diminished the need for maintaining the force structure required to address a Soviet blitzkrieg across Western Europe. As the force structure is reduced in size and changed in composition, the procurement needs will change as well, mandating a smaller and evolving industrial base to support them.

Richard T. Minnich works for a major defense contractor.

111

Defense reductions and conversion are not new problems. This is the fourth major downward shock in DoD procurement since the Second World War—the Truman cuts immediately after the end of the war, the reductions after the Korean and Vietnam wars, and now this period following the presumed end of the cold war.[3]

The effort to achieve a rational, controlled, systematic process for reducing the defense industrial base has been an acknowledged failure each time.[4] Current DoD planning for maintaining the continuity of the industrial base can only be described as minimal. The process of shrinking the Department of Defense is viewed by politicians of both parties as an opportunity for reallocating government expenditures to other, more popular programs or projects—"the peace dividend." Executives in the defense industry cannot hope to deal with the sudden, massive reduction in funding in a neat and orderly manner. Instead, they find themselves forced to hurriedly close entire divisions and production facilities to keep the firm afloat long enough to adjust to the new circumstances.

The consequence of this helter-skelter situation has been that each time the United States has suddenly needed to reequip military forces, the remaining capacity has been smaller, and the process required to reconstitute production has been more expensive and longer.

For industry, the problem is somewhat different. The defense industries contribute to national security, but, like all other firms, their primary responsibility is to provide an adequate return to their shareholders. The sudden change in "consumer preference" that has occurred since 1989 has left industry managers with significant challenges if they wish their firms to continue to grow or even, in some cases, exist. The questions that they must address involve charting a course that will maintain the asset value of the corporation in the short run, provide the wherewithal for future opportunities, and minimize the negative impact that the sudden decline in available procurement dollars imposes.

This chapter will evaluate these issues from an industry perspective. It addresses the uncertainty in the current situation and the difficulties of diversification, and it examines the path taken by several companies that have, over time, changed in their fundamental composition. A number of interrelated factors must be considered, including the financial status of the firms as they enter the 1990s, the different strategies that have been suggested for the industry, and an assessment of the strengths and weaknesses of the industry as it faces the transition.

This essay is not intended as a panegyric for defense industry management. At the same time, it *is* intended to provide an industry point of view, not to explore industry shortcomings; that aspect of the industry has been covered often and at great length elsewhere. Indeed, this essay begins with a key assumption: Defense industry managers act as managers do in any other industry—based on their perceptions of their own self-interest, making rational decisions based on the conditions and incentives of the business environment that confronts them.

What Is Conversion?

It will be worthwhile to consider the meaning of conversion and diversification, as some analysts have taken a very narrow view of what activities fall into these categories, while others use the terms in a broader way.[5]

The popular conception equates "conversion," or "diversification," with rebuilding specific facilities currently used for defense production, with a goal of producing commercial products at that facility using the same workers who had previously worked at the defense facility. This could be termed *plant-level conversion*. This is the most restrictive definition and, from the perspective of the industry, the least realistic.

This blueprint for conversion suffers from several practical flaws. World War II-vintage, hangar-sized facilities, with ceilings rising seventy-five or one-hundred feet above the ground, may be perfectly appropriate to assembling bombers or space shuttles, but they are completely inappropriate for high-tech manufacturing and assembly. Modern production requires a more controlled environment. Even to rebuild an existing heavy manufacturing plant into a more modern layout is not the trivial effort that is often envisioned—modern manufacturing equipment doesn't simply bolt into the floor.

The process of converting a plant often involves digging out the floor and rebuilding it from below ground level on specially hardened surfaces with shock and vibration dampers to isolate the equipment from passing traffic. A major plant rebuilding effort can take years.

If a defense firm were to make the decision to convert an existing facility, could management, anticipating a multiyear rebuilding effort, justify keeping highly paid defense workers on the payroll during that period? Clearly they cannot, and consequently, the notion of transferring workers directly from aerospace to commercial production is usually unrealistic.

Often, the emphasis on this direct plant-level conversion arises from an interest in the reconstitution question. From the DoD perspective, reconstitution is a vital consideration in any conversion effort.[6] Ideally, conversion should be done in such a way as to allow a rapid return to defense production should the need arise. In practice it would mean that defense industry firms would not strive to convert for maximum efficiency (which will almost certainly be irreversible), but should try competing in the commercial world with a less-than-optimally-efficient plant and facility, on the chance that at some future point in time national security needs will arise.[7]

Without a direct government policy that would provide funds for maintaining a reconstitution capability, it is unlikely that the companies can afford to take half-measures in the conversion process.

As a result of these difficulties, industry managers emphasize other conversion strategies—strategies that fall into a broader meaning of the word. These other strategies fall under the rubric *corporate-level conversion*, because they focus on efforts to change the nature of the entire corporation, as opposed to rebuilding specific plants and facilities. Corporate-level conversion is what is meant by "conversion" in this chapter.

The Government's Options for Defense Procurement

The government has a number of policy options for dealing with the new, lower level of procurement. Some of the options have a severe effect on the industrial base, while other options try to mitigate the impact. In the short term, at least, a firm's ability to convert to nondefense production is tied to the government's policy. The debate at the government level for dealing with the shrinking defense industrial base has focused on four broad approaches: the first is to let the free market decide; the second, termed the "roll-over approach," is a concept of engaging in technology research and development; the third approach is to maintain at least limited production of major systems ("roll over plus"); and the fourth is the concept of a national industrial policy (NIP) applied on a limited basis to national security.

Let the free market decide. The initial reaction of Bush administration officials was to rely on the free market to determine how the personnel, facilities, and resources of the defense industry firms would be efficiently reallocated.[8] The position articulated was that, although defense procurement would drop substantially from existing levels, in 1996 it would still be (if the administration's plans were adopted) $64.3 billion (in 1992 dollars).[9] This represents an almost 50 percent decline in procurement (in real terms) from the peak in 1985, but would still be $20 billion above the trough in procurement reached in 1975 under President Gerald R. Ford.[10]

This approach was in line with the economic philosophy of the Bush administration, although it was a somewhat curious position to take given the nature and history of defense procurement. The existing environment for defense firms is anything but a free market,[11] and even advocates of market systems from Adam Smith to Ludwig von Mises have recognized that national security is a sector in which the price mechanism does not operate.[12]

Upon reflection, its initial adoption of this position indicates that the Bush administration: (1) really had not considered the problem, having been just as shocked as everyone else at the rapidity with which the world situation changed in 1989; and (2) was opposed to alternative proposals for implementing a national industrial policy (NIP), a direction advocated by many prominent Democrats. The Bush administration didn't want to provide its political opponents with ammunition by proposing what would be seen as a de facto NIP for the defense industry.

Roll over—R&D prototyping without production. The current DoD policy, carried over from the Bush administration, has been called the roll-over approach. This approach, which is being reviewed by the Clinton administration, emphasizes continuing research and development to maintain a technological edge, funding systems to the prototype stage, but not engaging in full-scale production.[13] Existing systems would be upgraded and modified, and, in some cases an "arsenal" system, in which a single supplier would exist as a sole producer, would be used to acquire select supplies and systems.[14]

The precedent for this approach of producing prototypes but not advancing to full production is the series of supersonic fighters produced during the 1950s, in which only several examples of the type were produced and used for aerodynamic testing and advancing the technology. There are at least two intellectual difficulties with the analogy: full-size prototypes were needed for testing at that time due to a lack of alternative, less-expensive methods (such as computer simulation), and, although companies were producing these limited prototypes, there were also active production lines manufacturing an average of 2000 fighters a year![15] It seems likely that, without the profits from ongoing production to subsidize the research and development, and without the prospect that at least some of the new aircraft would eventually enter production, this approach could not have been sustained.

"Roll over plus"—limited production. A modified version of the roll-over approach was proposed by Les Aspin when he served as chairman of the House Armed Services Committee.[16] It adds to the roll-over concept by maintaining select "warm" production lines, combined with upgrades and modifications to existing systems. It goes beyond pure prototyping and includes an extensive program for proving manufacturing producibility and operational performance; that is, extensive field testing. For a few select systems of exceptional utility (the F-117 Stealth fighter, for example), a limited new production would be undertaken.[17] Advocates of this approach see it as a means of reducing the risk of having critical areas of defense production completely closed down; they regard the "pure" roll-over approach as one in which DoD is "satisfied to put the blueprints ... on the shelf after [the system] has been developed." [18]

One objection to the roll-over-plus approach is that it may retain production lines for certain weapon systems (such as M1A1 tanks and the F-16) which, according to the DoD, add little to the existing force structure. In addition, low-rate production of these systems results in a relatively high unit cost and takes money away from other, newer systems that DoD would prefer to acquire.[19]

National industrial policy. The final option under consideration is some variant on a national industrial policy (NIP). This approach would be far and away the most activist, creating a U.S. government office comparable to the Japanese Ministry of International Trade and Industry (MITI). In this para-digm, the government would take an active role in selecting "winners" or "losers" by providing direct support—regulatory and financial—for target technologies. It advocates a cooperative system in which private industry is guided by the government. This approach would have the government sup-port, with financial aid, the transition efforts of defense firms, preferentially directing R&D and production to dual-use technologies with both military and commercial applications.

Several prominent reports have been issued that advocate (to varying degrees) that major elements of an NIP be created to address the future of research and development funded through DoD.[20] The objections to this approach center on the appropriateness and ability of government planners to pick successfully winners and losers or to outperform the market in that function. Advocates paint a positive picture of the effectiveness of MITI and of European efforts (the joint Airbus consortium, for example). Critics believe that the impact of such joint government/industry efforts has been far less effective than proponents claim, and that using govern-ment subsidies inevitably costs an economy more than any offsetting gains that result.

This approach was opposed by the Bush administration, but support for such a plan could increase in the Clinton administration. Budget constraints may be a limiting factor to practical steps in this direction.

Options for the Firms

In general terms, the options for the firms fall into five categories, although companies may combine aspects of these strategies into a number of variants. The five major approaches are: 1) simple downsizing of the company to match supply to lower demand; 2) the reallocation of resources from defense production to existing commercial production; 3) diversifica-tion within DoD by pursuing new, nontraditional products and customers; 4) diversification within the government by pursuing new products and cus-tomers outside of DoD; and 5) diversification into commercial markets through acquisitions, mergers, start-ups, and joint ventures.[21]

Simple downsizing. This is not, strictly speaking, a conversion or diver-sification strategy, but a tactical decision taken by firms in the industry that have few alternative choices. In the short term it is difficult for a firm that is dependent on DoD business to do anything else.

The key feature of this tactic is to streamline the organization by cutting expenses and support and other staff—to do more with less. Of course, all of the firms are doing the same with their defense divisions. This approach strives to maintain profits (in relative terms) by shrinking the company in the face of lower sales.

One firm emphasizing this approach is General Dynamics, wherein Chief Executive Officer William Anders is actually concentrating more on defense rather than less by, among other things, selling the Cessna commercial aircraft division. The proceeds from this sale will be used to pay down the high debt load that the company accumulated in the 1980s and to boost the stock price. The rationale expressed by Mr. Anders is a "core competency" argument—defense is what the firm knows and does best, and it is best to stick to it.[22]

There is a presupposition buried in this approach: firms will be forced out of the defense market, leaving a larger share of a smaller pie to those firms that survive. Growth, therefore, will come at the expense of the firms that leave the industry.[23] Unfortunately, most of the major companies in the industry see themselves as the firms that should remain, and the "other guy" as the one who ought to take the losses and reduce industry overcapacity.

Reallocation of resources. The most straightforward true conversion tactic is to reallocate the firms' resources internally, from one existing product line to another. This is especially attractive to those companies, such as McDonnell Douglas or Boeing, whose commercial product is very similar to its major military systems.[24]

Alas, in most cases the reallocation of resources is not as benign as these scenarios in which technology (and presumably most of the work force) is transferred from one project to another. Most asset transfers are financial—that is, increasing a nondefense division's share of company financial resources while decreasing the share available to the defense groups, and effectively putting those divisions into a financial "sink-or-swim" situation.

"New" DoD customers. Another alternative strategy is to seek out "new" DoD customers. This is a zero-sum game in which the intention is to poach on customers that have traditionally dealt with other companies. This is like the simple downsizing approach in that it continues to rely on the same DoD customer base, but the distinction is between the company producing fewer units of its current product line and one that is willing to add entirely new products.

This strategy is more difficult than first reckoned because, although DoD is often regarded as a single customer with the same basic regulations and procedures, in fact there are often major differences between procuring service organizations.

As an example of the difficulties, consider Navy procurement. The Navy *must* procure some systems from the limited number of contractors with adequate facilities for their construction. In the case of submarines, for example, General Dynamics' Electric Boat Division and Tenneco's Newport News Shipbuilding are the only two facilities with the manufacturing capability.[25] Even when acquiring systems such as tactical missiles that could be manufactured by many of the industry prime contractors, the Navy may prefer to deal with a small group of firms with which it has had previous, successful relationships. These firms are already familiar with the particular service's procurement system, the people, the "hoops" that they must go through, and the design biases that are preferred. For an interloper, these present formidable obstacles to entry.

On the other hand, a new entrant may be willing to give a prospective new customer better value by accepting a lower profit rate for the initial contract or by bringing new skills, strengths, and technologies to bear. Another factor is, simply, that over time the relationship between the customer and the traditional supplier almost inevitably suffers from small frictions and disagreements that may lead the customer to believe that a new supplier, who brings a blank slate, may deserve a chance. Indeed, not only can the service anticipate that the new supplier will give it concentrated attention, but it will also serve notice on other suppliers that they can be replaced if they don't toe the line.

New government customers. A variant of the strategy of adding new DoD customers is trying to interest other, non-DoD government agencies in the firm's products or services. This strategy has several attractive features for traditional defense contractors. From one agency to another, government has the same basic regulatory, reporting, and accounting requirements. Defense industry firms suffer much less from a cost disadvantage than in a purely commercial environment, and it is a market that they understand. Additionally, the less technically sophisticated non-DoD agencies may rely on the contractor to provide a much wider range of services and support than that provided to traditional DoD customers.

Acquisitions, mergers, joint ventures, and start-ups in new industries. This last approach to conversion—acquisitions, mergers, joint ventures, and start-ups of activities unrelated to existing business lines—is not plant-level conversion but usually involves selling assets currently held and using the proceeds to purchase new, different assets. This is a "pure" conversion strategy, transforming the firm from a defense producer to a commercial producer.

In an odd way, this is the most controversial approach to diversification. There are two reasons for this: first, these strategies reassign financial assets from one activity to another without reassigning the existing people, facilities, and capabilities of the firm; and, second, there is a great deal of debate surrounding the ability of defense industry firms to succeed outside of a narrow range of ventures.

The first objection, that this kind of conversion does not take advantage of the existing industrial base of the company, is too often true. Making the decision to abandon a business area, to close facilities and lay off employees, is difficult, distasteful, and agonizing. But this situation is not unique to the defense industry: it is what economist Joseph Schumpeter called "creative destruction."

The second objection, the *ability* of companies in the defense industry to succeed in developing nondefense, commercial business will be covered at length below. But clearly no firm that tries to expand its business can be guaranteed of success, and, indeed, if the number of start-ups, joint ventures, and acquisitions are evaluated in total (that is, both defense firms *and* commercial firms), the chances of success may still be less than 50/50.

Suffice it to say that even a conversion strategy based on acquisitions, mergers, start-ups, and joint ventures still requires time, persistence, and a long-term singlemindedness on the part of management.

The Conversion Track Record: Is It Really So Bad?

Conversion, either on a plant or a corporate level, has been subject to criticism as inappropriate and ineffective, a path in which assets are wasted pursuing efforts in which defense industry firms cannot succeed.[26] This perception results from several factors, including a debatable interpretation of data and the adoption of a set of assumptions that are not entirely accurate.

Several studies support this pessimistic view of conversion, including a 1987 study by Michael Porter of the Harvard Business School and a 1986 study conducted by the McKinsey consulting firm for General Dynamics.[27] A more recent survey (1991) on commercialization of defense technology, conducted by DRI/Fraser Group/Winbridge Group, has shown startlingly different results.

The Porter study, among others, was characterized by William Anders of General Dynamics as showing "diversification acquisitions in the nondefense economy are economic failures 50-75% of the time." [28] The Porter study, however, does not make a value judgment by assigning the term "economic failures"—it merely assesses the percent of new businesses acquired and later divested.

This is a critical distinction: first because there are many reasons other than "failure" for divesting an asset; and, second, because an examination of the data shows that, of the thirty-three companies studied, there is no particular pattern that would indicate that defense firms are any worse (or better) than the other firms studied and, in fact, are widely distributed across the spectrum.

Indeed, a curious finding of the Porter study is that it shows two companies, Raytheon and General Electric, which are both considered to be among the defense industry's best managed firms, at opposite ends of the spectrum. Raytheon is among the companies that have had the lowest number of acquisitions later divested (implying economic success to critics), while GE, a commercial product powerhouse, ranks among the companies with the highest rate of divestitures (implying economic failure).

Just as the interpretation of the data is questionable, so is the supposition that firms divest businesses solely because they are economic failures.

Companies divest businesses for many reasons. Rockwell International divested its Measurement and Flow Control Division in 1989 even though it was considered to be the premier firm in that industry.[29] Boeing divested itself of a profitable division that manufactured fiberglass bathroom fixtures. Why? Even profitable divisions may be underperforming other parts of the corporation, and management may believe that by reallocating those assets they can raise the entire corporate return. According to one corporate executive, Boeing divested its fixtures business in the belief that a "low tech" consumer product did not fit well with its overall corporate culture.[30]

Management may perceive that the potential market for a product is smaller than initially forecast, or that the area is taking a disproportionate amount of executive time and energies, or that the peak product value has been reached, or that a large additional investment will be required to maintain the product's current position in the market over the long term. A defense firm may acquire a company in its entirety even though it only wants to keep several key divisions. In such a case, the defense firm may begin divesting the unwanted parts of the company soon after the initial acquisition.

This is hardly an exhaustive list of reasons, other than economic failure, for leaving a business area. Ironically, Mr. Anders was suggesting that defense firms divested businesses primarily as the result of economic failure, yet in the same speech he explained the divestiture of Cessna (the most profitable division of General Dynamics) as due not to failure, but to its asset value if sold. The proceeds from the sale would be used to reduce the corporate debt load and would allow management to focus more sharply on its remaining defense divisions.[31]

The 1991 DRI/Fraser Group/Winbridge Group study results are worth noting, in that they indicate that a significant number of companies in the defense industry are considering entering new business areas, and, among those that already have, the perception of a large percentage of the executives is that they have been successful. In addition, an even larger number of executives within the industry are considering diversifying into commercial areas, according to the survey.[32]

The data do not eliminate acquisition/mergers, joint ventures, and new start-ups as viable strategies for firms in the defense industry, but neither do they suggest that these are the appropriate paths for every firm. Indeed, the defense industry remains suspicious of the external diversification strategy for conversion because of the many seemingly viable ventures that have not succeeded.

Clearly, when a company decides to enter a new business area, the prospect of success will vary with the company's circumstances. Most new ventures take years to become profitable and to be completely integrated into the existing management structure of the parent company. Any company that expects otherwise is deluding itself. It is possible to buy into already profitable business areas, but that usually requires paying a premium.

The financial condition of the purchaser (or investor) in such ventures will also have an impact. A financially fragile company trying to acquire new assets may not have the wherewithal to buy into the top echelons of the target industry, instead opting to buy a second-tier player with potential, thus increasing the risk of failure. Such a venture is often doubly risky, since to bring a second-tier firm into the upper tier of the industry requires additional investment after acquisition and the financial staying power to remain in the game long enough to reach the goal.

The Defense/Aerospace Industry Today

Defining the Industry

The defense industry can be defined in several ways that give unique insights into the conversion potential of its firms.[33] One common approach for dividing the industry is to consider the percent of a firm's total sales that go to DoD.[34] This approach separates companies into those that have a high percentage of sales (in excess of 75-80 percent) to DoD and those that have a relatively low percentage of their total sales to DoD (less than 25-30 percent), with the rest of the industry falling into a broad middle range. These differences can arise from historical patterns—some firms like GE and Westinghouse were never *predominantly* defense firms, but rather were large conglomerates with many interests. Other firms have been predominantly defense-oriented, at least since World War II, and only a few (including Boeing beginning in the 1950s and United Technologies and Rockwell International beginning in the late 1960s) have made the conversion from a DoD to a commercial business base.

The validity of this analysis is borne out by the high inverse correlation between the percentage of total business that the companies were doing with DoD and the overall financial health of the firm. Companies like McDonnell Douglas, General Dynamics, Lockheed, and Northrop, which were very dependent during the 1980s on DoD contracts, were by the end of the decade in dire financial straits. High debt-to-equity ratios, low profitability, and negative cash flows characterized these firms. Such difficulties were not universal, though. Better managed firms, such as Martin Marietta, have maintained high ratios of defense work to total output and have remained financially healthy—but these were the exception, not the rule.)[35]

The opposite was also generally true: companies like GE, TRW, and United Technologies, with relatively low ratios of DoD sales to total sales, ended the 1980s with manageable levels of long-term debt, reasonable profitability, and positive cash flows. (Sales to DoD is a slippery measure subject to large fluctuations. For example, after the completion of the B-1B contract during the mid-1980s, Rockwell's percentage of DoD business dropped dramatically, from 50 to 26 percent.)[36]

From the perspective of diversification and conversion, it is intuitive that the financial health of the firms may be the single most important factor in the equation. While financially healthy companies in the industry are considering entering new business areas, other companies are selling still profitable divisions to reduce debt load and improve short-term freedom of action.

A second analytical approach is to examine the firms according to their structural role in the industry: prime contractors, major subcontractors, or parts and components suppliers. This was the basis for the recent evaluation of the industry by the Office of Technology Assessment and was used in studies of the industry in the late 1970s.[37] This approach allows several unique observations to be made using data on the concentration of the industry and on the exodus of parts and components suppliers.[38]

There are several striking difficulties with using this method: most of the large firms are prime contractors, major subcontractors, and, not infrequently, parts and component suppliers on different contracts all at the same time. Northrop, for example, is the prime contractor on the B-2 bomber, and is also a parts supplier to Boeing for structural members on the 747 commercial jetliner.

An important concern that arises from this structural analysis of the industry is the reported exit of parts and components suppliers in large numbers, perhaps as many as 80,000 during the past decade.[39]

Another way of analyzing the defense industry firms that has considerable merit is to examine the products and processes that are "typical" of the firm and then to categorize the firms on a scale of low-tech to high-tech. Clearly, firms like Hughes or TRW that manufacture satellites for communication, surveillance, and early warning have a very different corporate culture than manufacturers like FMC, which produces armored vehicles.

Conversion, seen from this perspective, has an almost contradictory result. The plants that are the most automated and designed for large-scale, mass production processes, similar to those found in commercial industries, are often so specialized that the task of converting them is economically implausible.[40] Facilities that are geared toward low unit output tend to be more flexible, equipped with a wide range of machine tools, and capable of producing any design—but are only profitable if they can produce a low-volume, high-cost-per-unit product.

Financial Status—Coming out of the 1980s

The 1980s were a paradoxical time for defense industry firms. The industry was in grave financial difficulty at the end of the 1970s, due to the 1968-1974 reductions in procurement spending.[41] The dramatic increase in funding for defense procurement (which started late in the Carter administration) created the impression that the 1980s would be a time of recovery and profitability, when the weak members of the industry could lick their wounds. Such was not the case.

In fact, unlike previous periods of defense spending increases, the 1980s did not result in defense industry firms acquiring new assets or having extraordinary profit rates. Indeed, the quip, "you can make a small fortune in the defense business—provided you start out with a large one" was unfortunately apropos.[42]

The financial facts. During the second half of the 1980s the financial condition of defense industry firms deteriorated significantly. According to an article in *Aviation Week & Space Technology*, during that period defense stock prices declined by 40 percent, forcing the firms in the industry to substitute debt for equity. Debt levels grew by 81 percent.[43] Many of the companies, reaching their borrowing limits, were forced to pay increased interest rates and were given lower debt ratings. Earnings declined by 45 percent, while the assets/sales ratio grew fourfold. Return on sales (ROS) dropped by 50 percent, and return on investment (ROI) dropped to about half of the prevailing industry cost of capital. Investment in inventories and receivables doubled, reducing available funding for other, profitable activities.[44] Several of the largest U.S. defense contractors had debt-to-equity ratios of 70 percent or higher.[45]

As noted earlier, as many as 80,000 firms left the defense industry during the 1980s. Companies that could easily find alternative products and markets got out of defense.

The reasons. Why were the 1980s such tough times for the defense industry firms? For several reasons, including a reduction in progress payments to 80 percent and the changes brought about by the Tax Reform Act of 1986, which eliminated the Contract Completion Tax Method. Using this method, defense contractors did not pay taxes on the profit earned on a contract until it was complete. The cost of this change was staggering. Imagine for a moment the interest earned (or saved) by a contractor on a ten- or fifteen-year contract producing a nuclear submarine or fighter aircraft involving billions of dollars. With a financial "float" of that magnitude, a great many costs could be offset.

The problem, though, was deeper. It started with the multiple, sometimes conflicting goals of the Reagan administration. In tune with the president's long-held conservative beliefs, the administration wanted a major increase in defense-related production, new weapon systems, and higher levels of munitions, spare parts, and supplies. The president himself provided the vision of an entirely new, additional area of defense spending: the Strategic Defense Initiative (SDI).

Along with this greater level of defense spending came another theme dear to conservatives: run government like a business; expose it, wherever possible, to the pressure of the market. One effect of this was an emphasis on fixed-price, in preference to cost-plus, contracts for defense procurement.[46] The shift was so pervasive that by 1989 almost 80 percent of the defense industries' business with DoD was done on a fixed-price basis.[47]

For the most part, the fixed-price contracts were not a problem. A large percentage of DoD procurement is made up of fairly standard items with predictable costs. It was the use of fixed-price contracts on research and development (R&D) projects—risky, uncertain technology efforts—that caused billions of dollars in write-offs in the decade.[48] In the late 1980s, several of the firms in the industry announced publicly that they would no longer bid on fixed-price R&D contracts.

The industry discovered a painful lesson: sales volume did not mean profitability or a bright future. As Bernard Schwartz, CEO of Loral, said: "The defense industrial base is no longer resilient, vital, or easily recoverable." [49]

A Strategy for Conversion—Case Study

Examples of Successful Conversion

There are two major conversion/diversification success stories among the large defense industry firms—Rockwell International and United Technologies Corporation (UT). In both cases, the process was accomplished over a twenty-year time span utilizing a combination of strategies. Based on available documents and discussion with observers inside the corporations, a number of general observations can be made.[50] There is no "cookbook" for diversification to guarantee success, but an examination of the track record of these firms may give some direction.

Acquisitions of and mergers with existing companies in commercial manufacturing. Both Rockwell and UT used mergers and acquisitions as the underlying strategy for achieving diversification.

Rockwell International is the result of a 1967 merger of North American Aviation and Rockwell-Standard Corporation and a later 1972 merger of

North American Rockwell with Rockwell Manufacturing Company (a second "Rockwell" company). The former North American Aviation (NAA), which constitutes the core of Rockwell's defense business, itself originated from a complex series of mergers of early airframe manufacturers. General Motors acquired a controlling interest in the company in the late 1920s and held it until 1948, when GM sold its remaining interest in NAA.

United Technologies began as Pratt & Whitney Aircraft, later becoming United Aircraft and Transport Corp.[51] Beginning in 1971, then-CEO Harry Gray undertook a series of acquisitions intended to reduce the 50 percent-plus dependence on DoD sales.[52] UT acquired Essex, a wire and cable manufacturer, in 1974, Otis Elevators in 1976, Carrier and Mostek in 1980, and two telecommunications groups from General Dynamics in 1982.[53]

An important factor in each company's success at using a strategy of diversification is good management. In the case of UT, both its Pratt & Whitney and Sikorsky divisions have products with obvious commercial applications, and the company has a long history of commercial production.[54] Consequently, the management was already accustomed to working in a commercial environment. In the case of Rockwell, the first two CEOs of the newly merged company came from the commercial, not defense/aerospace, businesses.

Reduce defense fixed assets, plant, and equipment. When procurement spending suddenly shrinks there are few short-term options available to managers to keep the business on a healthy footing. When the potential for additional sales is limited, the usual response, to maintain a healthy return on assets (ROA), is to divest assets. This is not really a solution, in that it almost inevitably means shrinking the company, but it may be necessary. Even companies that are not specifically trying to diversify, for example General Dynamics with its sale of Cessna, or those trying to bolster their finances to compete in an existing business area, like McDonnell Douglas, may have to sell assets.

There is a downside to adopting this course of action. Often the assets sold or scrapped are pieces of machinery or test equipment that would have great value in any new project that might be won in the future. But when managers cannot see the realistic possibility of capturing such a program in six months or a year, they can hardly afford to keep excess assets on the books.

Defense as "cash cow." In any long-term conversion program, the defense divisions of a firm must be used as "cash cows" to provide the financial backing for new nondefense activities. In technical financial terms, a "cash cow" is defined as a business in which the profit rate exceeds the anticipated growth rate. Today, with defense growth negative, any profitable activity is almost by definition a cash cow.

It is not easy, though, for managers to view their defense activities this way. Given the cyclical nature of the industry, the inclination during periods like the 1980s is to believe that potential growth and profit will be greatest in defense production. This leads managers to jettison investment-intensive, nondefense activities and to begin reinvesting profits in DoD ventures. Alas, at the end of the cycle, they find that their investment in additional capacity for supplying defense needs is of little importance when the customer is no longer interested in buying the product.

The main point is that the successful transition is made over a long period of time by managers who recognize the cyclical nature of defense procurement. This means that during the good times one must invest for the lean times, when the firm may have to rely on nondefense production. This is the case of Kavlico, a second-tier supplier that used its sensor business with DoD as a cash cow during the period while it was transforming itself into a producer of high-tech components for automobiles and equipment for the machine tool industry.[55]

Characteristics of Successful Conversion Ventures

Defense technology providing an edge.   Relying on defense technologies to provide the basis for success in the nondefense market seems to have limited potential. But to imply that defense technology cannot provide a real edge for a conversion venture would be to shortchange the possibilities.

Kavlico is one of the more direct examples of using defense technologies for nondefense production. Its application to the automotive and machine tool industries of sensor technologies that it acquired while supplying the military is one of the few cases where a firm was able to continue using the same facility and work force throughout the conversion process.

Another example was Rockwell's transfer to its Goss Colorliner printing press of imaging technologies developed for military applications. The press is considered to be the world leader in large-quantity, color printing for newspapers.[56] Indeed, this theme of transferring defense technology to non-defense production has been repeated often over a twenty-plus year timeframe, as shown in the Rockwell annual reports.[57]

When UT acquired Carrier Air Conditioning, part of the rationale was the potential for transferring advanced compressor technology to Carrier from the Pratt & Whitney jet engine division.[58] Otis Elevators has been incorporating advanced technology spinoffs from defense technologies, such as "fuzzy logic," artificial intelligence, and neural networks, into its products as well.[59]

Supplying intermediate users, not retail customers.   Critics of defense diversification often point to the inability of defense firms to compete in the end-user sector of the market.[60] While such generalizations must exclude consumer product giants GE (the second-largest U.S. defense contractor in 1990) and Westinghouse (the nineteenth-largest), it may contain a useful insight.[61] In the cases of Rockwell and UT, the most successful commercial projects have supplied intermediate users and not end markets.

In the early 1970s, for example, Rockwell produced some of the earliest integrated circuit-based calculators and a line of power tools for home use. Rockwell also acquired Admiral, with its line of consumer durables (refrigerators and stoves) and consumer electronics. None of these activities were highly successful, and some, like the Admiral consumer electronics, were very costly failures. On the other hand, Rockwell continues to be the largest producer of semiconductor data engines for high-speed modems. The Allen-Bradley division provides a wide array of control systems. And production of electronic components for commercial products that use the Global Positioning System (GPS) is a growing segment, as GPS units are making their way from military use to civil engineering, surveying, and navigation systems for automobiles.[62]

Market Niches That Grow

Just as uncertainty may work against companies trying to enter commercial businesses, it can also work for them, and they can find that a division that was in a stable, unexciting, low-growth market can suddenly take off.

The Rockwell/Goss Colorliner printing press is one example. A new technology infusion from the defense sector resulted in a substantial improvement in the color reproduction ability of high-speed printing presses, and the market grew as major newspapers acquired the new equipment.

The commercial use of GPS receivers, noted above, may in the future become an example of growth in an esoteric niche, as new uses, never contemplated by the original designers, are found.

Otis Elevator developed a market niche in Japan that grew beyond expectations when it entered a partnership with Matsushita. It increased its market share 500 percent, from 3 percent in 1973 to 15 percent in 1989.[63]

Large, complex projects. Another natural area for defense industry prime contractors is designing, creating, and maintaining large complex systems. Often such systems are comparable to systems produced for the military. Air-traffic-control systems would be an example. These systems are sold not only to the FAA but to foreign airports as well on a commercial basis.

Indeed, one of the reasons cited by GM management for the acquisition of Hughes was to tap into the systems engineering capability at Hughes as it was applicable to future intelligent vehicle highway systems, an area of great interest to GM as well as to several other firms in the aerospace industry.[64]

International market exploitation. UT and Rockwell receive a substantial part of their sales revenues from international subsidiaries and acquisitions.

Both Otis and Carrier have large foreign sales, and a large part of Carrier's sales increase abroad came from acquisitions made during the 1980s.[65] Carrier Air Conditioning is the number one company in the world in its field and expects to spend an additional $500 million for overseas acquisitions in the next five years.

Rockwell has a significant part of the drivetrain market for trucks in Europe and is expanding into central and Eastern Europe. The Collins Avionics division has a significant part of its sales outside the United States, as does the Goss division. Allen-Bradley is a global leader in control systems with facilities around the world.

In both cases, the international market share has developed through a combination of long-term presence in the market and selective foreign acquisitions.

Management persistence.   This discussion would be incomplete if it did not address the role of persistence among top management in the success of these ventures. The management of each company demonstrated a long-term objective of reducing its dependence on DoD sales and persisted in that thrust even during the times when defense divisions were able to achieve higher ROAs and ROEs than their nondefense divisions. Persistence also entailed running the defense-related businesses in a way that did not financially impoverish the company through the pursuit of high-risk, low-reward programs of the 1980s.

The Management Factor

Entrepreneurs to Manufacturers, Manufacturers to Bureaucrats

A gradual change in the nature of defense industry management has taken place since the end of World War II. The industry was started by classic entrepreneurs. Over time, as the firms grew, the entrepreneurs were replaced by professional managers who could competently run the large-scale production of manufactured goods. But as time has passed, the companies in the defense industry have come more and more to resemble the government agencies that they supply. And as that has occurred, the habits of bureaucracy characteristic of the government have led to similar behavior by defense industry management.

There are still exceptions in the industry. But when the system is structured to stifle risk-taking and creativity in favor of conformity and risk-reduction, it is inevitable that a different kind of manager will rise.

Such managers are not going to undertake a jump into the unknown, away from the comfort of inertia and onto the path of conversion. Conversion and diversification are paths of risk, stress, and uncomfortable times.

The Military/Industrial Revolving Door

One of the factors contributing to the management problem has been the close relationship of the defense firms with their military customers. Over time a large number of executive-level managers have gone directly from military careers into strategic planning and business development positions in the industry. Having spent their careers as managers in the government, an organization managed in the bureaucratic manner (rule-based and centrally controlled), they do not have the same market experience and background as managers who have spent careers in the private sector.[66] In many instances they continue to view the industry from the government's point of view: the industry exists solely to serve the needs of the government.

This is not a blanket indictment. Many ex-military personnel working in the defense industry, and especially in the technical specialities, perform their jobs admirably. But, as James Schlesinger is purported to have said, the problem with senior officers is not their uncontrollable desire to take initiative, but the opposite: "After a lifetime of taking orders, generals and admirals were, if anything, too compliant." [67] Eisenhower was wrong concerning the power of the military-industrial complex. The problem is not one of industry flexing its economic and political muscle to control the direction of policy, but instead of too often being prepared to follow the government's lead, even at the expense of the industry's long-term well-being.[68]

The Future

Some industry observers have attacked the "teaming" approach that has become increasingly common in the industry over the past several years. These critics believe, with some justification, that the government has encouraged teaming to keep financially weak companies in the industry, instead of confronting the reality of industry over-capacity.

Teaming has several advantages for the industry, some of which have unintended benefits for companies that are trying to convert their operations. A teaming arrangement spreads the market risk and allows many contractors to win a market share. Critic William Anders of General Dynamics also sees the potential of sharing the losses. But companies that don't receive at least some share of DoD sales will incur even greater losses (at least in the short term) than those that receive a less-than-maximum amount.

Teaming can provide a vital "bridge" for companies that want to turn away from DoD dependence by providing an income stream while the company finds alternative business areas. There are several companies, such as Grumman and Northrop, that may cease to be major prime contractors as their last large contracts wind down. Such firms can use teaming arrangements to evolve into major subcontractor roles.

The government has a substantial stake in promoting defense industry conversion: maintaining the "best" military capability within budget constraints, encouraging the growth of new jobs to replace those lost in the downsizing, ensuring that technologies developed in the defense sector are transferred to the private sector economy, and minimizing other national and regional effects.

One change that could be made, which would have an almost immediate impact on the ability of defense firms to enter into new business areas and markets, would be to reduce or eliminate export restrictions on U.S. firms.[69]

Government policies could be formulated to ease the transfer of technology from the defense sector to the private sector. This would include reducing the costs and legal barriers that prevent defense contractors from using technologies that were developed under government contract. Creating a uniform national system to provide access to technologies developed in the national laboratories is another specific concept that only the government can initiate.

Another suggestion is to overhaul the procurement process by eliminating the more expensive and onerous provisions that prevent companies from producing commercial and military products in the same facilities. Reasonable controls and audit procedures can be developed to reflect the changing environment and yet vastly reduce the time and expense of compliance. Surely some of the almost 850 steps in the procurement process can be eliminated.[70]

It is not the function of the government to redress all of the consequences that the sudden shift from defense production has caused. And the outlook for many of the white-collar defense workers is not as bleak in the long term as it has been in prior downturns. The short-term issue, beyond providing the normal social net, is another question. How can the United States continue to benefit from the skills and special insights that these people have developed during their years in the defense industry?

Many of the engineers and scientists have skills that are transferable to nondefense business. Their knowledge of science, mathematics, and computer programming could be put to productive use, adding to economic growth. Giving nondefense companies inducements for hiring these technical specialists would help to offset their lack of experience in the new industry.

Changing the rules that bar entry into such fields as the teaching profession is another possibility. Allowing former rocket and radar scientists to teach subjects in which they are well qualified without necessarily requiring them to become full-time teachers, might also be an attractive option.

Programs could be established through the Small Business Administration and DoD small business set asides to encourage former defense workers to establish their own businesses. Many of the people who are leaving the industry have creative ideas for new, unique products and services. They are highly trained, computer-literate people. Like all of us, though, they must feed their families and pay their bills. Finding ways to match the ideas and the capital, on a small, start-up scale, could result in an unimagined flowering of high-tech companies.

Can the government have its cake and eat it too? Can the firms in the defense industry be forced to convert away from defense production and also be expected to worry about the ease of re-entry? In the words of Les Aspin,

> This suggests there will be a kind of industrial triple somersault out of and back into the defense business. Why we should expect such a thing to happen is unclear. Why would anyone in their right mind go through the pain and expense of conversion and then go back to defense? [71]

Conclusion

Some may feel that this chapter presents a pessimistic outlook for conversion of defense industry firms. This is not entirely the case. The outlook for some aspects of the problem *is* pessimistic: reconstitution is a pipe dream; that firms will be able to directly convert specific plants, facilities, and labor force to commercial production (especially in the short term) is doubtful.

This analysis has led to several additional conclusions regarding the future prospects and requirements for transforming the defense industry.

Ten years from now companies that do not convert will either be out of business or will be a fraction of their current size. Although there is no reason to suppose that companies must entirely leave the defense industry to survive, they would be well advised to aim for a maximum sales reliance on DoD of 15-25 percent. This will reduce the impact of continuing procurement cycles to 7-13 percent of sales, an amount that most companies can handle.

There are many reasons to believe that defense industry firms that wish to make the transition away from DoD dependency to commercial activities have a higher probability of success today than at any time since the 1960s. With persistence, care, and a great deal of effort, conversion and diversification are possible. Large firms like United Technologies and Rockwell International have done it, and many smaller firms, an estimated 60,000, have also made the transition.[72]

The defense manufacturers have a surprisingly strong market to enter, one that can benefit from the characteristics of the industry: high-technology capital goods. According to recent research, there is a U.S. advantage in this sector, and it is the growth of this sector that has been fueling the recent export boom.[73] These goods take advantage of the very areas in which defense industry firms excel: advanced manufacturing, low unit production rates, high cost-per-unit, system complexity, and computer/control-intensive systems.

The markets for such capital goods are international. The fall of the former Soviet Union, the proximate cause for the decrease in sales to DoD, has simultaneously opened central and Eastern European countries that need to completely rebuild their industrial capabilities. China, the smaller countries of Asia, and Latin America are all developing markets for capital goods, willing and increasingly able to buy American manufacturing equipment.[74]

The United States itself may prove an interesting and expanding market for ex-defense firms' production. The issue of infrastructure in the United States is one of increasing concern, and, under a Clinton administration, funding for infrastructure projects may reach levels comparable to the DoD procurement that is disappearing.

New markets, new technologies, and new national priorities are the future for the defense industry firms. We may have entered a new phase, the beginning of a new Schumpeterian period of creative destruction in which the old industrial structure is swept away by a new, "smart" industrial revolution. And that revolution can be fueled by defense industry companies that seize the vision.

The most likely government policy is a roll over plus similar to that proposed by Les Aspin. As a consequence, the companies that are most likely to have significant DoD weapon systems business in the next five years are those that have active production lines today. The United States will continue to produce existing weapon platforms at low rates—replacement for normal attrition—rather than embark on new system acquisitions. Only a few companies, and only a few divisions of those companies, are likely to remain 100 percent in defense production. This is bad news for firms that do not have current production lines, because R&D and advanced technology demonstrator (ATD) programs will not provide enough business to support the existing, but currently unused, manufacturing capacity.

The new administration is also more likely to take an active role, including significant funding, in assisting technology transfer from DoD contractors and national labs into the private sector. Clinton appointees such as Robert Reich are among the architects of the national industrial policy movement and appear far more willing to implement programs that result in direct government interaction with the private sector. But, despite their willingness, budget considerations will likely limit the size and scope of these programs to providing information and accessibility—a national technology computer database, for example.

Companies that undertake a serious conversion effort need to undertake a major housecleaning of upper management. The current generation of top managers have too little salient experience outside of the government contracts world, and for the most part seem slow to recognize the need for change, much less understand how to go about making the changes.

Conversion requires managers who are willing to shake up the company and to take risks, but that requires changing the corporate culture in profound ways. Managers whose companies have already undertaken conversion efforts report that many of the most valuable employees in the conversion process are those who were once considered "boat rockers" and "mavericks." It is not clear, though, that the current top management of many of the defense firms recognize the value of such employees. As one industry observer has written, "employees who are terminated in the early stages of a downsizing are often the round pegs in square holes—the ones who don't quite fit into the corporate structure, but may be a likely source of alternative (read: entrepreneurial) ideas." [75]

The corporations need to rid themselves of the dead wood that has accumulated in upper management. When there isn't enough work, the blue-collar workers and middle-management are quickly laid off but the executives are kept on in corporate make-work positions. There is also a class of executives whose duties seem limited to attending industry meetings and sitting on various prestigious committees but who are never expected to bring in new business. In competitive environments, companies cannot afford the luxury of these superfluous executives.

Conversion can be successful, but if a path of least resistance is followed and the existing resources squandered through neglect and entropy, then the top managers may discover that all they can do is manage the gradual liquidation of the firm.

It is surprising how long it took for the defense companies to realize that a permanent decline in procurement was in the cards. Even after the effective fall of the Soviet empire, in 1989, they continued to pin their hopes on the production of new weapon systems—A-12, ATF, SDI—long after it had become clear that most of those programs would not survive, and those that did would be at dramatically lower funding levels.

Since 1989 a number of the financially weaker companies in the industry, notably General Dynamics, McDonnell Douglas, and Northrop, have significantly improved their balance sheets. They have done this by selling assets, shutting down unprofitable activities, becoming more selective of the programs they will pursue, and being wary of making up-front investments in DoD business. Whether or not this will give them the breathing room for conversion remains to be seen.

In sum, the conversion/diversification process will have successes and failures. The transformation of the industry will not be solved by quick fixes, but only through the determined and cooperative efforts of policy makers, the DoD, and the industry itself. But it *will* be a tragedy if, because the outcome is not certain and the process is difficult, the effort is not made.

Notes

1. Les Aspin (D-Wis.), "Tomorrow's Defense From Today's Industrial Base: Finding the Right Resource Strategy For a New Era," speech to the American Defense Preparedness Association, February 12, 1992.
2. Data taken from testimony of the Comptroller of Defense before Senate Armed Services Committee, January 29, 1992, "Comptroller Briefing Charts, FY1993 Budget."
3. Ethan B. Kapstein, *The Political Economy of National Security* (New York: McGraw Hill, 1991), 81.
4. U.S. Arms Control and Disarmament Agency, *Report to Congress on Defense Industrial Conversion* (Washington, D.C.: Government Printing Office, August 1990), 17. The report quotes Seymour Melman, a well-respected scholar, from 1983: "It is cause for very serious concern that, until now, no major military-serving enterprise has demonstrated the autonomous ability to carry out the sort of occupational switch that is needed to go civilian. Economic conversion is therefore an important policy idea that has yet to be proven in operation by American industry."
5. This is not an idle question nor unique to the U.S. context. Assessing conversion in the Soviet Union was the subject of an Air Force/CIA conference in June 1990. The author is indebted to the speakers at the conference for their insights into the many ways in which conversion can be undertaken.
6. This very point has been raised recently by Kenneth Adelman and Norman Augustine in "Defense Conversion," *Foreign Affairs* (Spring 1992): 26-47. "Defense conversion in the United States has been bedeviled by two conflicting objectives: how to shift firms out of defense and into civilian pursuits, and how to preserve a mobilization base to meet conceivable future defense needs" (p. 27).
7. Some analysts have suggested a flexible factory as a way of rapidly going back and forth between defense and commercial production. It is not so facile in practice. It might be possible in a few selected areas like electronic components to go back and forth between defense and commercial production, but that will be the exception, not the rule.
8. This position was articulated by Richard Mirsky of the Office of Industrial Base at a conference on defense downsizing and economic conversion held at Harvard University, February 4, 1991.
9. Ibid. Since early 1991, when the Harvard conference was held, the estimate for 1996 procurement has dropped by roughly $10 billion, to $54 billion.
10. Mark A. Forman and Charla Worsham, *Defense Industrial Base Implications of a Declining Defense Budget* (Joint Economic Committee Memorandum, December 9, 1991), 1-2.
11. Jacques Gansler, *The Defense Industry* (Cambridge, Mass.: MIT Press, 1980), table 2.1.
12. Adam Smith, *The Wealth of Nations* (Indianapolis, Ind.: Liberty Classics, 1981), 706-708. Ludwig von Mises, *Bureaucracy,* 2d ed. (Cedar Falls, Iowa: Liberty Press, 1983), 24-26.
13. Although advanced technology demonstrators (ATDs) have been presented as "prototypes," they are far less than what the industry understands the term to mean. The distinction was described at a recent conference ("Reconstitution: Force Structure and Industrial Strategy," May 7-8, 1992) by Gene Porter, a member of the Acqui-

sition Policy and Program Integration Office (Office of the Secretary of Defense) during the Bush administration. An ATD is limited to a "breadboard" or "brassboard" phase prototype. ATDs can be used as a proof of concept and for preliminary testing, but are far from full-scale engineering prototypes.

14. U.S. Congress, Office of Technology Assessment, *Redesigning Defense: Planning the Transition to the Future U.S. Defense Industrial Base,* OTA-ISC-500 (Washington, D.C.: U.S. Government Printing Office, July 1991), 10. Also, for a brief synopsis of this extensive document, see David F. Bond, "Report Urges New Strategy To Maintain Defense Industry," *Aviation Week & Space Technology,* August 5, 1991, 65.

15. Keith Hartley, *The Economics of Defense Policy* (London: Brassey's, 1991), 49.

16. Aspin, "Tomorrow's Defense From Today's Industrial Base," 1-8.

17. Ibid., 7.

18. Ibid., 6.

19. This may be the only means of keeping a "surge" capacity available; this author has a much more pessimistic outlook on the possibility for "reconstitution" than the planners and budget analysts in the Bush DoD.

20. See, for example, Carnegie Commission on Science, Technology, and Government, "Technology and Economic Performance: Organizing the Executive Branch for a Stronger National Technology Base" (New York: Carnegie, 1991); Council on Competitiveness, "Gaining New Ground: Technology Priorities for America's Future" (Washington, D.C.: Council on Competitiveness, 1991). In the Carnegie report the recommendation is made (p. 39) to transform DARPA (Defense Advanced Research Projects Agency) into "NARPA," that is, a "National" ARPA. The Council on Competitiveness recommends (p. 45) enhancing national competitiveness by "a five-year implementation plan to increase dramatically the percentage of federal R&D expenditures for critical generic technologies."

21. Increasing foreign sales of military equipment is not listed as a separate strategy because *all* of the companies that can increase efforts in this direction are doing so, and it is not exclusive to any one approach.

22. Mr. Anders' more recent sale of General Dynamics' fighter aircraft division to Lockheed raises the question of whether he isn't planning on liquidating most of the company, core competency or not!

23. This may also explain Mr. Anders' objections to the "teaming" arrangements that have become popular with DoD program management. From his perspective, it would be a better policy to encourage other, less defense-oriented firms, to leave the industry, rather than to keep a number of financially weak companies competing for future programs.

24. This is also the path frequently taken by the second- and third-tier firms that have undertaken the conversion process.

25. Aspin, "Tomorrow's Defense From Today's Industrial Base," 5-6. Aspin points out in the speech that there is just a single producer of the nuclear power systems used in U.S. Navy vessels.

26. In a keynote address to the twelfth annual defense week conference ("Rationalizing America's Defense Industry"), October 30, 1991, General Dynamics CEO William Anders states: "External diversification ... is usually a formula for disaster" (p. 13). Murray Weidenbaum made a similar point in a paper presented to the annual meeting of the Western Economic Association ("The Future of the U.S. Defense Industry," July 1, 1991), in which he stated: "Most of the diversification ventures outside of the defense and aerospace markets have been abandoned or sold off. The remainder generally operate at marginal levels" (p. 2).

27. Michael E. Porter, "From Competitive Advantage to Corporate Strategy," in *Michael E. Porter on Competition and Strategy* (Boston: Harvard University, 1991), 15-31.

28. Anders, "Rationalizing America's Defense Industry."

29. Rockwell International, *Rockwell International Annual Report 1990*, November 29, 1990, 38.

30. Boeing vice president Perry Sykes at the Air Force/CIA conference (1990) referenced in n. 5, above.

31. Anders, "Rationalizing America's Defense Industry," 15. See also Rick Wartzman, "Divestiture of Cessna is Planned," *Wall Street Journal*, October 18, 1991, A3.

32. David Hughes, "Survey on Defense Firm Commercial Efforts Shows Surprising Success Rate, Activity," *Aviation Week & Space Technology*, December 9, 1991, 21-22.

33. One reader of an early draft of this chapter pointed out, correctly, that it mainly addressed prime contractors and did not cover in depth the subcontractors and parts-and-component suppliers. Length considerations are partly at fault, but in addition, the largest one hundred contractors represent almost 80 percent of the total sales in the sector (Gansler, *The Defense Industry*, 37), and can fairly represent the industry.

34. Murray Weidenbaum used a similar methodology in "The Future of the U.S. Defense Industry," table 2.

35. In 1989 Martin Marietta was the sixth largest DoD contractor, with an estimated 92 percent of its business with the government. But it maintained a remarkable 23 percent return on equity and a low 35 percent ratio of long-term debt to equity.

36. James Flanigan, "Rockwell Sees Role for U.S. Defense in the Next Century," *Los Angeles Times*, November 3, 1991, D1.

37. Office of Technology Assessment, *Redesigning Defense*, 41-43.

38. Gansler, *The Defense Industry*, figure 2.1, figure 2.2, figure 2.3.

39. John T. Correll and Colleen A. Nash, "Declining, Diversifying and Disappearing," *Air Force Magazine*, October 1991, 38. "Some (including 20,000 small firms) went out of business, but most simply moved to nondefense markets." See also Center for International Studies, "Deterrence in Decay: The Future of the US Defense Industrial Base" (Washington, D.C.: CSIS, 1989.)

40. This view was offered by Richard Barnett of the Army Materials Command (AMC) at the Air Force/CIA conference. AMC studied automated munitions facilities for their conversion potential and concluded that they were so specialized that little, short of tearing them down and starting over, could be done with them.

41. Gansler, *The Defense Industry*, 21-28.

42. Correll and Nash, "Declining, Diversifying and Disappearing," 38, quoting Kenneth Adelman and Norman Augustine.

43. In the 1980s the trend of increasing debt-to-equity ratios was pervasive throughout U.S. business. According to a study by Frederick Furlong, the book-value debt-to-equity ratio for nonfinancial firms had risen to slightly above 50 percent in 1989. The 81 percent average of the defense industry firms is still significantly higher. See Frederick Furlong, "Tax Incentives for Corporate Leverage in the 1980s," in *Economic Review of the Federal Reserve Bank of San Francisco* (Fall 1990, no. 4).

44. Anthony Velocci, Jr., "U.S. Defense Industry Must Change Ways To Stay Out of Financial Emergency Room," *Aviation Week & Space Technology*, December 24, 1990, 16-17.

45. Ira E. Cornelius and Richard H. Young, "Competitor Assessment—Major Aerospace Prime Contractors" (Seal Beach, Calif.: Rockwell International, September 1990). This study drew on a number of sources, including *Defense News, Space News, Aviation Week & Space Technology, Value-Line*, and other financial services.

46. The use of fixed-price contracts, especially for development programs, is generally considered the brainchild of former Navy secretary John Lehman.

47. Velocci, "U.S. Defense Industry Must Change Ways."

48. Ibid.

49. Quoted in Velocci, "U.S. Defense Industry Must Change Ways."

50. This case study began as an analysis of Rockwell International's diversification effort

undertaken by the author for the Air Force/CIA Conference (1990). At that time the similarity of the strategy used by UT was observed.

51. A.G. Edwards & Sons, Inc., "United Technologies—Company Report," March 28, 1990.

52. Ibid.

53. Ibid.

54. In fact, recently UT named Karl Krapek, the former president of Carrier Air Conditioning, as the new president of the Pratt & Whitney jet engine unit. ("UT Names 3 Executives To Jet Engine Unit," *Wall Street Journal*, December 14, 1992, B5.)

55. Joel Kotkin, "How to End Pentagon Dependency and Thrive," *Los Angeles Times*, February 9, 1992, M3. See also U.S. Arms Control and Disarmament Agency, *Report to Congress on Defense Industry Conversion*, August 1990, 17.

56. The "transfer" of technology was accomplished by assigning a cadre of engineers from the defense electronics division to Goss. Lest it be trivialized, it took several years for this to be accomplished.

57. Rockwell International, *Rockwell International Annual Report 1972*, 9: "Major emphasis is given to the transfer and utilization of technology between the Aerospace and Systems Group and the Commercial Products Group." *Rockwell International Annual Report 1990*, 4: "We share and apply advanced technologies across our Electronics, Aerospace, Automotive and Graphics sectors." Similar statements are made throughout the period 1967 through 1991.

58. According to a statement by James Martin at the Harvard conference, February 1991 (see n. 8). Mr. Martin had been the director of international marketing at UT.

59. United Technologies, *United Technologies 1991 Annual Report*, 18.

60. Murray Weidenbaum, *Small Wars, Big Defense* (New York: Oxford University Press, 1992), 44-49.

61. "Top 100 Worldwide Defense Firms," *Defense News*, July 22, 1991, 6.

62. Rockwell International, *1991 Annual Report*, 4: "The GPS engine is one example of what we call 'leveraging technology'—taking technology that exists in one Rockwell business or product area and extending it into another for competitive advantage."

63. Richard McCormack, "UT's Strategy for the 1990s: Take on Japanese in Japan," *New Technology Week* 4, no. 22 (May 29, 1990).

64. In addition to GM/Hughes, similar projects are also under way at Lockheed, Northrop, and Rockwell.

65. The first major section of the *United Technologies 1991 Annual Report* (pp. 6-9) is called "Global Strategies, World of Opportunity."

66. von Mises, *Bureaucracy*, preface to the 1962 edition: "There are two methods for the conduct of affairs within the frame of human society. . . . One is bureaucratic management, the other is profit management." Also, pp. 66-69: "Armies are certainly the most ideal and perfect bureaucratic organizations."

67. Robert Woodward, *The Commanders* (New York: Simon and Schuster, 1991), 80.

68. von Mises, *Bureaucracy*, 70-71.

69. Richard Burt, "Drop Barriers To Defense Trade In the West," *Wall Street Journal*, May 22, 1991, A12.

70. This figure is from Mark Forman, senior economist, Joint Economic Committee. Only a few of these steps are legislated requirements; most are DoD initiated regulations.

71. Aspin, "Tomorrow's Defense From Today's Industrial Base," 4.

72. Correll and Nash, "Declining, Diversifying and Disappearing," 38.

73. Lawrence Lindsey, "America's Growing Economic Lead," *Wall Street Journal*, February 7, 1992, A14. See also, Karen House, "Japan's Decline, America's Rise," *Wall Street Journal*, April 21, 1992, A18. U.S. exports have increased by 13 percent a year from 1986 to 1990.

74. Ibid. Capital equipment exports from the United States have risen from 30 percent of total exports (of a smaller base) in the late 1960s, to 41 percent of exports today.
75. Robert J. Schlesinger, "For intrapreneural conversion," *San Diego Daily Transcript*, July 28, 1992, 6.

7

Adjustments to Reduced Domestic Defense Spending in Western Europe

Bernard Udis

The dramatic changes in the security environment in Europe have raised hopes across the continent of peace dividends and widespread disarmament. Reductions in defense spending, however, will bring short-term economic burdens along with long-term benefits. This chapter addresses the situation facing defense producers and governments in Western Europe. It is based on conversations and exchanges with more than twenty-five individuals representing industry and government in eight European countries.[1] The focus of the chapter is on the empirical issue of how firms adjust to reduced spending for military equipment and the role, if any, assumed by the government in facilitating the adjustments.

One might begin with an obvious point; namely, that any such adjustment will be more easily accomplished in a period of strong economic activity in which available labor and other resources are straining to meet the demand for goods and services. Economists might argue about the most propitious mix of fiscal and monetary policies to absorb the resources newly released from the military sector but there would be little cause for debating the "proper" government role. In this chapter, however, emphasis will be placed on the microeconomic considerations surrounding an individual firm's reactions to a loss of some part of its traditional market.

In setting the stage it might be useful to examine recent changes in levels of military spending in neutral and allied countries.

Table 7-1 presents data for the fifteen NATO members that maintain military forces plus three traditional neutrals. Of the eighteen countries, thirteen reduced military expenditures in the 1985-1990 period.[2]

Table 7-2 presents the percentage distribution, by category, of total defense expenditures of NATO member countries for each half of the decades of the 1970s and 1980s and annually for 1987-1991. The percentage

Bernard Udis is professor of economics at the University of Colorado at Boulder.

devoted to equipment expenditures is the most relevant to this discussion since this influences the economy and industry most directly. Since the 1991 figures are estimates, not too much credence should be paid to the 1990-1991 changes. Over the second half of the 1980s there is a gradual decline, at least among the major industrial states, in the share of defense budgets devoted to weapons procurement. Current budget discussions in these countries suggest rather strongly that procurement of military equipment will fall noticeably in the near future. For example, the German government is expected to reduce its procurement expenditures by approximately 40 percent between 1990 and 1994.[3]

A military producer facing the reduction of domestic defense spending can react in a number of ways. To the executive, the alternatives fall into such categories as seeking to expand the market for the products facing reduced domestic demand or, possibly, attempting to diversify production by offering new products. Economists see such policies as attempts to retain or expand economies of scale or of scope. If successful, such policies would replace declining defense markets at home. This inquiry identified few efforts to diversify but found major efforts to preserve or expand scale economies, suggesting a preference in many firms to maintain their traditional lines of business.[4]

Export Enhancement and Collaborative Ventures

The search for scale economies takes two forms: an effort to expand exports and an effort to fashion collaborative ventures with firms in other countries so as to yield a significantly larger product run than would be possible for a single firm working in one country. In the case of the smaller European states the collaborative approach often is combined with an effort to carve out a special niche in which comparative advantage can be developed.[5] This effort, in some cases, also involves the staff cutbacks associated with abandoning a wider product line and moving toward specialization.

In both Eastern and Western Europe a common policy seems to have emerged—a drive to expand weapons exports. This will doubtless be disappointing and perplexing to the observer hoping to see a rapid move toward disarmament. However, the fighting that has erupted in the former Soviet Union and Yugoslavia reminds us that not all hostilities in the world were consequences of the cold war. There is concern in Europe over the possibility of violence spilling over national frontiers and involving other countries in the fighting. Deep hostilities continue to exist in other parts of the world and it would appear that the disappearance of a bipolar world dominated by the United States and the USSR has in some ways heightened the danger.[6] The persistence of such hostilities and suspicions frustrates the

Table 7-1   Defense Expenditures of NATO Members and Selected
European Neutrals, 1985-1990 ($, millions)

Country	1985	1989	1990
NATO			
Belgium	$2,428	$1,597	$1,558
Denmark	1,259	1,264	1,253
France	20,780	18,025	18,113
Germany[a]	19,922	17,122	16,940
Greece	2,331	2,191	2,209
Italy	9,733	9,690	9,320
Luxembourg	38	50	52
Netherlands	3,884	4,218	4,134
Norway	1,797	1,826	1,880
Portugal	654	768	753
Spain	3,969	3,752	3,742
Turkey	1,649	1,424	1,600
United Kingdom	23,791	20,451	19,574
NATO Europe Total	92,235	82,378	81,128
Canada	7,566	6,996	7,064
United States	258,165	260,024	249,149
Total NATO	357,966	349,398	337,341
Neutrals			
Austria	892	790	752
Sweden	3,192	2,735	2,916
Switzerland	1,930	1,974	2,047

Source: *The Military Balance: 1991-1992* (London: Brassey's for the International Institute for Strategic Studies, Autumn 1991), 212.

Note: Figures are in constant 1985 dollars. Some military expenditures include internal security expenditures; in other cases these and research costs are borne by other ministries' budgets.

[a] Data is for former FRG only. Excludes aid to West Berlin.

hope of a neat falling into place of the elements necessary for a peaceful environment.

In Eastern Europe, states with capability in weapons production and low reserves of hard currency find willing customers hard to turn down.[7] In Western Europe a similar situation has evolved, although the details are somewhat different. Here, the problem is to find a way to adjust to the high unit costs caused by the widespread reduction in domestic weapons acquisition. The countries of Western Europe with significant arms production capacity are also pursuing a policy of increased military exports. Even erstwhile neutrals that have long restrained arms sales abroad have indicated that they too will be competing to export arms.[8] Table 7-3 presents the percentage of total exports represented by arms exports in the period 1979-1989 for NATO member states, the former Soviet Union and its allies, and three traditional Western neutrals.

Table 7-2   Distribution of Total Defense Expenditures by Category

Country	Average 1970- 1974	Average 1975- 1979	Average 1980- 1984	Average 1985- 1989	1987	1988	1989	1990	1991[a]
	Percentage devoted to personnel expenditures								
Belgium	62.4	62.9	61.8	63.4	62.1	63.7	67.1	68.4	67.4
Canada	65.6	60.8	50.7	46.2	46.1	45.4	47.9	50.0	49.3
Denmark	58.9	58.0	54.6	56.6	55.2	58.0	59.8	58.4	58.3
Germany	50.5	49.8	46.6	48.9	49.2	49.7	51.1	52.1	56.6
Greece	66.8	57.6	54.6	60.5	61.7	58.2	61.5	64.1	63.9
Italy	59.9	61.9	59.1	57.8	59.0	57.8	58.7	61.6	—
Luxembourg	82.2	85.5	77.5	76.9	76.8	74.7	77.1	79.6	74.5
Netherlands	65.4	61.2	55.3	52.8	53.6	54.3	53.7	53.9	53.6
Norway	52.1	52.9	48.8	43.9	43.3	45.6	42.6	43.3	43.8
Portugal	50.8	68.8	66.6	67.7	65.7	66.3	71.4	73.1	73.5
Spain	—	—	—	—	49.7	54.5	57.3	62.0	64.2
Turkey	66.7	47.6	45.3	37.1	34.7	35.6	46.1	48.3	49.3
United Kingdom	48.8	44.6	37.4	38.6	39.0	40.7	39.5	42.2	42.4
United States	—	—	41.9	37.0	35.9	37.6	38.2	36.6	37.7
	Percentage devoted to equipment expenditures								
Belgium	10.7	11.7	13.8	12.1	13.1	12.0	9.9	7.9	7.7
Canada	7.3	9.0	17.8	19.7	21.4	20.1	18.4	17.0	16.1
Denmark	16.4	18.4	16.9	14.0	14.9	14.4	13.1	14.9	15.9
Germany	16.4	16.8	20.0	19.6	20.1	19.3	19.0	17.7	16.6
Greece	8.2	19.3	17.4	18.2	17.2	23.3	21.9	21.4	22.8
Italy	15.3	14.7	17.4	19.7	20.6	20.5	20.5	17.5	—
Luxembourg	1.5	1.9	1.8	3.5	3.9	2.8	3.8	3.2	4.9
Netherlands	12.8	18.0	20.5	19.8	17.8	20.4	17.6	17.9	16.3
Norway	15.2	16.0	19.4	21.7	20.4	18.8	24.8	22.6	22.7
Portugal	7.1	2.2	5.5	7.6	10.1	10.5	11.9	10.3	8.1
Spain	—	—	—	—	24.7	20.7	18.3	12.7	14.9
Turkey	3.9	19.2	9.1	18.2	21.1	22.5	17.2	20.0	20.7
United Kingdom	16.6	21.6	26.2	24.8	24.7	25.4	22.0	19.5	20.1
United States	21.4	17.6	21.9	25.6	26.5	24.8	25.3	24.8	24.3

The case of Sweden is particularly interesting, especially in the interaction of political and economic forces. For almost sixty years Sweden pursued a policy of political neutrality. This neutrality was reinforced by the military capability to defend itself with its own weapons free of dependence on foreign military suppliers. The result was the development of a relatively large, subsidized military equipment sector. The economic cost of maintaining the capability to design and produce advanced military products has become

Table 7-2 (Continued)

Country	Average 1970-1974	Average 1975-1979	Average 1980-1984	Average 1985-1989	1987	1988	1989	1990	1991[a]
Percentage devoted to infrastructure expenditures									
Belgium	5.5	6.5	5.5	4.0	4.6	3.9	3.0	3.8	4.3
Canada	2.8	2.5	2.3	2.8	2.6	2.9	3.7	3.9	2.4
Denmark	3.3	2.4	2.8	3.4	2.8	3.4	4.0	3.4	4.3
Germany	6.3	6.3	5.4	5.9	5.8	5.6	5.8	5.9	5.0
Greece	5.8	5.3	2.8	2.2	1.9	2.3	2.6	2.1	1.8
Italy	1.6	1.8	2.3	2.6	2.4	2.5	2.3	2.8	—
Luxembourg	4.9	3.2	10.3	7.3	8.9	5.5	7.1	7.0	10.0
Netherlands	2.8	3.2	3.7	5.2	4.7	5.2	6.6	5.9	6.6
Norway	4.4	4.3	5.0	8.2	9.7	8.2	8.7	9.8	10.8
Portugal	2.3	3.4	5.9	3.7	3.7	4.1	2.8	3.4	3.0
Spain	—	—	—	—	4.0	3.2	3.1	2.3	2.2
Turkey	5.5	7.3	13.2	5.4	5.9	4.5	3.8	3.2	3.3
United Kingdom	2.4	1.7	2.7	3.9	3.7	4.1	4.1	5.8	5.0
United States	1.5	1.9	1.6	1.8	2.0	2.0	1.7	1.7	1.5
Percentage devoted to operating expenditures									
Belgium	20.9	18.9	18.8	20.4	20.3	20.4	20.0	19.9	20.6
Canada	24.0	27.3	29.0	31.2	29.9	31.6	30.0	29.2	32.2
Denmark	21.2	21.0	25.7	25.8	27.1	24.2	23.1	23.4	21.5
Germany	26.7	27.0	27.9	25.5	24.9	25.5	24.0	24.3	21.7
Greece	18.5	17.0	24.9	18.4	19.2	16.1	14.0	12.3	11.6
Italy	23.0	21.5	21.0	19.8	18.0	19.2	18.5	18.1	—
Luxembourg	11.1	9.1	10.2	11.9	10.3	16.9	11.9	10.2	10.7
Netherlands	18.9	17.3	20.3	22.0	23.9	20.1	22.2	22.3	23.5
Norway	28.0	26.6	26.7	26.0	26.5	27.4	24.0	24.3	22.6
Portugal	37.9	25.1	21.9	19.8	20.6	19.0	14.0	13.3	15.4
Spain	—	—	—	—	21.6	21.6	21.3	23.0	18.7
Turkey	22.6	23.7	30.1	38.4	38.3	37.5	32.9	28.5	26.7
United Kingdom	32.0	31.9	33.5	32.5	32.6	29.7	34.4	32.5	32.5
United States	—	—	34.5	35.5	35.5	35.6	34.9	36.9	36.4

Source: "Financial and Economic Data Relating to NATO Defence," NATO Press Release M-DPC-2(91)105, 12 December 1991, p. 7.

[a] Estimated

oppressive. The Swedish minister of defense, Anders Bjorck, recently observed: "No other small nation makes the same kinds of aircraft, submarines, missiles, and radar we do. It is a technology and an expertise that we must keep alive, if necessary, by finding new partners in Europe." [9] Mr. Bjorck, in proposing the first increase in Swedish military spending in nearly twenty years (5 percent), largely targeted on equipment, emphasized that he could not permit Sweden's advanced military industry to decay.[10]

The Swedish prime minister, Carl Bildt, has emphasized the importance of the arms industry because of its involvement in high technology; he hopes that sophisticated technology developed in electronics and aircraft, and the precision tools and skills that produce them, will spill over to Swedish industry in general, strengthening the country's competitive position.[11] The prime minister also focused on recent political changes in Europe and their implications for traditional Swedish foreign policy. Thus: "The policy of neutrality no longer applies to the policies we intend to pursue, when we are actively seeking to take part in foreign and security preparation with the rest of Europe." [12]

Sweden has applied for membership in the European Community and hopes to establish collaborative ventures with defense producers in the community. Studies of Sweden's relatively tough restrictions on arms exports are now under way with a view to their liberalization in order to facilitate such partnerships.[13] Sweden would appear less attractive as a potential partner if its own rules inhibited exports to third countries.

The Russian government provides a highly interesting case of a government adopting a specific policy of encouraging military exports to earn the funds needed to cover the costs of converting a significant share of its military industry to civilian production. This position was spelled out at a Moscow press conference on May 7, 1992, by Mikhail Maley, President Yeltsin's adviser on conversion and defense industry matters. Maley complained of "unfair quotas and restrictions on Russian arms trade and high technology export in the international markets." He specifically criticized the Missile Technology Control Regime and the International Atomic Energy Agency.[14]

The Swedish case also illustrates another form of adjustment to reduced domestic military spending—the conscious decision to sacrifice a domestic weapons capability across a wide range of weapons and seek alternate sources abroad. This path has been taken by other European countries. The British long ago made that painful decision in aircraft. However, as part of the NATO alliance Great Britain was able to count on foreign weapons to fill the need. Sweden's neutrality made such a decision more difficult. This may also be an element in the Swedish decision to consider distancing itself from such extreme self reliance. Sweden will no longer design and produce its own main battle tanks. It is now considering a tank purchase, and U.S., British, and German models are competing for the sale. This is the latest example of an attempt to specialize across a shorter range of products and fill the remaining needs from abroad.

With the development of aerospace capability in an ever-widening circle of countries, competition to export has grown more keen. Some observers see the development of consortia as a way to limit this competition. The various consortia would still be interested in exports, but combining the needs of the armed forces of the members would provide scale economies.

Table 7-3 Arms Exports as Percentage of Total Exports

NATO

Year	Belgium	Canada	Denmark	France	W. Germany	Greece	Italy	Netherlands	Norway	Portugal	Spain	Turkey	U.K.	U.S.
1979	0.1%	0.3%	0.0%	1.7%	0.7%	0.1%	1.0%	0.2%	0.4%	0.6%	0.3%	0.4%	1.3%	3.2%
1980	0.2	0.2	0.1	2.4	0.7	0.0	1.0	0.3	0.5	1.1	0.3	0.3	1.8	2.9
1981	0.6	0.4	0.2	4.0	0.9	0.0	1.8	0.5	0.4	0.7	0.5	0.2	2.7	3.6
1982	0.4	0.7	0.3	4.2	0.6	2.8	1.5	0.6	0.4	2.6	2.8	0.3	3.4	4.3
1983	0.7	0.5	0.2	4.2	1.2	0.2	1.8	0.3	0.3	1.5	2.0	1.6	2.1	5.6
1984	0.8	0.7	0.2	4.5	1.7	2.3	1.7	0.4	0.2	2.1	4.3	2.2	2.2	4.7
1985	0.7	0.6	0.1	5.3	0.8	0.7	1.6	0.2	0.2	3.7	2.2	1.5	1.5	5.1
1986	0.3	0.6	0.1	3.9	0.5	0.7	0.7	0.1	0.2	3.0	0.6	0.0	3.5	4.1
1987	0.1	0.6	0.2	2.0	0.5	0.6	0.5	0.7	0.2	0.6	1.3	0.1	3.6	5.6
1988	0.0	0.6	0.1	1.4	0.4	0.6	0.3	0.7	0.2	0.9	0.7	0.1	1.1	4.6
1989	0.0	0.3	0.1	1.5	0.4	0.0	0.0	0.1	0.1	0.3	0.3	0.0	2.0	3.1

Warsaw Pact Organization

Year	Bulgaria	Czech.	E. Germany	Hungary	Poland	Romania	USSR
1979	0.6%	7.3%	0.5%	0.4%	3.4%	0.8%	25.6%
1980	0.7	6.2	1.0	0.4	4.8	0.8	22.2
1981	1.6	5.3	0.7	0.1	7.3	3.9	22.5
1982	3.7	5.3	0.7	0.6	6.1	6.7	21.7
1983	2.9	5.3	0.9	1.8	6.7	3.3	21.2
1984	3.7	3.9	1.6	1.5	5.8	2.5	21.2
1985	4.3	5.4	2.3	1.6	7.3	3.6	19.6
1986	3.2	4.0	1.1	1.0	6.4	2.5	21.9
1987	3.5	3.5	1.0	1.3	5.3	1.6	21.0
1988	2.1	2.4	1.4	0.8	3.9	NA	19.5
1989	1.0	6.6	NA	0.2	1.4	NA	17.9

Selected European Neutrals

Year	Austria	Sweden	Switzerland	Yugoslavia
1979	0.6%	0.4%	1.9%	2.6%
1980	0.2	0.4	2.3	2.9
1981	2.0	0.6	1.3	3.0
1982	0.5	1.0	1.5	3.5
1983	0.8	0.4	1.7	3.8
1984	1.4	0.5	2.2	6.3
1985	0.9	0.7	1.2	3.9
1986	1.2	0.7	0.8	3.5
1987	0.2	0.7	0.9	2.8
1988	0.2	0.9	0.4	1.8
1989	0.1	1.1	0.1	1.1

Source: *World Military Expenditures and Arms Transfers* (Washington, D.C.: U.S. Arms Control and Disarmament Agency, November 1991), table II.
Notes: Luxembourg and Albania omitted. NA: Not available.

Thus, some nine hundred Tornado aircraft were produced by the Panavia consortium, a much larger number than any of the three partners (U.K., Germany, and Italy) alone could afford to produce.[15] All benefited from scale economies due to specialization in production and lower design costs than any one of the partners would have experienced alone.

Consortia like Panavia have been criticized for being unwieldy, bureaucratic, and slow, but the hope has been that "economies of experience" exist which would lead to lower costs on subsequent projects. The European Fighter Aircraft (EFA) was conceived as such a project. The Panavia consortium was enlarged by one member (Spain) and under the new name Eurofighter was to undertake the project. Although the project is still in the design phase, the costs have escalated substantially and German unhappiness over cost inflation was the principal reason for a decision by the German cabinet on July 1, 1992, to eliminate production funds for the EFA from the 1993 budget.[16] In late November 1992 air force commanders of the four partner states were reported to have agreed to a revised design for the EFA that would lower its costs sufficiently to bring Germany back into the program.[17]

It is now clear that all future aircraft development in Western Europe will be, to some extent, collaborative. Participation in such projects will be viewed as essential by all European states that have some aerospace capability and a desire to retain it. This position is now widely held in all the countries and companies surveyed.[18]

Here again, political and economic factors combine to present a dilemma. As the European Community matures, the question of its military dimension becomes more difficult to sweep under the rug. Article 223 of the Treaty of Rome stipulates that military industry be excluded from the Common Market and declares as individual state responsibility the production, procurement, and export of armaments. Yet, the topic of a common European defense and foreign policy arises repeatedly, as it did at the recent Maastricht meeting. A common European organization to oversee military research and development and procurement appears to hold real appeal to most of the member states. The Western European Union has been the focus of such discussions. This organization numbers among its members Belgium, Britain, France, Germany, Italy, Luxembourg, the Netherlands, Portugal, and Spain. The formal rationale for the discussions is to open up the European military marketplace and combat protectionism.[19] Whether, as some fear, this presages a Fortress Europe from which the United States is to be consciously excluded as partner or supplier is yet to be seen.[20]

Taking stock of the foregoing, what do we conclude? The early reactions to reduced domestic defense spending will surely include redoubled efforts to export armaments and to form international partnerships and collaborative ventures to produce them. To predict the outcome one must balance the decline in domestic orders against the increase in orders from abroad. It is unlikely that the net demand will rise sufficiently to utilize the available productive capacity. Even assuming a highly efficient restructuring into international consortia and carving out of specialized niches in the process, one may reasonably expect a reduction in the number of producers in world markets.

Such downsizing is not a new phenomenon in Europe. Stronger firms (such as Thomson in France) will continue to absorb the weak, or at least their military divisions. It would not be surprising to find an increase in the ratio of defense sales to total turnover in firms that visualize themselves as having a comparative advantage in military output and that position themselves to survive in the defense market.

For the past two decades there has been a reduction in the number of new military aircraft introduced and a lengthening in the interval between their introduction. This trend will likely continue, with a shift from the design and development of new weapon systems to a focus on their maintenance, modification, and renewal. Military aircraft will increasingly become older than their pilots. Maintenance and modification capabilities will become increasingly important and sales contracts that provide for the acquisition of those skills will become standard. Many direct offset arrangements make such provision, and their popularity should continue to grow.[21] Firms like Volvo Flygmotor in Sweden, SABCA in Belgium, and Alenia in Italy have all emphasized the importance that they place on repair, refurbishment, and modification of existing aircraft and their engines.

Diversification and Conversion

An additional adjustment path exists which has been widely discussed but little practiced: defense conversion or industrial diversification among military producers. "Conversion" and "diversification" are similar but not perfectly synonymous. Conversion suggests a replacement of sales to the military sector by sales of civil products. Diversification refers to the addition of new products. Thus a declining share of military sales may represent no change in the monetary volume of sales to military customers but rather the more rapid growth in sales of other products or acquisition by the parent firm of new product divisions. Diversification is a more commonly encountered approach.

Contributions of Modern Economic Theory

A branch of economic theory has evolved gradually over the last several decades—following in the pioneering footsteps of Ronald H. Coase and Oliver Williamson—that is relevant to these issues. The fundamental questions asked by Coase: "What determines what a firm does? Why isn't General Motors a dominant factor in the coal industry, or why doesn't A&P manufacture airplanes?" are most relevant to the economic conversion question.[22] Coase moved away from traditional theory by rejecting the view that the limits of the firm were a parameter and by arguing that the firm's limits were themselves a decision variable requiring economic evaluation. The issue then is identifying "efficient boundaries" for the firm so that questions of what activities should be performed within the firm, which outside it, and why, can be answered.[23]

Recent developments in the theory of transaction costs and economies of scope have substantially advanced our ability to define efficient boundaries. The most fundamental work is that of Williamson,[24] and Baumol, Panzar, and Willig.[25] An important extension is provided by Teece.[26]

The challenge facing the management of military-dependent firms in their efforts to diversify may be described as that of defining efficient borders or limits to their activities. The concepts of transaction cost economizing and economies of scope provide useful guidance in meeting that challenge. Transaction costs are those costs associated with negotiating and monitoring of agreements. Scope economies are said to exist when conditions are present that make it cheaper for one firm to produce several products than for each of the products to be produced by separate firms. Such conditions may involve the availability of excess capacity that incorporates a common technology or group of skills. As David J. Teece argues, "diversification based on scope economies does not represent abandonment of specialization economies in favor of amorphous growth." [27] It reflects, rather, a redefinition of the firm's comparative advantage, shifting away from a focus on products to one based on capabilities. In his words, "The firm [establishes] a specialized know-how or asset base from which it extends its operations in response to competitive conditions." [28] This would appear to be a fair description of what Saab-Scania of Sweden attempted when it established the new Combitech division to undertake the commercialization of innovations developed in its aircraft division. Here, certain familiar characteristics of the aerospace industry may be seen as encouraging scope economies. Such phenomena as a well-developed ability to deal with the contracting authorities of the government; a sizable stable of scientists and engineers engaged in current production and maintained in anticipation of future contracts; and the high variability of production in the industry all argue for diversification and scope economies.[29]

Diversification Experience in Western European Aerospace

The evidence gathered during this study reveals very little success or even effort at diversification in Western Europe.[30] At one end of the spectrum is the blunt statement of a Swedish defense firm executive: "Diversification is not a reality." At the other are the observations of a former Dornier executive in Germany, who stresses the patience, careful attention, and willingness to bear risk necessary for successful diversification:

> This increase of share of civilian market sales—as you can well imagine—did not just happen by chance. It was part of our company policy during the last 10 years. The long-term planning of our DoD gave enough early warning that missing defense business had to be compensated by other and, therefore, civilian programs. This policy meant taking in subcontracting work in Airbus on not too advantageous and risk-sharing terms conditioned to many millions of Marks of investment in infrastructure, special machinery and tooling out of our own pocket (these kinds of costs normally are carried by the government, if military programs). It meant also to invest heavily not only for R&D, series preparation and all the work in process to run a program like our Dornier 228 Commuter Aircraft with a return on investment (break-even-point) in a very distant and uncertain future and it also meant to push ahead with the [kidney stone] Lithotripter entering a so-called "new game" like the medical market (diversification). To expand our traditional textile machinery field is a comparatively easy "game." Therefore, yes, the company has plans to increase the civilian market share and will have to continue in the future to do so.[31]

These words were written several years ago. The interim developments are most interesting, particularly in the case of the Lithotripter, since it appears to be further removed from the military aviation side of the firm than efforts in civil aviation. Initially, Dornier's Lithotripter enjoyed a monopoly in the medical equipment market. Its successes became well known and Siemens, which traditionally had been a market leader in the field, entered the market a few years later with a somewhat different machine. Dornier's medical equipment division found itself facing increasingly serious competition from Siemens and responded by establishing a subsidiary in the United States and investing in a second generation of medical equipment designed to treat gallstones. The Dornier operation thus far has been able to maintain its position in competition with Siemens. In the interim, Dornier has been absorbed into the newly formed Deutsche Aerospace giant. This may strengthen Dornier's hand in the medical equipment market if Deutsche Aerospace maintains its interest in medical equipment.

There are several lessons in this episode. First, innovative use of aerospace technology—in this case expertise in the use of sound waves—does not assure success in the new market. Other traditional leaders in the field are unlikely to sit back and allow the upstart to progress very far without a major counterattack. Unless the new entrant has access to significant financial backing it may be forced to license its technology to established leaders in the applied field. This may still be socially desirable in terms of bringing a new and useful device into public use but there is no guarantee that the innovating firm or division will succeed.

This example indicates the difficulty of attempting to "convert in place," as it were, where the success of the venture is measured by the financial success of a particular plant and its existing work force and community base.[32] In the above case one might be impressed with Dornier's imaginative use of some of its expertise and be drawn by emotion to hope for its success. There is no guarantee of such success in the competitive market, however, and the complete adjustment may require the mobility of both labor and capital. For the government to act to avoid such an eventuality would require its intervention for an indefinite period via some form of industrial policy.[33]

Another interesting case of innovation in the medical area is found in Sweden. Several years ago Bofors developed a process for implanting teeth. Recently the operation stopped losing money but a series of corporate reorganizations has now removed that activity from the Bofors group. Again we see a case of a potentially useful innovation leaving the defense establishment where it began. Society may still benefit but the development fails to provide the innovator with an alternative market.

Even should such activities remain within the innovating defense firm, a fundamental question remains. How realistic is it to assume that such new markets will develop an adequate turnover to match the losses on the military side of the house? [34] One cannot completely eliminate the possibility of such a volume in the new product area but it would appear highly unlikely in the short run. Thus, some downsizing of military equipment firms seems inevitable, even if they successfully innovate outside of the defense market.

The experience of Britain's Vickers Defence Systems in locating nondefense work is more traditional. As a major producer of battle tanks, Vickers sees its comparative advantage in performing precision machining on large metal parts. There is a certain logic therefore in its working on offshore oil facilities and building large steel frameworks for the Hong Kong and Shanghai Bank Building. This strategy of moving into technologically similar areas may be a useful short-term activity. A Vickers executive observed that they were not planning to change drastically the skills of their work force to attract nonmilitary business. Rather, they preferred to do it the reverse way—that is, locate activities for which their skills were already appropriate. They also are seeking markets in which cost is not the only criterion.

A recent United Nations study of conversion experience in several countries casts some doubt on the long-term viability of the Vickers approach. A Japanese case reported in the study sounds remarkably similar to that of Vickers. Here, also, the management first tried to maximize the use of its skills and equipment in technologically similar areas. The markets found that way did not provide profitable opportunities. A shift in strategy followed. The new approach first located potentially profitable opportunities and only then considered the capabilities of work force and capital equipment. This approach involved much retraining, job mobility, and investment in research and development but resulted in an expansion in product mix, a doubling in revenues, and continuous productivity growth.[35]

The foregoing section has focused on efforts by a firm to diversify through the use of its existing resources of technology, capital, and labor. There is, of course, another route to altering the product line of the company: acquisition of another firm, or division of a firm.

An interesting example of a defense-oriented firm attempting to buy its way into civilian markets was the purchase by Northrop in the United States of 49 percent of the aircraft segment of the bankrupt LTV Aerospace and Defense Co. Northrop's interest in the aircraft segment of LTV Aerospace was reputed to be in the latter's substantial work on commercial transports.[36]

Such a strategy is not unheard of in Europe but there is reason to believe that the process is somewhat less frequently encountered there than in the United States. Especially in older, tradition-oriented firms, the concept of what is an "appropriate" activity for the firm is still encountered.[37] Nevertheless, such attitudes are changing and this is reflected by the declining relative significance of military sales since 1980 in important European firms.[38] Table 7-4 provides data on the military share of the total sales for fourteen Western European companies for selected years since 1980. A necessary caveat in interpreting this trend is the recognition that several possible alternative explanations exist for the general declining share of military sales—other than an *absolute* decline in military sales.

The Role of Government

One of the truly remarkable findings of this study was the infrequency of active government policy to aid the transfer of resources from defense to civil sectors. The Swedish government apparently made a direct loan to Saab to assist in the development of the Saab 2000 civil airliner. The French government is supporting a policy of early retirement to reduce employment in French defense firms. British respondents were particularly cynical, pointing to government orders in marginal constituencies prior to the recent national elections. Such actions hardly suggest a comprehensive policy of government assistance.

Typically, governments assume that defense industry managers will behave as rational capitalists and will adjust to cycles in military markets by developing alternative products and markets. In other words, governments

Table 7-4   Military Share of Total Sales

Country	Company	1980	1983	1985	1987	1989	1990	1991
Belgium	SABCA	90%		75%				60%
France	Aerospatiale	60		65				41
	Dassault	85		77				70
	Matra	80		55				33
Germany	Deutsche Aerospace:							
	Dornier	63		39			25%	
	MBB	67		54			60	
	MTU	86		68			48	
	Rheinmetall GmbH	100		92				85
Italy	Alenia	70		65				60
Netherlands	Fokker				34%		9	6
Sweden	Saab Aircraft			91%		48%	32	
	Volvo Flygmotor	62	55	41			24	38
U.K.	British Aerospace	73		71				39
	Vickers Defence Systems			11				31

Source: Company annual reports and data provided directly by corporate officials.

take for granted that in a dynamic economy managers will take responsibility for making the adjustment.[39]

This observation would appear still relevant in 1992. This may reflect in part the slow movement of policy through a series of stages. Some defense producers would be happier with government policies that liberalize export restrictions and encourage multinational collaborative ventures. As noted above these measures are also government efforts to help firms adjust to reduced domestic military expenditures. The move to diversification may be awaiting the success of the less extreme efforts. As the United Nations study referenced above emphasizes, the role for government in aiding diversification clearly varies with the political philosophy of the government and its degree of dependence on the market mechanism.

There is still another possible explanation. European industrial policies cover a multitude of areas such as low-interest loans to industry, aid to research and development, aid to the unemployed, retraining, aid in support of exports, regional development policies, and so on.[40] In no case are such policies identified as a package in aid of military downsizing or diversification per se. Yet, they are all capable of aiding that process. If all or many of the problem areas likely to be encountered are covered by *general* policies, the absence of specifically tagged conversion policies may be largely a semantic issue.

The logical question one would ask is which policy measures work and which do not. Unfortunately, the answer is more complex than that. There is no exact formula for successful economic conversion. Thus, similar measures in the different countries do not yield similar results. Conversion, or transfer of resources from military to civilian use, is an example of adjustment to changing market pressures. Since the challenge to firms in this situation is often to adapt or die, one may reason that national environments that encourage such adaptation will enjoy higher success rates. Therefore, the society's views and attitudes to adaptability and change may be as important as specific policy measures in explaining differential success.

In this context, the views of French scholars were particularly interesting. They expressed concern that the French economy's adaptability to change would remain low as long as French society continued to draw its leaders essentially from two institutions of higher education: the Ecole Nationale d'Administration and the Ecole Polytechnique. While acknowledging their excellence as educational institutions, they saw them as stifling new ideas with their oppressive application of the old boy network, thereby effectively locking the door to the self-made executive who might be more inclined to consider less traditional approaches to problem solving.

The importance of flexibility applies to workers as well as to managers. European workers have long been noted as tradition-bound and resistant to geographical mobility. Sweden's active labor market policy appears to deal with these issues directly. An impressive program to subsidize geographic mobility exists. It includes actual moving expenses, starting grants, and per diem allowances to cover additional costs of double residency. Labor market training and extensive vocational counseling are provided to participants. It should be noted, however, that while Sweden's unemployment benefits are among the most generous to be found anywhere, they are accompanied by strict rules governing eligibility. There is a ceiling of three hundred days on the receipt of benefits and a strict work test to discourage shirking. Recipients who refuse training or appropriate jobs face the immediate loss of benefits.[41] There is also an effort to improve the state of information in the labor market. Thus, Swedish law requires that almost all job vacancies be registered at the local employment service office. While firms are not required to hire all referrals from the service and may recruit labor without involving the service, the listing requirement helps to rationalize the matching of job seekers and vacancies.

Many of the policies noted above such as low-interest loans to industry, aid to research and development, aid to the unemployed, retraining, aid in support of exports, and regional development policies are also found in the United States. The principal differences appear in the area of labor market policy and training. Sweden's active labor market policies provide useful and current information on job vacancies and might well provide a model for the U.S. system to emulate. In furtherance of the goal of work force flexibility, a program of industrial apprenticeship training such as that in Switzerland and in several other European states might also be considered. It would provide an alternate career path for young persons not oriented toward university education and provide them with genuine craft skills widely used in modern industry. Persons with such training require much less supervision and could more easily adapt to changes resulting from reduced military spending.

In the modern industrial world, change in markets and products appears to be inevitable. Any policies that enhance the flexibility of management and labor would clearly ease the adjustment to lower military spending and indeed to other challenges that may lie in the future.

Notes

1. This effort follows two prior inquiries in Western Europe and Scandinavia. See Bernard Udis, *From Guns to Butter: Technology Organizations and Reduced Military Spending in Western Europe* (Lexington, Mass.: Lexington Books of D.C. Heath, 1978); and *The Challenge to European Industrial Policy: Impacts of Redirected Military Spending* (Boulder, Colo.: Westview Press, 1987).
2. The five states that increased defense outlays were among Europe's smaller countries: Luxembourg, the Netherlands, Norway, Portugal, and Switzerland. It is likely that the reasons for such increases deal less with the security environment in their regions than with such random elements as the delivery of new weapon systems and other aspects of modernization programs already under way.
3. See Hans Ambos, "Is a Rationalization of the Western European Armaments Industry Possible Without Supranational Authority?—A View from German Aerospace Industry." Presentation before the Quatrième Session Européenne des Responsables d'Armament, Paris, March 17, 1992.
4. Indeed, one of the reasons given by officials of Sweden's Volvo Flygmotor for acquiring the military engine maintenance facility previously operated by FFV at Arboga was to prevent their balance between military and civilian operations from tilting too far to the civilian side.
5. An interesting example of the identification of such a niche and a rapid effort to benefit from it is the development of the ATR regional commuter aircraft by Alenia of Italy and Aerospatiale of France. The niche evolved when U.S. passenger airlines adopted "hub and spoke" flight routes after deregulation of the industry and the traditional American aircraft producers virtually ignored their need for short-range aircraft.
6. For example, the Pakistani finance minister recently observed that security concerns did not permit his country to make the military budget cuts demanded by aid donors. In defending his recommended 8.4 percent increase in the military budget he stressed the overwhelming importance of national security and said that Pakistan's military capabilities would receive top priority as long as his country feels threatened by India. See "World Briefs," *International Herald Tribune,* May 16-17, 1992, 2.
7. For a discussion that identifies Czechoslovakia as a country facing such a dilemma, see Kenneth L. Adelman and Norman R. Augustine, "Defense Conversion: Bulldozing the Management," *Foreign Affairs* 7, no. 2 (Spring 1992): 26-47, especially pp. 37-38. See also John Tagliabue, "Czechoslovaks Find Profit and Pain in Arms Sales," *New York Times,* February 19, 1992, A11.
8. See, for example, William E. Schmidt, "Neutral Sweden Pursues Arms Sales," *New York Times,* February 17, 1992, D1; and Michael J. Witt, "Sweden May Ease Export Rules," *Defense News,* April 6-12, 1992, 38.
9. Schmidt, "Neutral Sweden Pursues Arms Sales."
10. Ibid.

11. Similar motives underlie Sweden's offset policy. See "Re: Industrial Collaboration in Procurement of Defence Materiel from Abroad" (Stockholm: Ministry of Defense, Defense Materiel Administration), transcript. Government Decision, 1983-09-22, signed by Anders Thunborg, minister of defense, and assistant undersecretary of defense Christer Dahlberg. This statement is partially duplicated and discussed in Bernard Udis, *The Challenge to European Industrial Policy*, 103-105.

12. Quoted in Schmidt, "Neutral Sweden Pursues Arms Sales."

13. In the past, Sweden has exported military aircraft but only to small and essentially neutral or Nordic countries such as Austria, Denmark, and Finland. It had negotiated a sale of its Viggen military aircraft to India but the United States prevented the sale, considering it destabilizing. The basis for U.S. intervention was the presence in the Viggen of U.S. parts. This potential veto power over third-country sales was a condition of the original sale to Sweden.

14. See Sergio Rossi, "Russia to Fight Weapon Sales Curbs," *Defense News* 7, no. 2 (May 18-24, 1992): 1, 53.

15. An interesting question is whether the partner states could have met their respective needs for such an aircraft more economically by direct purchase from a foreign source. The U.S. F-111 is a similar aircraft and the first models were delivered in 1964-1965. Deliveries continued through November 1976. [See Jane's, *All the World's Aircraft: 1978/1979* (London: S. Low, Marston, and Co., Ltd.), 334.] The Tornado project began in July 1968 with the first flight in August 1974. [Keith Hartley, *The Economics of Defence Policy* (London: Brassey's, 1991), table 9.4.] Thus, a purchase of the U.S. F-111 would have been possible, and deliveries to the three European partners' air forces probably would have begun several years earlier than the Tornado was delivered. However, each partner's goals in the program went beyond the acquisition of an aircraft capable of meeting the needs of its air force at an "acceptable" cost. Questions of domestic jobs, technology acquisition, and economizing on foreign exchange all played a role. One can only speculate about whether an acceptable offset deal might have been negotiated.

16. Giovanni de Briganti and Charles Miller, "EFA Partners Work to Salvage Program," *Defense News* 7, no. 27 (July 6-12, 1992), 1, 21.

17. Alessandro Politi and Michael J. Witt, "New EFA Design May Lure Germany," *Defense News* 7, no. 47 (November 23-29, 1992), 1, 20.

18. The same situation prevails with commercial aircraft. Aside from the case of Airbus, countries producing commuter, regional, or executive aircraft, such as Sweden and Holland, are seeking partners.

19. Another organization, the Independent European Program Group, within NATO, existed to accomplish similar purposes but some observers questioned its effectiveness on the grounds that it had failed to bring about agreement on unified military requirements and common weapon systems. See Theresa Hitchens, "EC Officials Seek to Boost Defense Competition," *Defense News* 7, no. 13 (March 30-April 5, 1992), 10. The absorption of the IEPG's functions by the Western European Union in late May 1993 may be the first step toward the ultimate transfer of some NATO functions to the European Community.

20. Statements made in early June 1992 by French government and industry leaders make the case that the United States has never allowed European industry access to its defense markets in any way comparable to the openness encountered by American sellers in European markets. Therefore, Serge Dassault, writing in *Le Monde* of June 3, 1992, argues that "the European Community should not allow its members, or even its prospective members such as Switzerland and Finland, to buy American weapons. . . . Buying a U.S. weapon system is a betrayal of Europe's industry, and allows U.S. industry to take its place. . . . It means European taxpayers are funding U.S. industry." Though less dramatic, French defense minister Pierre Joxe also has

called attention to the lack of reciprocity that he sees as a barrier to participation in an integrated European defense market. A Western European Union report of June 3, 1992, recommends that the WEU Council "give priority to European space industries." See Giovanni de Briganti, "Europeans Demand Better Access to U.S. Defense Market," *Defense News* 7, no. 23 (June 8-14, 1992), 33.

21. An offset is a contractual agreement imposing performance conditions on the seller of a good or service so that the purchasing government can recoup, or offset, some of its investment. In some way, reciprocity beyond that associated with normal market exchange of goods and services in involved. Offsets may be direct or indirect.

   Direct offsets require the participation of industry in the buying country in the manufacture or assembly of the item around which the sales contract is written and may include licensed production, coproduction, or subcontractor production. Indirect offsets involve goods and services unrelated to the exports referenced in the sales agreement and may include some forms of foreign investment, technology transfer, and countertrade. The last of these, countertrade, may involve mechanisms for barter, counter-purchase, compensation, or buy-back. See Bernard Udis and Keith E. Maskus, "Offsets As Industrial Policy: Lessons From Aerospace," *Defence Economics,* 1991, Vol. 2, 151-164.

22. Ronald H. Coase, "Industrial Organization: A Proposal for Research," in *Policy Issues and Research Opportunities in Industrial Organization,* ed. Victor H. Fuchs (New York: Columbia University Press, 1972), 59-73, especially 63 and 67.

23. Oliver E. Williamson, "The Economics of Organization: The Transaction Cost Approach," *American Journal of Sociology* 87, no. 3 (November 1981): 548-577, especially 549.

24. Oliver E. Williamson, *Markets and Hierarchies* (New York: Free Press, 1975); "Transaction-Cost Economics: The Governance of Contractual Relations," *The Journal of Law and Economics* 22, no. 2 (October 1979): 233-261; "The Economics of Organization"; "The Modern Corporation: Origins, Evolution, Attributes," *Journal of Economic Literature* 19, no. 4 (December 1981): 1537-1568; "The Incentive Limits of Firms: A Comparative Institutional Assessment of Bureaucracy," *Weltwirtschaftliches Archiv* 120, no. 4 (1984): 736-763; and "Asset Specificity and Economic Organization," with Michael H. Riordan, Working Paper Series D, no. 6 (New Haven: Yale University School of Organization and Management, May 1985).

25. William J. Baumol, John C. Panzar, and Robert D. Willig, *Contestable Markets and the Theory of Industry Structure* (New York: Harcourt Brace Jovanovich, 1982); also John C. Panzar and Robert D. Willig, "Economies of Scope," *American Economic Review* 71, no. 2 (May 1981): 268-272.

26. David J. Teece, "Economies of Scope and the Scope of the Enterprise," *Journal of Economic Behavior and Organization* 1, no. 3 (September 1980): 233.

27. Ibid.

28. Ibid.

29. These final points were suggested by Loren Yager of the Aerospace Research Center of the Aerospace Industries Association of America, Inc.

30. This finding is remarkably similar to that of a study of the plans and experience of southern California aerospace companies. See Michael C. Lambert, "Defense Contractors Use Down-Sizing, Not Diversification, to Maintain Profits," *Aviation Week & Space Technology,* March 9, 1992, 61-63.

31. Private correspondence with the author.

32. Of particular relevance is a study of conversion in the United States. It concluded:

> The compositional differences across defence and non-defence production, and the fact that firms tend to be specialized in defence at the establishment level, imply that the bulk of conversion efforts are unlikely to take place at the establishment level—unless establishments shift the

focus of their activities rather substantially. The more common occurrence in the United States is for employees to leave their old places of employment to seek opportunities in new economic fields and different geographical areas, and for firms to reduce their activities in defence by shutting down or selling off their idle facilities, by selling equipment, or by running plants with excess capacity. Therefore, a good deal of conversion in the United States occurs through the mobility of workers and capital equipment, rather than through diversification at the establishment level.

See Arthur J. Alexander, "National Experiences: A Comparative Analysis," in *Disarmament: Topical Papers 5, Conversion: Economic Adjustments in an Era of Arms Reduction,* Vol. II (New York: United Nations, 1991), 3-60, especially p. 47.

33. Despite its appeal to journalists [see "Industrial Policy—Call It What You Will, the Nation Needs a Plan to Nurture Growth," *Business Week,* April 6, 1992, 70-76] careful studies of industrial policy in France, where it may be said to have begun, indicate that it has been successful—defined as achieving a strong technological and commercial position—only with high dependence on government procurement policy and continuous state intervention. See Christian Stoffaes, "Industrial Policy in High Technology Industries: The French Experience," paper presented at Brookings Institution conference on industrial policy in France, and its implications for the United States, September 27-28, 1984, p. 15.

34. Very relevant here are the comments of a Fokker official made in a letter to the author several years ago:

> As far as my experience goes, the spin-off we have had from commercial aircraft business has been marketable in a limited number of cases. However, these spin-offs, so far, have been special technical applications of which the market in the world is very small indeed. For example, we have developed, because of our metal bonding expertise, certain non-destructive testing devices, which we market worldwide; also we were able to develop certain devices to improve flight simulation. All in all, the turnover in these areas is about 2% of our total business and one wonders whether that is worth the effort.

35. See Alexander, "National Experiences," 11-12.

36. See Anthony L. Velocci, Jr., "Northrop Eyes 49% of LTV's Aircraft Business in Move to Diversify," *Aviation Week & Space Technology,* April 27, 1992, 25.

37. That such an attitude may be based on experience rather than simply reflect a conservative, static view is suggested by the comments of a Dutch aerospace official in a letter to the author several years ago:

> In the past . . . our management thought that we should enter into markets like caravans [trailers], vending machines, light lifting equipment and such kind of commercial goods. Our practice has [taught] us that our marketing was unable to handle [such] commercial goods in a satisfactory manner, that our manufacturing organization was too expensive and our internal accounting system not suitable to market these commodities in a heavily competitive market.
>
> Since that time we have avoided [entering] into markets which are unknown to us as an aircraft company; however, it could not be excluded that, if our present products will be successful in the commercial market and sufficient money can be generated, we will acquire other companies in aircraft related or high technology areas in order to broaden our business base. However, that would mean also that we would have to restruc-

ture the present Fokker company to a holding with divisions which are reasonably independent in these operations in the world market.

The corporate cultures in this case would remain in the original companies forming the total corporation. The management in the holding will have to become a far more general business-oriented management than the present one which is oriented to the aircraft business only.

With regard to the present Fokker company, there is of course some diversification in the sense that we ... have entered [some] years ago into the space business and at the present time are trying to expand this business with related products in the field of missile systems or components thereof. We do this in such a way that our efforts are directed to those kind of specialties which (1) have an affinity and may support our main objective, i.e., our commercial aircraft business and (2) have an affinity to our Space business. In this way we hope to obtain synergetic effects which could be beneficial to our total business volume and at the same time increase our technological knowhow in really advanced fields.

38. An interesting case of relatively successful adjustment by a European firm is provided by Matra of France. Two decades ago Matra was completely dependent on defense contracts. The chief executive was aware of the risks involved and began a campaign of diversification funded largely by profits from defense contracts. The strategy was to buy or create new companies in which the common link was familiarity with the high technology used. Several of the early efforts failed. These involved clockmaking and the manufacture of automobile carburetors, dashboard instrumentation, and computers. Matra made an imaginative attempt to market the company name by sponsoring a Formula 1 racing car team. The subsequent development of a sports car was also effective in developing or improving public awareness of the company. More recently, Matra was responsible for the design of the highly successful "Espace" vehicle distributed by Renault. This has a Renault engine that is manufactured at a Matra factory. Matra has also bought the major publishing firm of Hachette. This gave Matra a presence in publishing and press technology. Closer to its original work in missiles, Matra also has developed a role in space. Also, the firm bought into telecommunications and into the design and production of unmanned metro trains (successfully operating in Lille, and soon to start in Chicago). As a result of this conversion, by 1993 Matra was only 20 percent dependent on defense-related contracts. The general lessons to be drawn from this case are: 1. Successful conversion is likely to take considerable time, effort, and investment; 2. In this case it was accomplished largely without direct government support but did benefit from security of public contracts in the transition—there was no sudden ending of defense contracts; 3. The conversion benefited from the continuous commitment of the top executives of the firm; 4. Companies were acquired that had a different culture from that of the military industry mentality. They brought a market understanding with them that assisted in the process of changing the culture.

39. See Udis, *The Challenge to European Industrial Policy*, 2.
40. Ibid.
41. See "The Swedish Economy: A Survey," *The Economist*, March 3, 1990, 6.

8

Downsizing the Defense Industry in the Former Soviet Union: Implications for the United States

Yevgeny Kuznetsov

Given the magnitude of change in the Russian, Ukrainian, and other successor states' economies, it is meaningless to interpret the turmoil in the defense industry as a conversion. Rather, one has to focus on its downsizing, which would involve the closing of some enterprises, the diversification of others, and the formation of new ventures on the basis of defense industry human capital, but would not involve conversion per se. An unbalanced growth strategy—favoring investment in certain targeted sectors—is needed to make the process of reducing the defense sector self-sustaining.[1] This chapter will focus on various scenarios of reducing the defense sector.

The machine-building output of the former Soviet Union in 1988, if estimated in world prices, would break down as follows: capital goods 32 percent, consumer durables 6 percent, and military hardware 62 percent.[2] Domestic price estimates yield somewhat different figures: capital goods 50 percent, consumer durables 20 percent, military hardware 30 percent.[3] Two conclusions may be drawn from these estimates. First, the size of the defense sector ensures the central role that defense cutbacks will play in the current economic restructuring in the successor states of the USSR. Second, because of the chaotic price structure, the macroeconomic indicators of downsizing are generally unreliable, and only disaggregation to the level of specific factors of production can create a convincing picture of the conversion efforts.

These two circumstances—let's call them the size effect (the broad variety of conversion experiences) and the observability effect (the difficulty of aggregating a wide range of microefforts into the macropicture)—produced a sense of bewilderment in the Russian and Western research communities that were studying the Soviet conversion efforts of 1988-1991. Some observers questioned the motivation behind numerous cases of factory-level conver-

Yevgeny Kuznetsov is a research fellow at Cornell University Peace Studies Program. This research was partially supported by the SSRC-MacArthur Foundation in International Peace and Security.

159

sion; they tended to interpret the turmoil in the defense industry as a restructuring aimed at weeding out obsolete technologies rather than as a true reduction of military industrial capabilities.[4] This particular concern is less relevant for the current Russian defense industry adjustment. In an attempt to reduce government expenditures, defense procurement was supposed to be cut by 75 percent. In 1992 the output of weapons and military hardware was 77 percent of 1991 levels. While cuts in defense production were quite dramatic, they were lower than initially announced, in part because military-related exports did not decrease as drastically as domestic procurement. According to First Deputy Minister of Defense A. Kokoshin, the procurement budget in real terms will be 13-17 percent higher in 1993 than in 1992. Nonetheless, other methodological, theoretical, and empirical challenges arise.

The post-Soviet defense industry is experiencing many macroeconomic problems typical of any less-developed country that tries to minimize imports during industrialization. External strangulation—decreased imports of critical spare parts or primary inputs because of depleted foreign exchange reserves—and a pervasive need for unforeseen state subsidies are the most noticeable of these. Furthermore, in addition to reduced demand for defense products one must consider the shock caused by the collapse of civilian demand, which is very important for the diversification potential of individual defense enterprises. Thus, the microeconomic perspective is blurred: a variety of factors affect a defense enterprise's adjustment, and factors other than cuts in procurement may dominate its economic behavior.

The macroeconomic perspective is also not well defined. Cuts in procurement are made by the newly emerging Soviet states in an ad hoc manner as a matter of short-run crisis management rather than as a well thought through response to the more friendly international climate. As such the cuts are erratic and correlate hardly at all with the industrial policy of the governments; consequently, large sections of society are disillusioned with the state, which in turn makes the elaboration of a coherent strategy of defense industry adjustment in particular, and industrial policy in general, all the more difficult. A discredited state and economic crisis are the unavoidable context of the Russian defense cutbacks. In such a fluid and chaotic economic environment, the relationship between defense procurement cuts and welfare gains, which is relatively well established otherwise, is subject to such a formidable number of obstructive or intervening factors that one has to elaborate a number of qualitatively different scenarios to gain an understanding of the possible social, political, and economic consequences of defense cuts.

Given this background, defense downsizing will be examined here as a development problem rather than a restructuring problem. The latter implies a neoclassical view of conversion as reallocation of resources from military to civilian use, while the former is rooted in early development economics, which would view conversion as the release for civilian use of latent resources locked into defense production. An entrepreneurial mindset and high-tech production routines are the most important of these latent resources, yet in the Soviet context they also were the most military-specific. Thus certain incentives are needed to shape their evolution in a commercially viable direction. This evolution will be a long process of learning-by-doing.

The developmental outlook also allows for a Russian-American comparative perspective that otherwise would be difficult to establish. We will look at the reasonably successful postwar classical conversion experiences in the United States, USSR, and Japan in order to identify the essential prerequisites for conversion. Then we will compare that early postwar environment to the current conversion environment in Russia and we will outline what might substitute for the missing prerequisites in both the post-Soviet states and the United States.

Out of the total Soviet arms industry labor force, 72.5 percent was concentrated in what is now the Russian Federation.[5] Together with Ukraine and Belarus, the total employment figure is 93.5 percent. Throughout the text we will refer to the Russian defense industry, which was in fact the core of the old Soviet military-industrial complex. Most of the conclusions are valid for the other two Slavic successor states of the Soviet Union.

The Evolutionary Perspective of Russian Defense Industry Cutbacks

Soviet defense conversion between 1988 and the attempted hard-line Communist coup of August 1991 is generally regarded as a complete failure. The Soviet and Western press were full of examples of such inefficient conversion as when nuclear missile manufacturing facilities were converted to the production of washing machines.[6] The most telling indicator of failure was the skyrocketing cost of the civilian output produced at the former military plants. After the defense industrial complex took over the ministry responsible for producing consumer durables and machinery for light-industry, the cost of the output increased in many instances by a factor of ten without substantial quality improvement.

However, that interpretation of the Soviet conversion experience was unduly harsh. There were in fact elements of both failure and success.

Critics blamed the defense industrial complex for the failures of conversion. They assumed that the defense industrial complex on the macrolevel and defense enterprises on the microlevel have modern capital stock and skilled labor and therefore can produce any output. If they do not produce the required civilian output, then one should look for powerful military-industrial interest groups resisting downsizing or a lack of market incentives for efficient conversion.

No doubt the vested interests of pressure groups and lack of adequate incentives were important variables shaping the Soviet conversion effort. However, no less relevant factors were problems with the availability of productive opportunities and investment resources for conversion.

In the United States the average time from go-ahead to having a product on the market as the result of commercial downsizing is eighteen months, and that is in a country with a highly developed capital market and elastic product and factor markets.[7] Given the pervasive supply rigidities of the Russian economy, one should wonder how Russian defense enterprises were able to increase the production of certain high-tech consumer durables such as television sets within the first three months after conversion. Inside stories of successful conversion experiences, which usually go unreported, provide evidence that defense industrial managers are gradually becoming risk-taking entrepreneurs who perceive and take advantage of rare business opportunities. The real problem was that conversion was constrained by the need to preserve the technological integrity of defense industry capacities (should reconversion to military production be required) and the indivisibility of many defense technologies (which means that a decrease in military output has no direct opportunity cost because joint civilian and military production is impossible).[8]

Defense industry conversion should be viewed as a learning-by-doing development process that is characterized by certain prerequisites needed to make learning (just like development and growth) sustained and by certain factors affecting its speed. Thus the availability of short-term production opportunities and entrepreneurial ability on the part of defense industry managers are the prerequisites of efficient conversion, while inadequate incentive structure and resistance to change from interest groups are the factors influencing its speed.

The conventional points of reference in discussions of the current conversion efforts are postwar conversions in the United States, USSR, and Japan. The American conversion not only provided reemployment within a year for 10 million people released as the result of defense industry reductions, but also was able in a year to absorb the same number of soldiers returning home in 1945-1946.[9] The Soviet postwar economy also proved to be rather elastic and susceptible to change. The following factors were particularly important for the post-Second World War economic adjustment.

Ample availability of dynamic entrepreneurs ready to assume the business risk of conversion. In the immediate postwar years in the United States there was an upsurge of new small businesses. Results of military-related research were declassified and many engineers involved in military R&D started their own businesses or found employment in commercial firms. Defense industry conversion was fueled by entrepreneurial spirit and might be considered a classical example of what Joseph Schumpeter called "growth through creative destruction." [10] It is important to note, however, that the entrepreneurial spirit was often subsidized by the Pentagon itself in an implicit industrial policy. The role of military spending in postwar American recovery is well known. [11]

In Japan the purge of zaibatsu officials provided an opportunity for young and able businessmen to start their careers, and this became an important factor in defense industry conversion. [12]

Large demand for capital goods and consumer durables. Pent-up demand that had accumulated in the United States during the war not only provided an extremely favorable economic background for defense downsizing, but also to a certain extent lowered the sensitivity of demand to price-cost-quality characteristics of output. This contributed to a narrowing of the gap between military and commercial technologies. In the Soviet Union, demand was virtually insatiable because of the vast reconstruction that was needed. That demand resulted in high short-term growth rates because it was relatively easy to find a civilian counterpart for almost any military technology. By the same token, postwar conversion itself became a handicap for long-run economic growth. Postwar conversion decisions shaped the technological development of the Soviet capital goods industry, which still has distinct generic features of military technology. For example, some models of tractors are not actually tractors but semi-tanks in terms of their excessive weight and their effect on the soil.

Broad variety of efficient conversion opportunities on the supply side. In the postwar years military and civilian technological paradigms were quite similar. In fact, civilian technological change was military-driven in the semiconductor and nuclear industries. In addition, postwar downsizing was actually reconversion, that is, the return to civilian production of industries temporarily converted to military manufacturing. This is in stark contrast with the present-day situation, with military technology becoming increasingly "baroque" and military industry becoming institutionally and culturally isolated from civilian industry. [13]

Availability of external resources (capital, entrepreneurship, skilled labor) to alleviate supply rigidities in the course of conversion. In the case of the USSR, postwar reparations from Germany and the other defeated powers provided important structural assistance for conversion, a fact that is not yet fully appreciated. The salvage value of dismantled plants was at least $10 billion (at 1938 prices), which is comparable to the total value of the first phase of Marshall Plan aid, which was about $13 billion. Whole new industries were established on the basis of German equipment, with the electronics industry being the most notable example. [14]

The United States, which experienced a shortage of highly skilled labor, benefited from European emigration. Japan received major entrepreneurial assistance from the American military administration, which broke up local monopolistic structures. Japan also enjoyed generous technology transfer from the United States. To be sure, the long-run effects of such assistance were not necessarily favorable in any of the countries. In the United States there was prolonged underinvestment in human capital. This trend was reversed after the shock of Sputnik. The availability of capital because of reparations retarded the formation of an indigenous Soviet capital goods industry.

In the current downsizing none of these prerequisites exist. Russian monetary overhang (when the amount of money in circulation exceeds the value, under fixed prices, of available consumer goods) could provide an exception in the case of the second prerequisite (large and growing demand), but the restrictive monetary policy and resulting stagflation eliminated even this factor. How will the business community learn to adjust? Which success factors will have to be invented to substitute for those that are missing? Or is massive unemployment, rather than conversion, the likely outcome?

What Conversion Strategy Is Viable in the Russian Case?

Three reference points were of primary importance in shaping Soviet defense/civilian industrial relations: the creation of a consumer durables sector as a result of Khrushchev's decision to launch a large-scale housing construction campaign in the late 1950s; the Soviet-American nuclear rivalry of the 1960s; and windfall oil revenues of the 1970s. The first process was the dawning of modern economic growth in the USSR in the sense that consumer demand became as important as defense demand in making growth self-sustaining. The nuclear rivalry resulted in the formation of a high-tech defense industry, the technological level of which was much higher than that of civilian industry. In that sense the Soviet economy became "dual," with a well-developed defense-related sector and a less technologically developed civilian sector.[15] Windfall oil revenues of the 1970s and mid-1980s allowed the Soviet Union to meet demand for high-tech capital goods (civil as well as military) with purchases from the West.[16]

This last factor changed the structure of the economy, and thus civil-military industrial relations, in two important ways. A civilian high-tech sector was created on the basis of foreign capital (financed by oil revenues) and on the diversification of defense firms into civilian businesses. Since high technology is successfully applied only through learning by doing, technology transfer within multinationals rather than the trade of goods became the major vehicle of its diffusion. Because skilled labor in the Soviet Union was concentrated in defense enterprises, their diversification into the civilian sphere followed economies of scope and scale, and the process of diversification was functionally equivalent to the entry of multinationals into a less-developed economy.

The mentality surrounding the presence of multinationals in a less-developed economy applies equally to the Soviet version of high-tech dualism. Defense firms were reluctant to commit a substantial share of their R&D budget to civilian manufacturing, instead relying on technology transfer from the West. Transfer pricing between military and civilian divisions financed defense production.[17] There were recurrent attempts to "indigenize" high-tech and consumer durables manufacturing; that is, make it independent from defense business. That was typically approached in two ways. Civilian capital goods industries created enclaves under their own auspices based on capital stock acquired, installed, and maintained by a Western partner. No learning is generated in this way. When Western maintenance expires, the plant in question either deteriorates or seeks the protection of experienced high-tech producers.[18] Another way is through the takeover of a civilian sector of a defense complex by a powerful civil industrial monopoly. Thus a separate ministry was created on the basis of defense industrial plants producing consumer durables and capital goods for the light and food industries. It lacked indigenous R&D capabilities, and in 1988 it was taken over once again by defense industries under the pretext of conversion. This organizational dynamic indicates that a high-tech sector producing civilian goods, while having clearly different organizational routines from its military counterpart, was not capable of self-sustained growth. Without infusions of foreign capital it tended to shrink. This was the first vicious circle of the Soviet economy: transformation from military to civilian high-tech industry becoming locked into a low-level equilibrium trap.

In addition to the dichotomy between the defense and civilian high-tech sectors, a duality within high-tech civilian industry also developed. Expanded oil production contributed to the growth of only technologically undemanding industries geared to simple civil construction techniques. Interest groups perpetuating obsolete technologies created profound institutional rigidities that stand in the way of eroding this high-tech/low-tech duality of civilian industry.

The dual-dual economy has become locked into two low-level equilibrium traps.[19] Because of institutional rigidities and the defense industry's priority, the civilian high-tech sector remains small, being unable to exploit economies of scale and scope. This is one trap. Because of the underdeveloped high-tech industry there is no downsizing of obsolete (traditional) industry. The transfer of resources to high-tech (both civilian and military sectors) is then limited. The modern sector of the economy remains small and dependent on foreign supplies. This is a second trap interlocked with the first one.

Gorbachev's economic restructuring and acceleration policies, which during the first two years led to a dramatic increase in investment in high-tech, were from the perspective of development economics an attempt to rescue civilian industry from the underdevelopment trap with the help of a "big push"—a simultaneous increase of high-tech investment in the whole economy.[20] When these policies failed, the vague suspicion arose that another trap existed: in our terminology, the defense-civilian trap. Another "big push" was attempted: the high-tech sector was bolstered by transferring resources from the military subsector of high-tech industry to the civilian subsector.

Our development analysis provides some clues as to why "big push" had unavoidably to fail. A dual-dual economy locked in the low-level equilibrium traps described above, just like any developing economy, becomes plagued by supply rigidities. Structural dependence on foreign equipment and intermediate supplies is the most important of these. In development economics it is recognized as a two-gap model: internal investment alone does not guarantee growth because equipment (capital) from abroad is required to utilize domestic capital.[21] This was the case in the Soviet conversion. It turned out that the civilian sector of the economy was unprepared to provide inputs for conversion precisely because it was so underdeveloped. The press was full of reports that conversion had to be halted because civilian enterprises were unable to supply certain mass-produced intermediate parts (microengines for home appliances, for example) that accounted for no more than 3-5 percent of the value of the output in question.[22] Defense managers (or newly emerging cooperatives on their behalf) had to resort to all kinds of risky devices to supply required intermediate parts from abroad or to find substitutes on the internal market (an equally complex strategy).

The agency responsible for conversion (the Military Industrial Commission) quickly came up with its own "big push" to rescue a failing conversion. A proposal was made to pump 40 billion rubles in investment into the civilian economy within the span of five years just to mitigate its supply rigidities.[23] When it became clear that there was no money for such a push, discussion shifted toward the problem of how to finance it. The idea emerged of gearing the military sector of high-tech industry toward the foreign market to generate hard currency so as to make the growth of its civilian sector self-sustaining. Soviet policy makers involved in conversion planning succumbed to the whole set of romantic prescriptions of early development economics, which were devised for a "capitalist" developing economy! Revealing the same "big push" mentality, a variety of market economists in the West joined the Soviet planners in advocating large-scale foreign aid to the Soviet economy to assist in the conversion of its military industrial facilities.

The moral of this story is clear. Instead of looking for yet another "big push" to make defense industry conversion a reality, one should gradually eliminate the interlocking vicious circles of the economy as a whole. If the major problem is the supply rigidities of the civilian economy, then they should be the primary focus of attention, rather than the defense industrial complex per se. This conclusion is all the more relevant given the current supply disintegration in Russia and other post-Soviet states. Before 1989 the problem was the rigidities retarding growth. Now the problem has shifted to mitigating the supply rigidities precipitating economic collapse. This is an issue of short-run crisis management.

A strategy of unbalanced growth rather than a "big push" should be applied to mitigate numerous supply rigidities and thus create a favorable economic environment for cutting back the defense industry.[24] The unbalanced growth doctrine holds that vicious circles of underdevelopment can be overcome by uneven development of various sectors of the economy, which necessarily creates new imbalances and strains. Its main thrust is the assertion that incentives and strains generated by imbalance can induce entrepreneurship. On the other hand, all the bottlenecks and development prerequisites that failed to materialize are boiled down to one major prerequisite: aggressive, but not necessarily profit-motivated, entrepreneurship. Available evidence of efficient conversion fully supports this approach. Let us discuss an example.

The major problem confronting conversion of manufacturing processes in the short run is the lack of profitable production opportunities. In a rapidly disintegrating economy this problem is crucial. The major goal of production cooperatives established by defense manufacturers is to establish the whole technological chain embracing the slack industrial capacities of one defense-oriented enterprise, the unused inputs from another, excess labor from a third, and so forth. This semi-market behavior might entail converting defense manufacturing processes into civilian ones. Such cooperatives, however, would be heavily dependent on the parent defense-oriented company that instituted them. That is why one would consider it a profit-maximizing internal venture rather than an independent economic agent.

Desperate to find satisfactory conversion technologies, constrained by numerous restrictions imposed by planners, unable even to disclose their company's identity because of secrecy limitations, those defense industry managers who are shrewd and far-sighted would establish a cover company. This company would seemingly be independent (and thus free from the usual behavioral constraints), but in fact would perform functions during conversion that are vital for the parent company. The major objective of the cover firm would, of course, be production of civilian goods on the basis of unutilized capacities of the parent firm. Thus something very important for genuine market transition would emerge: organizational competition between a large-scale firm and its own internal venture—a market cooperative. If the "market" organization turned out to be more efficient in the search for new civilian production routines, the wages of its employees would be higher, and one might expect the transfer of labor from the state-controlled part of the large plant to the market-oriented (internal venture) part. As long as the internal venture produces civilian output utilizing the slack capacities of the defense firm that otherwise would have been idle, and the output of the internal venture counts for the conversion effort of the defense firm, its manager would support such resource transfer. In evolutionary terms, the internal venture performs the Schumpeterian creative destruction of the state-controlled part of the large plant. Significant wage differentials in state-controlled and market sectors of the enterprise in question provide the labor transfer incentive.

The objection may be raised that in the current Russian economic environment the establishment of cooperatives is quite often a stealthy form of asset-stripping in which a group of managers takes the potentially profitable shops of a plant and leaves the rest to be supported by state subsidies.[25] However, this is not an argument against the transfer of resources from established state to start-up private enterprise, but rather an argument for very strong control (including that of privatization) of the state sector of the economy.

In the first phase of the postsocialist downsizing, which is driven by short-run crisis management, none of the prerequisites or conditions for efficient conversion outlined earlier are relevant except for the first one—the need for dynamic entrepreneurs ready to assume the risk of conversion. The economy is so unbalanced that there are always some goods (for example, spare parts for agricultural machinery) where the demand is virtually unaffected by price and cost no matter what the level of aggregate demand is (thus the second prerequisite is irrelevant). The peculiar characteristics of demand make the conditions of availability of efficient (low-cost) civilian manufacturing opportunities (prerequisite three) somewhat irrelevant: any cost might be accepted. Certainly this would create cost-push and possibly structural inflation, but it should be judged as a lesser evil compared to the threat of economic collapse.

The Russian case is extreme, but it does show how certain allegedly rigid prerequisites can be avoided or made much less binding. We turn now to an analysis of our remaining prerequisite of efficient entrepreneurship and to an analysis of subsequent phases (which will follow the short-run crisis management) of the Russian downsizing.

Two Contrasting Entrepreneurial Mentalities

The growth of small enterprises within large defense production associations will ease some supply rigidities and will stimulate economic growth in the long run. But the Russian military-industrial complex employs 6.5 millior people in 2,000 enterprises (on average 3,000 are employed per enterprise), at least half of whom are expected to lose their jobs in 1992-1993. Thus one should concentrate on the entrepreneurial evolution of decision making in large enterprises.

The business acumen of defense managers is mixed. The chief designer of a weapons system was traditionally viewed as the broker between the military's requirements and the far inferior capabilities of the industry.[26] Under pressure exerted from both sides, he had to be entrepreneurial, at least to a certain extent. In addition, in a few defense industries such as aviation there was some competition among design bureaus. Business routines in the high-tech design bureaus may be described as a blend of intense lobbying of the government for privileges and innovative activity, with a substantial correlation between the intensity of innovative behavior and rewards (the amount of hard currency available for the design bureau, quality of equipment received, welfare gains for employees).

To a lesser extent, the same is also true of high-tech defense manufacturing. Here too there is a striking imbalance between defense requirements and inferior technological capabilities, partly because of the weak civilian high-technology base and partly because of Western restrictions on exporting high technology to the USSR. Thanks to Western export restrictions, enforced by the Coordinating Committee on Multilateral Export Controls (CoCom), some Soviet defense enterprises became capital-stretching "aggressive" monopolies rather than "lazy" monopolies that resorted to quality deterioration.[27] From this standpoint, managers of the enterprises that were engaged in technologically undemanding tasks were less likely to display profit-oriented entrepreneurship.[28]

As an example, let us outline the emerging conversion strategy within the framework of unbalanced growth in the Soviet aviation ministry. The ministry comprises nine design bureaus and about twenty large vertically integrated manufacturing associations.[29] Its output in 1989 was estimated in the range of $23-28 billion,[30] which is comparable to the combined military and civilian sales of McDonnell Douglas ($14.6 billion) and Boeing ($20.3 billion).[31]

Since the ministry apparatus has been dissolved recently in preparation for market shock therapy, manufacturing associations have started to form business alliances with the design bureaus in order to produce civilian aircraft and other high-tech equipment. There will be approximately ten aviation firms, some of which seek to eliminate defense orders completely. These large firms are expected to pursue first a strategy of producing aircraft for Russia and other states of the newly emerging Commonwealth. All associations seek the assistance of Western companies to enhance efficiency and international competitiveness. Thus Pratt & Whitney is working with the Tupolev and Ilyshin design bureaus on installing PW2037 engines on the

Soviet aircraft Tu-204 and Il-96M. Both planes are expected to fly with Pratt & Whitney engines in 1993.[32] The credits needed to finance the Western equipment can be covered by proceeds from international flights of Russian air carriers, which have a severe shortage of modern aircraft.

The next step is to diversify into production of capital goods that were previously imported from the West. Oil drilling equipment is one example. This is essentially an import substitution strategy, which might be efficient in the medium term by virtue of the vast Russian market. The experience acquired in import substitution may be used to penetrate the less quality-conscious markets, such as the Chinese market. Eventually, with the accumulation of experience and in partnership with Western companies, entering the international marketplace seems quite likely. In the last stage, export will be based on the low cost of labor in Russian aircraft companies.

The institutional evolution of Soviet defense companies is likely to be based on large, diversified, growth-oriented groups. Growth itself is supposed to produce a virtuous circle: economies of scale and scope generate technical efficiency (X-efficiency), which is further enhanced by top managers attracted by growing, diversifying businesses. John D. Morrocco, in his review of the Soviet aerospace industry, specifically noted the business qualities of enterprise managers, many of whom displayed ingenuity in discovering profitable conversion technologies even when the economy was in chaos.[33]

Restructuring of diversified companies and the formation of small, innovative private enterprises represent two approaches to business. The latter is the classic "creative destruction" based on individual entrepreneurship resulting in innovation. The former is entrepreneurship within diversified business groups (prevalent in late and "late-late" industrialization), the essence of which is learning rather than innovating. Both embryos are clearly present in the current conversion attempts, the further dynamics of which will be determined by the extent of cross-fertilization between these two business approaches.

Almost every enterprise has to face the virtual collapse of defense-related demand for its output because of the program of fiscal adjustment started by the Russian government on January 2, 1992. Yet evidence from the first three months following implementation of this program showed that managers of defense enterprises capable of such cross-fertilization did surprisingly well. For example, 80 percent of the output of the electronic components plant in Viborg, which employs more than 4,000 workers, went to the military in the middle of 1991. By the end of April 1992 this share shrank to 30 percent, with only occasional lay-offs. Moreover, despite the collapsing economy, the enterprise continues to invest. Its success is based on aggressive export promotion. Rapid growth of exports is possible because of a very undervalued ruble and because of the exploitation of large-scale innovative civilian R&D available elsewhere in the Russian defense industrial complex. Thus the company offers very cheaply various intermediate products for Finnish, German, and French machine-making firms. Each of these products contains some innovative component. It is noteworthy that the enterprise in question has itself offered credit to support its partner's R&D, which it will incorporate into its own products later. Thus the firm has to perform functions of Schumpeterian supply-inducing finance, risk assessment, and profit sharing. There is a clear understanding among the top management of the enterprises that this export-dependent strategy is very sensitive to the exchange rate. Once the ruble's value becomes close to equilibrium, the company will have to diversify into domestic civilian business, with extensive long-term opportunities such as production of capital stock for nascent private farming. Profit from export revenues that is not going toward external R&D or to support the home-based R&D is allocated for investment in agricultural machinery. Managers envision the enterprise as a highly diversified business group in which the electronic components division will not necessarily play a substantial role.

We have illustrated through this example the first two steps of an unbalanced strategy of downsizing and growth on a microlevel. This strategy is inherently imbalance-generating. For example, the successful transfer of labor to export manufacturing is based on a number of conditions, such as a favorable exchange rate and a large market, that tend to disappear as one advances in a certain export market. Initial success contains the seeds of possible failure. But the failure is by no means predetermined, as imbalances create pressure to seek new business opportunities (in this case, retreat into a specific sector of the internal market), the exploitation of which results in a subsequent new "act of discovery." Thus a self-propelling growth process is launched where downsizing generates growth, growth generates imbalance, and vice versa.

The Alliance among Local Interest Groups, Foreign Capital, and the State

No doubt the transition from import substitution to export promotion will produce further imbalances. For example, the balance of payments may deteriorate initially to finance the supply of capital goods. But this is the essence of unbalanced growth, which proceeds from one evil to another presumably less dangerous one. An alliance among the local entrepreneurs organized into interest groups, foreign capital, and a strong state capable of implementing its own policies is the vital prerequisite for this strategy to succeed. We now proceed to a discussion of the main actors in the unbalanced strategy of defense downsizing and Russian economic development in general.

Large industrial enterprises. Neoclassical economics regards monopoly or limited oligopolistic competition as uniformly inferior compared to (the unrealized ideal of) perfect competition. However, downsizing and the process of forming market institutions, which are both emphatically processes of disequilibrium, impose their own criteria of efficiency. For example, in unbalanced growth the guarantee of freedom of entry and exit becomes the only important indicator to watch for, irrespective of the current degree of market power. Temporary or transitory monopoly should be permitted or even encouraged as long as rivals who are alert to new opportunities are not prevented by purposive restrictions from entering the market and thus driving prices down.[34] The issue is then "lazy" monopoly, not aggressive monopoly, which would take advantage of the new opportunities. The available anecdotal evidence shows that even the current downsizing produced a shock strong enough to "awaken" lazy monopoly and make it, if not profit-oriented, at least capital-stretching.

The chaotic macroeconomic environment promoted by short-run crisis management poses another problem. In a chaotic market there will be extremely large costs associated with failure and exit from the business. Thus, very high profit may be required to encourage entry of a transitory monopoly. It is this monopoly profit that was the incentive for the relatively efficient conversion of small-scale ventures of the type described earlier. If the authorities had tried to restrict profit by progressive taxation or price control, the new entrepreneurs of defense enterprises would have abandoned at once any attempt to enter new civilian business. If a strategy of unbalanced growth is pursued, then the transition to a market economy is bound to be highly inflationary.

Another problem is that of transaction costs. How is one supposed to break up the nuclear power industry into smaller units if virtually all its capital is highly partner-specific and thus transaction costs in the case of breaking the monopoly will be prohibitively high? In this case, the criterion of transaction cost economizing is the most essential one. One should gear this industry toward the foreign market with the help of a strong industrial policy to enhance competition rather than putting into effect standard antitrust measures. By world standards, Russian industrial conglomerates are small. For example, the output of the whole ministry of aviation industry, which gave rise to at least ten associations, is roughly the same as the output of the leading Korean business group, Samsung.

Foreign business. Russian defense enterprises are often diversified on the facility level, but their defense and civilian outputs are produced within unified technological processes. On the accounting level there is no distinction between military and civilian business. Foreign companies are extremely reluctant to invest in such enterprises, however advanced they might be, since one never knows the final destination of investment. Thus one should expect increasing specialization of the diversified Russian defense-related enterprises, either on civilian or military business, much like in the United States.

Three patterns of foreign capital involvement are emerging (see Table 8-1). The "Brazilian" pattern amounts to encouraging the entry of multinationals into domestic industry. Multinationals bring modern production and organizational routines that are to a certain extent indigenized. There are also profound and well-known disadvantages associated with the broad involvement of multinationals.[35] The most likely candidates for this pattern of foreign involvement are obsolete sectors of the defense industry that are subject to closure. The value of such capital stock (taking into account the debt toward the environment) is negative, the labor force is as highly skilled as it is underpaid, and interest groups are relatively weak. One could expect multinationals to take advantage of these essentially static comparative advantages and to acquire the relevant enterprises through privatization (perhaps not right at the start). It is only labor (after retraining) and part of the real estate that will be used for the manufacturing of such goods as machine tools.

If, however, the linkage to domestic production or the indigenous labor force is negligible, one might expect an "Argentinean" type of foreign involvement, where foreign business is an enclave within the highly inefficient domestic industry. An enclave type of development is likely to occur within the R&D sector of the Russian defense industry. Now it is frantically seeking sources of financing from the West and often finding them. Internal brain drain is emerging concomitantly with the classic form of brain drain. In the former case the "brains" in question do not leave the country, but results of their research are targeted exclusively to more advanced Western economies. The signs of "internal" brain drain are noticeable in some aviation research institutes.[36]

Finally, the Korean type of foreign investment entails strict state-imposed limitations. Learning from the outside world is tremendous but it takes the form of learning-by-doing through the purchase of foreign equipment and licenses.[37] This pattern might emerge in politically powerful defense industries such as nuclear power and aviation.

Interest groups. With the emergence of a market economy and profound defense reductions the defense industrial groups will not disappear, nor will they resist conversion. The conservative image that is usually ascribed to them should be attributed more to the stagnant if not collapsing economy, with its absence of avenues for transformation of these groups, rather than to their alleged ingrained attachment to defense production. The likely scenarios of interest group transformation are the following.

In a "Brazilian" transformation, former defense industrial groups would push for a strong market-reserve policy in the high-tech area. The infant-industry argument would be used but protection would be much stronger than would be required in the case of infant industry. Inefficiency again is an issue, but it is second-best inefficiency because high-tech firms under the

Table 8-1   Stylized Scenarios of Russian Defense Industry
Downsizing and Emerging Development Strategies

	"Brazilian"	"Korean"	"Argentinean"
Development strategy	Gradual transformation from import substitution to export promotion: export-adequate strategy.	"Targeted" development strategy encouraging diversification and export orientation of the existing chaebol-like diversified enterprises.	Lack of consistent development strategy. Constant (albeit chaotic) short-run crisis management.
Transformation of defense industrial interest groups	Transformation into high-tech pressure groups that seek to protect existing high-tech industries from competition (infant industry argument).	Expansionist and 'aggressive' pressure groups seeking to obtain more investment or favorable terms in return for high performance standard.	Fight for power and prestige. Engaged in redistributional conflict for higher wages.
The role of the state	Developmental but segmented state under the influence of various, primarily former, defense industrial interest groups. State-induced capital formation is essential.	Developmental and strong state capable of imposing strong performance standards on recipients of government subsidies. State = national entrepreneur.	The state, similar to the Soviet state before 1990, is completely captured by various interest groups.
Bureaucratic authoritarian tendencies directed at:	Political stability to escape labor unrest and encourage entry of multinationals.	Enforcing low (but presumably growing) real wage.	Coping with increasing, from time to time drastic and unbearable, deterioration of economic situation.
Foreign capital participation in conversion and growth	Very broad. Some industries are taken over completely by foreign capital.	Mainly indirect forms of participation or through joint ventures and foreign trade.	Lack of incentive for foreign capital to enter. In the cases it does enter, the foreign enterprise remains an enclave in the national economy.

(Continued on next page)

Table 8-1   (Continued)

	"Brazilian"	"Korean"	"Argentinean"
Role of defense downsizing in economic growth	Defense industry is supplier of private entrepreneurs. Some limited provision of capital as a result of conversion.	In the short-run downsizing mitigates supply rigidities. In the long run, it is the major determinant of market structure.	Conversion and downsizing are viewed as a campaign to extract revenues to cover government deficit. Change of policies is erratic, e.g., from outright privatization of defense enterprises to halting privatization campaign.
Pattern of diversification of defense industrial companies	Vertical and horizontal disintegration (Stigler, 1951). Defense companies specialize in defense business only.	Nonlinear (Amsden, 1989) diversification: facilitation of creation of dynamic comparative advantages by large enterprises by diversifying into technologically dissimilar business.	Diversification into marginal and technologically undemanding markets (such as toys, umbrellas).
Defense industry after downsizing	Small defense industry with highly specialized plants, some of which are explicitly export-oriented.	The absence of institutional dichotomy between civilian and military industry. Military output is included in large enterprises' output mix for business cycle consideration.	Downsizing without conversion. Substantial (2-3 million) downsizing-induced unemployment.
Transformation of technological duality (modern defense-oriented vs. less modern civilian sector)	Industries catering to lower-income groups are less technologically advanced than those catering to higher-income groups. The latter industries are former defense industries that have undergone conversion.	Uniform and well-integrated technological structure.	Enclaves comprising large-scale foreign enterprises vs. relatively small and inefficient domestic enterprises. Domestic vs. foreign capital dichotomy.

(Continued on next page)

Table 8-1   (Continued)

	"Brazilian"	"Korean"	"Argentinian"
Determinants of military budget	1. The need to improve the well-being of the military. 2. Dual-use military-civilian R&D. Defense budget as a cover for the support of civilian R&D.	1. Requirements of minimal low-cost "alternative" defense. 2. The need to improve the well-being of the military.	1. Interests of the powerful defense industrial pressure groups. 2. Possible (or "would-be") civil and ethnic unrest. 3. Social security of the military.
Conflict of short-run and long-run interests: Conversion as part of short-run crisis management vs. defense downsizing as a component of development strategy	*Short-run crisis management* Much higher protection for the converted enterprises. Weak antitrust policy and toleration of "transitory" monopoly. Widespread mark-up pricing and structural inflation as a result of conversion. Participation of multinationals in privatization of defense enterprises and conversion without any restrictions. *Development strategy* Selected protection, strong antitrust policy, selective entry of multinationals.	*Short-run crisis management* Pervasive and inefficient bailing out of enterprises in which conversion is in progress by the state. Bolstering of weapons sales. Mergers and acquisitions of defense enterprises to exploit economies of scale and scope. *Development strategy* Limited bail-out, regulated mergers, strictly limited weapons export dependence.	No difference.

market reserve policy are supposedly acquiring valuable experience. Thus Soviet defense space programs before the shock of price-liberalization were being transformed into civilian space programs, the efficiency of which was highly questionable.

The former military industry also may be at the core of the coalition pushing for inflationary consumer-credit-based economic growth. In this way the problem of effective demand for output (not just for consumer durables, but capital goods such as passenger aircraft) would be mitigated. This is also a distinctly Brazilian type of economic growth.[38] There is evidence that many defense managers, like the manager of the Viborg plant mentioned earlier which switched swiftly to civilian export, see the problem not just in the collapse of defense demand but also in the collapse of civilian demand. They are currently organizing into groups which will pressure the Russian government to stimulate (by credit expansion) civilian demand, and in particular high-tech demand, making the process of civilian diversification easier.

The most discouraging outcome is an Argentinean scenario of interest group evolution, which is chaotic and disorderly because every actor in the interest group coalition has the power of veto but none is able to impose its own scheme. Competitive pressure for wage increases would likely emerge. One possible outcome is wage-led growth accompanied by structural inflation.

Finally, the Korean type of interest group evolution would push for selective credit policies from the state. It would result in the creation of a highly fragmented capital market with negative real interest rates for the privileged. Numerous conversion banks emerging now in Russia on the basis of former defense industrial ministries are prototypes of such a fragmented capital market. However, fragmentation is not necessarily indicative of inefficiency.

The state. The continuing erosion of state authority in Russia and the other newly emerging nations evidently is over. Disillusionment with the state and the dismantling of governmental industrial policy should give way to a slowly emerging image of a developmentally strong state capable of setting up and implementing development goals.

Modern economic theory tells little about the conditions under which the state plays a positive role in economic transformation. Paradoxically, in both Marxist and neoclassical theoretical frameworks the state is incapable of setting up, let alone implementing, its own policies because it is effectively "captured" by vested interests and pressure groups. The performance of the Russian government after the 1992 price liberalization may appear to support this view.

In private conversations government officials confess that they feel themselves to be hostages of the military-industrial complex, implying that collapse of defense-related employment will result in an overthrow of the government. The statistical data is quite alarming too. In spite of the fact that only 6.5 billion rubles were allocated for the first quarter of 1992 for military hardware procurement, the actual output was 20 billion.[39] Enterprises are still able to rely on credit expansion (which for the defense sector for the same period amounted to 20 billion rubles) rather than resort to layoffs and enterprise closure.

These figures tell little indeed about the ability of the Russian government to implement its own industrial policies. What they reveal is the insufficiency of monetary austerity to induce downsizing. Monetary austerity fails when confronted, for example, with the closure of the defense enterprise in a one-company town. Industrial policy is needed to ensure the peaceful transition of military-related to alternative employment.

The Russian government began to display some awareness of the need for an industrial policy targeted to military industries only in March-April 1992. So far the record is mixed. What is noteworthy, however, is that the informal networking between business and government (usually associated with the Japanese or Korean type of developmental state) seemed to be more efficient in inducing the transformation at the enterprise level than financing the conversion projects through government institutions like development banks (the latter is the hallmark of the Brazilian type of developmental state). Informal networking and more formal institutions clearly complement rather than exclude one another in implementing industrial policy. Evidence indicates, however, that a Korean type of strong developmental state that extracts high performance from business is unlikely to emerge, for it clearly requires authoritarianism. The other extreme case, the Argentinean state which is neither developmental nor strong because it is completely captured by various interest groups, is also unlikely, at least in Russia. The Brazilian scenario is the most likely: the state is extensive and developmental (in the sense that it sets and to a certain extent implements developmental goals), but it is segmented because of the extensive "capture" of the government by the numerous interest groups.

Emerging "Korean type," "Brazilian type" or "Argentinean type" trends can be viewed as stylized extreme scenarios of future growth. The possible scenarios of evolving alliances between states, local interest groups, and foreign business and their implications for the conversion in the Russian Federation are summarized in Table 8-1.

Lessons from Russian Downsizing for Western Democracies

At first glance it seems improbable that the strategy of unbalanced defense reductions devised within a framework of short-run crisis management could be of any relevance for market economies, and yet the strategy was at least partly fueled by the conversion experience of a postwar market economy. Finland, the case in question, had none of the prerequisites for conversion stated above, with the exception of a large but very peculiar demand from the Soviet economy. It had never received any assistance from abroad. On the contrary, it had to pay war reparations to the Soviet Union. It had to suppress temporarily private entrepreneurship and put much greater emphasis on the state as the "obligatory" major entrepreneur because of the exceptionally heavy toll of reparations. In fact, payment of the war debt was considered so urgent that a special war reparations agency, with far-reaching authority, was set up for its administration. Armaments and munitions factories had to be converted rapidly by the state because initially there was inadequate capacity to meet war reparations.[40]

The initial stage (1945-1947) of war reparations, which were repaid completely only in 1952, involved standard short-run crisis management with broad central intervention and pervasive inefficiencies. What is interesting, however, is how short-run crisis management was transformed into efficient long-term development policy. War reparations were used to gain a strong foothold in the Soviet market: the productive output of conversion and post-war investment was not competitive on Western markets, but it was readily absorbed by the Soviet market. Gradually, with the accumulation of experience Finnish firms diversified into more demanding markets. Thus the trade with the Soviet Union that followed the war reparations served as a stepping-stone for export to other countries.[41]

Likewise, American military contractors trying to diversify into civilian business might themselves have a comparative advantage in certain segments of Russian and East European markets. They can team with Soviet defense companies to produce goods with infinite opportunity cost whose price might be very high. Some guarantees on investment from the federal government will be required to put forward this strategy. For the United States, the formation of an alliance between local business, government, and foreign capital is the major precondition if conversion rather than unemployment is to result from a reduction of military industry.

The Soviet conversion can provide lessons, based on the conditions for efficient conversion established above, for downsizing the American defense establishment.

One lesson stems from the notion that a lack of productive opportunities and diverging military and civilian technological trajectories are the major barriers in military-civilian technology transfer. Technological and cost-price rigidities in technology transfer from military to civilian business are well known. But sometimes technological problems are confused with institutional rigidities; that is, the lack of will to adjust commercial and military mentalities to each other to devise new products or processes. The magnitude of this entirely institutional problem can be illustrated by the almost nonexistent technology transfer within military industries, where the traditional argument about contrasting requirements of the commercial and military business does not apply.

A second lesson relates to lack of demand for high-tech civilian output and the issue of demand creation. For the United States, just like for the Russian Federation, one of the main issues in downsizing is the transformation of interest groups that had flourished on government business. If the direction of their lobbying shifts toward government support of R&D in the precompetitive stage, the conversion of military R&D will be much easier. This is why the ideologically sensitive question of supporting Sematech, which required amending the antitrust law, sets an important precedent.[42] After all, precompetitive R&D support (which may take the form of federal assistance to the conversion of military R&D) is one of the instruments of targeted demand creation, which as far as high-tech demand is concerned is much more efficient than standard fiscal and monetary instruments.

The issue of American industrial policy invariably emerges when acquisition of Russian high technology is concerned. The Bush administration's failure to define such a policy resulted in a windfall for Europe and Japan, which are forging strong high-tech ties with the former USSR.[43] France, which has been a partner in the Soviet space program for years, is making particularly good progress. NASA officials believe that Russian aerospace capabilities "could be crucial to the U.S. in gaining an advantage over Western Europe and Japan." [44] The increasing awareness that Russia is doomed to a strategic alliance with the United States, which is experiencing increased competition from Japan and Western Europe, prompts U.S. investment companies to start investing in Soviet defense enterprises that are undergoing conversion.[45] The whole process would have gone much further, however, if the Bush administration had guaranteed support for private investment in certain sectors of the post-Soviet economy, or at least abolished unnecessary restrictions on R&D cooperation with Russia.

As Richard Minnich rightly notes, defense companies' opportunities for diversification are rich on the capital goods market, and in particular in designing, creating, and maintaining large complex systems.[46] The unbalanced growth approach, emphasized throughout this chapter, suggests that the international market could exploit the Third and former Second World. This conclusion implies that the successful conversion of high-tech military industries in Russia and the United States will result in stiff competition in certain segments of the world market, with potentially very unpleasant retaliatory measures.[47]

The problem is that in the market for strategically sensitive equipment there is a temptation to use the unavoidable ambiguities of treaties on nonproliferation of sensitive technology in such a way as to exclude a competitor from a growing market. CoCom, for example, was used by the United States against Japanese high-tech expansion. Currently, the American space industry—the monopoly supplier of space services in the world market—faces competition from the cash-starved Russian space industry. No wonder Russia's sales of cryogenic-technology engines for the Indian space program provoked great controversy as allegedly violating a relevant nonproliferation treaty. The Russian side claimed that there was no such violation, citing the reluctance of the American side to discuss technical details of the technology transfer in question, which would have provided an answer.[48]

The recent history of the Japanese-American high-tech rivalry indicates the magnitude of the problem of coordinating export policies. In the Russian-American rivalry there is a need for an institution to resolve high-tech trade controversies. This may become the major function of CoCom which, in this case, should undergo substantial transformation.

Conclusion

Competition in weapons procurement with the West and the imbalance between the Soviet defense and civilian technology base created specific incentives and strains for high-technology generation in the Soviet economy. Even over the long term it is unlikely that limited competition in the emerging post-Soviet market will provide sufficient pressure to innovate. Erosion of the Russian high-technology base is in the offing, as is large-scale brain drain. This does not mean, however, that one should rule out the emergence of some pockets of high-tech excellence in current conditions of short-run crisis management. These pockets of excellence will be maintained by certain entrepreneurial business managers: as in any development process, people matter more than institutions in the current Russian downsizing.

This fluid economic environment provides unique opportunities to Western business for investment in Russia no matter how developments unfold. We outlined three scenarios—the "Brazilian," "Korean," and "Argentinean"—all three based on semi-industrialized countries. Downsizing was explicitly viewed as a development rather than just a restructuring process. The development economics approach suggests an "unbalanced growth" strategy concentrating on conditions that generate motivated entrepreneurship to make conversion self-sustaining.

The most important of these conditions is the alliance between local entrepreneurs, the state, and foreign business, which we showed was vital in such diverse cases as postwar reconstruction, conversion in Finland, and the downsizing attempt in the former Soviet Union. The United States can learn from these and other cases how to create and maintain such an alliance in order to influence large-scale development processes (of which downsizing defense is just one example), that generate substantial disparities between private and social return, provoking profound market failures.

The success of converting defense business in a commercially viable direction will result in stiff competition between American and Russian producers, notably in developing countries' markets. There is a need to institutionalize a process for resolving already emerging controversies in the area of strategically sensitive high-tech trade.

Notes

1. See A.O. Hirschman, *The Strategy of Economic Development* (New Haven: Yale University Press, 1958).

2. A. Ozhegov, Ye. Rogovski, and Yu. Iaremenko, "Konversia Oboronnoi Promyshlennosti i Preobrazovanie Ekonomiki SSSR," *Kommunist* 1, 1991, 54. ["Defense Industry Conversion and its Role in the Transformation of the USSR Economy."]

3. Ibid.

4. Ozhegov, Rogovski, and Iaremenko, "Konversia Oboronnoi Promyshlennosti i Preobrazovanie Ekonomiki SSSR," in *Problemy Prognozirovania* 1, no. 1, 22-38.

5. Julian Cooper, "Defence Industry Conversion in the East: The Relevance of Western Experience," paper prepared for the 1992 NATO Economics Directorate colloquium, "External Economic Relations of the Central and East European Countries," Brussels, April 8-10, 1992. Cooper reports that in 1985, 5,416,800 "industrial productive personnel" were employed in the defense complex in the Russian Federation (which is 24.9 percent of total industrial employment). This is not the only estimate. Iablokov, a journalist, in an April 23 *Izvestiia* article, cites estimates ranging from 7.3 to 16.4 million. Malei, an adviser to President Yeltsin on conversion issues, quotes a figure of 4.4 million, which increases to 12 million if workers in industrial subsidiaries of the military-industrial complex are counted (*Izvestiia,* March 31,1992). Much of the discrepancy is attributable to classifications of what precisely is a worker in a military-industrial complex. We will stick to a range of 5-7 million. I am indebted to Patrick Flaherty for providing me with the above citations.

6. Julian Cooper, "Military Cuts and Conversion in the Defense Industry," *Soviet Economy* 7:1 (January-March, 1991).

7. David Hughes, "Survey on Defense Firm Commercial Efforts Shows Surprising Success Rate, Activity," *Aviation Week & Space Technology,* December 9, 1991, 21-22.

8. This is a characteristic of semicontinuous, large-scale manufacturing processes. Tank production is an example.

9. Hugh G. Mosley, *The Arms Race: Economic and Social Consequences* (Lexington, Mass.: Lexington Books, D.C. Heath, 1985), 167.

10. J. Schumpeter, *The Theory of Economic Development* (New York: Oxford University Press, 1934).

11. Gregory Hooks, *Forging the Military-Industrial Complex: World War II's Battle of the Potomac* (Urbana: University of Chicago Press, 1991).

12. Zaibatsu were large, diversified firms with interlocking ownership of each other's assets. They monopolized the prewar Japanese economy and blocked the entry of new businesses.

13. Mary Kaldor, *The Baroque Arsenal* (New York: Hill and Wang, 1981). Kaldor defines "baroque" technology as a technology that provides increasing levels of sophistication and cost without corresponding improvement in performance.

14. Anthony C. Sutton, *Western Technology and Soviet Economic Development 1945 to 1965* (Stanford: Hoover Institution Press, 1973).

15. Ronald Amann, Julian Cooper, and R. W. Davies, eds. *The Technological Level of Soviet Industry* (New Haven: Yale University Press, 1977).

16. The Soviet case is special because it was not the whole industry that was affected, but rather only the high-technology segment of it. S. Glaziev, *Ekonomicheskya Teoria Tekhnicheskogo Razvitiya* (Moscow: Nauka, 1990). [The Economic Theory of Technological Development].

17. Yevgeny Kuznetsov and F. Shirokov, "Naykoemkie Proizvodstva i Konversia Oboronnoi Promyshlennosti," *Kommunist* 10, 1989, 15-23. [An English translation is available: "Science Intensive Output and Defense Industry Conversion," Joint Publication Research Service-UKO-89-016, 21 September 1989, 8-13.]

18. Yevgeny Kuznetsov, "What is the Impact of the Military-Industrial Complex on the Emerging Russian Development Strategy? Soviet Defense Industry Build-up and Post-Soviet Demilitarization from a Development Economics Point of View." Paper

prepared for the John M. Olin Institute Consensus Project, Harvard University.

19. On the supply side, the equilibrium traps are similar to the underdevelopment trap described by R. Nurkse in *Problems of Capital Formation in Underdeveloped Countries* (Oxford: Basil Blackwell, 1953). Nurkse was concerned with a situation where market limitations made it unprofitable for any single producer to increase production, and yet if all producers increased production they would all profit from it. In the Soviet case the amount of resources available for the high-tech civilian sector does not allow utilizing economies of scale and scope, keeping the social rate of return low. If there were a nonmarginal impulse to overcome the efficiency threshold, the civilian modern sector would evolve from low-level to higher equilibrium.

20. Paul N. Rosenstein-Rodan, "Problems of Industrialization of Eastern and South-Eastern Europe," *Economic Journal* 53 (1943), 202-211.

21. K. Basu, *The Less Developed Economy* (Oxford: Basil Blackwell, 1984).

22. D. Pipko, "Conversion in Aviation Industry," *Socialisticheskya Industria,* August 28, 1989, 2.

23. Ohzhegov, Rogovski, and Iaremenko, "Konversia Oboronnoi Promyshlennosti," in *Problemy Prognozirovania.*

24. Hirschman, *The Strategy of Economic Development.*

25. I am indebted to P. Flaherty for making this point.

26. Thane Gustafson, "The Response to Technological Change," in *Soldiers and the Soviet State: Civil-Military Relations from Brezhnev to Gorbachev,* ed. Timothy J. Colton and Thane Gustafson (Princeton: Princeton University Press, 1990), 192-238.

27. The distinction between profit-oriented (high cost but stable quality of output) and "lazy" monopolies (quality of output is deteriorating) is proposed by Albert Hirschman in *Exit, Voice, and Loyalty: Responses to Decline in Firms, Organizations, and States* (Cambridge: Harvard University Press, 1970) in conjunction with the "exit-voice" concept. In an economy where price-mediated competition is weak, *voice*—"any attempt at all to change, rather than to escape from, an objectionable state of affairs"—might be as effective in enhancing allocation efficiency as *exit* (switch of demand to another producer). Hirschman noted that limited competition is able to suppress "voice" and bolster a monopoly by unburdening it of its more troublesome customers, in this way providing freedom to deteriorate. For the majority of Soviet civilian enterprises, windfall oil revenues of the 1970s provided this "freedom to deteriorate," since inputs of high quality could be obtained from the world market. This was not the case with the high-technology sector, however. Because of Western export controls on high-technology goods and because of strict Soviet military requirements, both civilian and military enterprises had to learn how to produce high-quality output themselves. The dichotomy between the modern and traditional sectors is also a dichotomy between "aggressive" and "lazy" monopolies.

28. Their comparative advantage is low-cost skilled labor. The burden of learning and maintaining quality management fell on the shop floor engineers and workers rather than new product designers and top management in the high-tech case.

29. Peter Almquist, *The Red Forge* (New York: Columbia University Press, 1990), 68.

30. My own estimate. Procurement of aircraft and engines by the Soviet military in 1989 was 3.1 billion rubles, according to the Stockholm International Peace Research Institute, *SIPRI Yearbook 1991* (Oxford: Oxford University Press, 1991), 149. Taking into account military aircraft export, the total military output is 4.0-4.5 billion rubles. Purchasing power parity for aircraft is $4-6 per ruble. Thus military output is estimated to be $18-22 billion. Civilian output was approximately 40 percent of the total (civilian and military), or 2.5 billion rubles. Assuming purchasing power parity for civilian aircraft and other output adjusted for quality ($2-3 per ruble), civilian output will be in the range of $5-7 billion.

31. *SIPRI Yearbook,* 311.

32. John D. Morrocco, "Avionics Firms Diversify, Seek Western Investment," *Aviation Week & Space Technology*, November 18, 1991, 55, 57.
33. Ibid.
34. O. E. Williamson, *The Economic Institutions of Capitalism* (New York: The Free Press, 1985).
35. See, for example, Werner Baer, *The Brazilian Economy: Growth and Development* (New York: Praeger, 1989), chap. 10.
36. Internal brain drain is somewhat self-contradictory. Why do the scientists not emigrate if they are alienated from the indigenous "mainstream" research community? However, this is typical for any semi-industrialized country. Michael P. Todaro, *Economic Development in the Third World*, 4th ed. (New York: Longman, 1989) cites numerous examples of internal brain drain in India where, for example, medical scientists are involved in research on certain cardiac diseases common to old age because it is considered to be prestigious in the West, although it is totally irrelevant to local health care problems. See also John D. Morrocco, "Avionics Firms Diversify, Seek Western Investment"; Morrocco, "Five Research Facilities Band Together to Form Independent Association," *Aviation Week & Space Technology*, November 18, 1991, 48-49; Morrocco, "Soviets Grope for Order with New Industry Alliance," *Aviation Week & Space Technology*, November 18, 1991, 42-44; Morrocco, "Yakovlev Banks on New Transports to Ensure Design Bureau's Survival," *Aviation Week & Space Technology*, November 18, 1991, 50-51.
37. Alice H. Amsden, *Asia's Next Giant: South Korea and Late Industrialization* (New York: Oxford University Press, 1989).
38. Baer, *The Brazilian Economy*.
39. V. Golovachev, "The Collapse of The Defense Complex May Cause the Crash of the Economy," *Ekonomika i Zhizn* 18 (May 1992).
40. Tarmo Haavisto and Ari Kokko, "Politics as a Determinant of Economic Performance: The Case of Finland," in *Diverging Paths: Comparing a Century of Scandinavian and Latin American Economic Development,* ed. Magnus Blomström and Patricio Meller (Washington, D.C.: Inter-American Development Bank, 1991), 181-212.
41. In hindsight this strategy has obvious flaws. Because of dependence on exports to the Soviet Union the GDP dropped by 6.1 percent and unemployment rates tripled from 3.4 to 11.5 percent. William E. Schmidt, "Finland Struggles to Overcome the Soviet Fall," *New York Times*, May 28, 1992, A11. Finnish manufactured goods are not very competitive on Western markets. The Soviet trade that started the growth later became a handicap. Such tradeoffs often emerge in the development process.
42. Sematech is a consortium of major American semiconductor manufacturers. It was established, in response to Japanese competition, to pool the R&D resources of its members. Results of the joint R&D efforts are shared by all consortium members.
43. Craig Covault, "U.S., Europe, Japan Vie For Russian High Technology," *Aviation Week & Space Technology*, January 27, 1992, 37.
44. Ibid.
45. For example, Batterymarch Financial Management intends to invest $500 million to $1 billion in the near future (*Financial and Business News*, 1991).
46. Richard T. Minnich, "Defense Industry Conversion: An Industry Perspective," page 127 in this volume.
47. At a recent meeting of Russian and American nuclear industry officials, the head of a Russian nuclear laboratory allegedly exclaimed on seeing his American counterpart, "Well, finally I see who was supposed to be my enemy." The latter was quick to respond, "You were never an enemy. Los Alamos was an enemy." Rivalry in market share has more far-reaching consequences than superpower competition. The newly emerging competition for the civilian high-tech market in the developing countries implies that while Los Alamos will continue to be an "enemy," a dozen or so nuclear

research establishments in Russia will indeed become strong competitors for the American head of the nuclear laboratory just cited.

48. S. Glaziev, "Why are the Americans Irritated?" *Rossiskie Vesti* 8, May 1992; and Fred Weir, "U.S. Tries to Erase Russia's Place in Space," *Guardian,* May 20, 1992, 13.

9

Acquisition Policy for a New Era

Murray Weidenbaum

The continuing military power of the United States depends on a secure industrial base that can meet three key requirements. It must have the capability to supply current forces. It must have the ability to sustain military operations and to sustain expansion of the military force structure. Finally, it must be able to design and produce new weapon systems if and when that becomes necessary.[1]

The juxtaposition of declining military budgets and the continuing requirements of national security makes more urgent than ever the need to get more military output per dollar of cost. This chapter presents the case for trying to achieve that objective by means of a fundamental overhaul of the entire process by which the defense establishment acquires weapon systems and other specialized equipment. A warning is also offered against the notion that a new layer of bureaucratic paper shuffling should be added to the process in the name of "conversion planning."

It is ironic that, during the 1980s when many federal departments and agencies focused on deregulation, the procurement rules of the defense establishment became increasingly byzantine in their complexity and burdensome to the companies designing and producing weapon systems.[2]

Although most studies of government regulation of business ignore this important sector, defense contractors (and major subcontractors) are subject to more detailed government control than any other branch of the American economy. Those who have worked on defense studies, however, have no doubt about the degree of government involvement. Gen. George Sammet, Jr., formerly commander of the Army Materiel Command, and Colonel David Green, former Army program manager, describe the nature of military procurement succinctly and accurately:

Murray Weidenbaum is director of the Center for the Study of American Business at Washington University in St. Louis; he is a former chairman of the Council of Economic Advisers.

> Although defense is not called a regulated industry, it is controlled by the government as though it were. All effort is controlled through congressional legislation and regulations such as the Federal Acquisition Regulation. . . . The defense buyer is in fact a regulator.[3]

Because the military market is so completely subject to the changing needs of its one primary customer, relationships between buyer and seller differ fundamentally from those in civilian sectors of the economy. By its selection of contractors, the government controls who enters into and who leaves this market. It also determines the potential growth of these firms, and it is in a position to impose its ways of doing business on them and it surely does so.

Although the status quo is accepted as a simple matter of fact by the many participants in the process, it is useful to remind ourselves that the officials of the Department of Defense (DoD) make many decisions that are normally the responsibility of business management. In the words of one knowledgeable analyst, "private firms in the American defense industry are subject to public controls of unequalled scope and complexity." [4]

Unlike other government involvement in private business, there is no separate regulatory commission to point the finger at. The most pervasive way in which the military establishment shares the management decision-making functions of its contractors is through procurement legislation and rules governing the awarding of contracts. These regulations require private suppliers to "take it or leave it" when it comes to standard clauses in their contracts, clauses that give the government sweeping surveillance and often veto power over the internal operations of these companies.

The authority assumed by the government customer is extremely wide-ranging, including power to review and veto a host of company decisions: which activities to perform in-house and which to subcontract, which firms to use as subcontractors, which products to buy domestically and which to import, what internal financial system to utilize, what minimum as well as average wage rates to pay, and how much overtime work to authorize. Thus, when a business firm enters into a contract to produce a weapon system for the military, it takes on a quasi-public character. This is implicitly recognized by requiring the firm to conduct itself in many ways as a government agency—to abide by equal employment, depressed area, buy-American, prevailing wage, environmental, and similar statutes and regulations.

Rarely if ever are the bits and pieces of federal regulation of military production seen as a total process. Unusual insight can be gleaned from Table 9-1, which contrasts the paperwork required of a major aircraft manufacturer for the development of a new military plane with that for the development of a jet airliner. The latter included the needs of both the airlines and the Federal Aviation Administration.

Table 9-1   Military Versus Commercial Paperwork for Development
of New Aircraft

Category of Paperwork	Military (no. of documents)	Commercial (no. of documents)
Program plans:		
Management systems	20	0
Other	20	1
Specifications	210	9
Data item descriptions	300	0
Total Documents	550	10
Paperwork consequences:		
Pages of specifications	16,000	400
Separate data submissions	30,000	250

Source: McDonnell Douglas Corporation, "Federal Government Business Aspects Which Entail Unnecessary Expense," October 27, 1975.

The differences between the military and civilian buying procedures are staggering. The 400 pages of specifications required for the commercial market contrast with the 16,000 pages for the military; likewise, the 250 separate commercial data submissions are very modest compared with the 30,000 that the military needed.

Unlike private business practice, the identification of the smallest "goof" in military purchasing quickly results in another round of regulation. In the words of Norman Augustine, former undersecretary of the Army and currently chief executive of Martin Marietta, defense companies do no worse than other industries in terms of ethical lapses. In his view, the perception of abuse has gone too far in the direction of making sure that nothing can go wrong. As a result, "we are paying inordinate amounts of money to prevent small misdeeds." [5]

A series of widely publicized shortcomings in specific military procurements arose during the rapid buildup of the 1980s. Items such as hammers, toilet seats, and coffee makers were alleged to have been purchased for prices far exceeding those charged in the commercial marketplace (in most cases, careful analysis shows that the taxpayer was not "overcharged").[6] Nevertheless, the adverse publicity resulted in numerous changes in federal procurement policy, virtually all in the direction of tightening controls over contractors. Some examples provide an indication of the overall trend:

- The Pentagon has imposed higher administrative costs on defense contractors by virtue of more stringent government record-keeping requirements.

- Recent changes in the *Federal Acquisition Regulation* shift the burden of proof on the reasonableness of contractor costs from the government to the contractor. Also, they abolish the presumption of reasonableness previously attached to incurred costs.
- Defense contractors are now required to provide warranties for aircraft engines and for all new systems generally.
- Frequent delays occur in awarding new contracts because of new procedures that give losing firms more opportunities to protest the awards. Many federal procurement offices now regularly extend their acquisition schedule to allow for the virtually predictable delays that result from contract protests.[7]
- Contractors must fund a greater share of initial research and development (R&D) costs. They now share a substantial portion of development costs with the Pentagon, which means that they often incur a loss on these development contracts (in the past, R&D contracts were at times a minor source of profit). Moreover, the contractors no longer have a virtual assurance that, if the program goes into production, they will be awarded the follow-on production contracts. In addition, the prospect of cancellation of large production runs in midstream has increased substantially with the end of the cold war.
- Contractors must now pay for about one-half of their expenses for tooling and test equipment. In the past, these expenses were reimbursable under procurement contracts as they occurred.
- In addition, the Tax Reform Act of 1986 repealed the completed contract method of accounting for taxes. Defense contractors are now required to pay taxes annually on a portion of their completed contracts, regardless of whether they actually realize a profit on those contracts in a given year. The tax deferral permitted by the completed contract method had been in effect a significant source of cash financing or working capital for major contractors.[8]

This increasing bureaucratization of the defense acquisition process and resultant increase in overhead costs of government and contractors alike are in stark contrast to the almost universal downsizing and streamlining that have been occurring simultaneously in the civilian sector of American industry. Spurred on by virulent foreign competition, companies in a great variety of commercially oriented industries have chopped out layers of overhead, reduced internal reporting requirements, and given more discretion to operating managers. By doing so, they have lowered their costs and raised their productivity. There is a cogent lesson there for defense decision makers.

Attempts at Reform

Fairness requires us to acknowledge that the Department of Defense has tried repeatedly to reform the military procurement process. All sorts of efforts have been made over the years, ranging from introducing new purchasing concepts (such as total package procurement) to altering contractor incentives (with a variety of contractual forms). Unfortunately, by and large the past attempts have increased the paperwork flow and raised, rather than lowered, the overhead costs of producing goods and services for the military establishment. Incremental changes will not suffice.

For example, several years ago the three major federal procurement agencies—the General Services Administration, NASA, and the DoD—replaced their individual procurement guides with a jointly issued *Federal Acquisition Regulation (FAR)*. This one "regulation," it turns out, is a massive two-volume handbook. Although *FAR* limits DoD and other agencies to issuing only those additional procurement instructions necessary to implement *FAR* in their agencies, inevitably the Pentagon bureaucrats took full advantage of that loophole. The DoD's *FAR* supplement (known as *Defense Acquisition Regulation,* or *DAR*) is even larger than *FAR*.

The patient reader of *DAR* must begin with Part 1, describing the federal acquisition regulation system, and continue through Part 70, covering the acquisition of computer resources. In addition, *DAR* contains twelve appendices, two manuals, and six supplements! Daunting in their own right, *FAR* and *DAR* are amplified by a massive body of auxiliary regulatory rules that includes court decisions and directives on the part of each of the military services and operating commands. According to former Navy secretary John Lehman, Jr., existing legislation and case law governing Navy procurement alone occupy 1,152 linear feet of library shelf space.[9]

Every serious examination of the military procurement system concludes that—even when it achieves its substantive objectives—it is excessively bureaucratic and needlessly costly. Robert Costello, former undersecretary of defense for procurement, lamented that the Department of Defense wastes twenty-to-thirty cents of every dollar it spends on procurement.[10] The success of American arms in the recent Gulf War may be cited to justify this high cost. Yet, the delays resulting from the extended paperwork flow are hardly positive contributions. Worse yet, the overhead costs eat up dollars that otherwise could be used to buy more equipment or to develop more advanced systems.

A panel of senior government and business officials convened by the Center for Strategic and International Studies echoed Costello's sentiments: "About 25 percent of the cost of research, development, and procurement of military products is wasted as a result of unnecessary oversight, auditing and regulation; program instability and poor estimates; excessive performance requirements; and overspecification of product and process in defense acquisition." [11] Although comparable estimates are not available for the private sector, those who have been involved in both areas of the economy are keenly aware of the differences. When the outside auditors report some deficiency in corporate performance, the management—and often the audit committee too—will ask whether the cost of eliminating the defect is worth it. Very frequently, the answer is that the current procedure, with all its shortcomings, is the sensible approach.

In its own way, the military acquisition establishment has tried to be responsive to criticisms about the complexity of its procurement system. For example, *Defense Acquisition Regulation* permits contracting officers to use simplified order forms, but it needs an eleven-line sentence to explain when the basic ordering agreement can be used:

> A basic ordering agreement may be used to expedite contracting if after a competitive solicitation of quotations or proposals from the maximum number of qualified sources, other than a solicitation accomplished by use of Standard Form 33, it is determined that the successful responsive offeror holds a basic ordering agreement, the terms of which are either identical to those of the solicitation or different in a way that could have no impact on price, quality or delivery, and if it is determined further that issuance of an order against the basic order agreement rather than preparation of a separate contract would not be prejudicial to the other offerors.

Not surprisingly, many contracting officers prefer to bypass the "simplified" alternative.

To sum up the lessons from previous acquisition reform efforts, new requirements and reviews are typically added to the existing bureaucratic routine. Little if any effort is made to scrape off the old paint and varnish before applying new layers. Thus, the size of the regulations, the number of officials with review power, the overhead cost imposed, and the length of time required by the entire process simply expand over time. Moreover, the ability of entrenched management to sandbag the reforms cannot be ignored. As we will see, reductions in their numbers and a basic change in their composition and outlook are vital.

Major Shortcomings of the Acquisition Process

The fundamental shortcomings of the military acquisition process are well known. Four basic problems are reported in virtually every study of the process:[12]

1. The congressional tendency to micromanage the specifics of defense decisionmaking

2. The excessive variety of socioeconomic (that is, nonmilitary) objectives superimposed on the process
3. The deficiencies of existing acquisition personnel
4. The shortcomings in the performance of defense contractors

The Congressional Desire to Micromanage

Much of the procurement complexity and cost result from the tendency of Congress to get involved in operational details, often referred to as "micromanagement." Back in 1970, the Blue Ribbon Defense Panel reported the existence of forty separate statutes governing defense procurement in addition to the basic armed services procurement legislation. The statutes cover such detail as assignment and adjudication of claims, judicial review of agency contract decisions, performance bonds, labor standards, antikickback provisions, conflicts of interest, use of convict labor, and procurement of supplies made by prisoners and the blind.[13]

Since 1970 the tendency for Congress to pass such legislation has accelerated. Each legislative enactment generates a wave of implementing regulations. Between 1983 and 1988 alone, Congress enacted sixteen "micromanagement" types of provisions that complicate the military procurement process.

A sampling of these special provisions gives the flavor:[14]

- Providing for the placement in each major defense acquisition center of a representative to oversee the participation of small business in the procurement of spare parts
- Codifying and then repeatedly revising the description of allowable costs under DoD contracts
- Establishing requirements for the use of prequalification procedures
- Setting rank and grade for competition advocates
- Establishing tours of duty for program managers
- Setting rules for allocating overhead to spare parts
- Directing the use of work measurement standards in various contracts
- Establishing rules governing contract costs for special tooling
- Revising repeatedly the "synopsizing" requirements in the announcements of requests for proposals

Micromanagement, however, is not the result of mere congressional whims. At times, the adoption of these special provisions reflects the loss of congressional confidence in the candor and cooperation of the Pentagon, especially in responding to legislative mandates with which it does not agree. With a higher level of mutual trust, much of the congressional second-guessing would not be necessary. But without that trust, all of the legislative mandates and restrictions are ultimately unsatisfying.

Much of the congressional interference results from the desire to please constituents who want some special favors. One former deputy secretary of defense reports that, in a recent three-year period, Congress asked the Pentagon to produce 2,198 reports at an average cost to the taxpayer of $50,000 a study. Each day Congress is in session, the Department of Defense is asked to respond to 450 letters and 2,500 phone calls from Capitol Hill.[15]

An example of a congressional query on defense matters in behalf of special interests was the request for an examination of the reduction in defense procurement of fresh fruits and vegetables from New Jersey sources. It turns out that weather conditions were an important explanation as well as a shift in military preferences to fruits and vegetables that are grown in other states.[16]

The Variety of Socioeconomic Provisions

Another problem is the excessive number of extraneous socioeconomic provisions that are included, usually by statute, in the procurement regulations. In 1988 the House Committee on Armed Services listed thirty-three different "social and economic programs" that generate requirements affecting military procurement. The requirements range from governmentwide provisions, such as labor standards and equal employment opportunity, to restrictions on purchases for the military assistance program.[17] (See Appendix for a more complete tabulation). Many of the congressional "add-ons" are designed to shelter an industry from foreign competition. For example, Public Law 102-202 (1987) prohibits imports of selected types of machine tools, mooring and anchor chains, and equipment for manufacturing textiles. Many of the special provisions are advantageous to specific groups or interests (such as small businesses, the blind, labor surplus areas, Vietnam veterans, and residents of Alaska and Hawaii). Public Law 99-661 authorizes DoD to pay a 10 percent premium in order to achieve the goal of awarding 5 percent of procurement, R&D, and construction awards to minorities.

All the socioeconomic provisions share one common and negative characteristic: none are related to enhancing national security. On the contrary, they avoid the need to request a separate appropriation to help a favored group by burying the favor in the military procurement budget. In earlier periods, when military budgets were rising rapidly, such luxuries may have been affordable. But the widespread belt-tightening now being administered to every service and command should surely extend to these peripheral and clearly nonessential elements of cost. In a report on the defense technology base, the Congressional Office of Technology Assessment (OTA) concluded that the defense acquisition system is "a major contributor" to the long delays in getting new technology into the field. There are formidable barriers to exploiting technology developed in the civilian sector. OTA noted that, "While Congress did not intend the system to be slow, cumbersome, and inefficient, laws passed to foster goals other than efficient procurement have made it so." [18]

Although it is difficult to quantify the cost of meeting the numerous regulatory requirements imposed on military procurement, researchers at the RAND Corporation did identify influences that could be measured: the increase in the number of congressional staff who work on procurement issues; the increase in the restrictions that Congress adds to the annual defense authorization and appropriation bills; the increase in administrative obstacles that prevent acquisition personnel from accomplishing their program objectives in a timely and efficient manner. There was widespread frustration among project-level personnel who believe they could do their jobs more rapidly and at less cost with fewer controls.

However, the RAND researchers found almost no evidence that regulatory activity had affected the performance or quality of the final product, either favorably or adversely.[19] Given the overall positive assessment of American weapon systems in the recent Gulf War, that assessment comes as no surprise. However, in view of the substantial time and resources devoted to meeting regulatory requirements, the case for a dose of deregulation or at least substantial regulatory reform seems compelling.

Deficiencies of Acquisition Personnel

Much of the verbosity and specificity of military procurement regulations is an attempt to deal with the lack of training, technical skills, and experience of procurement officers.[20] The shortcomings of quality are thus overwhelmed by sheer quantity. Prior to the recent cutbacks, over one-half million military and civilian personnel spent all or a substantial part of their workday on acquisition activities.

The turnover rate for key procurement managers is awesome. One General Accounting Office survey found that the average tenure of a military program manager (including experience as a deputy program manager) was slightly over two years. During the eight-to-twelve years of its development, a typical weapon system may have four or five different military officers in charge.[21]

Then-defense secretary Dick Cheney concurred with the conclusion of the Packard Commission that, compared to its industry counterparts, the DOD's procurement staff is "undertrained, underpaid, and inexperienced." [22] Identifying these shortcomings is much easier than rectifying them. For example, it would take an act of Congress to permit the military establishment to do something that is standard for private business—to reimburse its civilian personnel for tuition to take courses that would enhance their job skills.

To deal with the qualitative shortcomings of its procurement people, the Department of Defense has inserted into the *DAR* pages and pages of the most naive and elementary language. For example, Section 16.101(a) instructs acquisition personnel that "Profit, generally, is the basic motive of business enterprise." We must wonder how people who need to be reminded about such a fundamental matter are assigned to the procurement function. Then, consider Section 9.1-7(4)(1), which informs the reader that "In certain instances, a sound decision may be possible after a simple review. ... Under other circumstances, a more comprehensive review and analysis will be required." The inclusion of such basics in the regulation itself is very revealing as to the presumed intelligence of the people who are given purchasing responsibility.

Another shortcoming of the traditional method of staffing the military procurement function is that the bureaucratic routine attracts bureaucratically oriented people. The result is that many forward-looking reforms are lost in the paperwork maze. For example, the current bureaucratic interpretation of the Truth in Negotiations Act virtually guarantees a vast paper-shuffling exercise every time a contract is awarded. The law recognizes that competition is the best assurance that the government will pay fair and reasonable prices. When adequate price competition is found to exist, there is no statutory requirement for the submission of the elaborate cost and pricing data otherwise required. However, unless the contract was awarded exclusively on the basis of the lowest evaluated price, the *Federal Acquisition Regulation* says that adequate price competition does not exist and all the special paperwork must be filled out. Even when adequate price competition is found to exist, the contractor must perform "cost realism analysis," which is almost as involved as in the uncompetitive case. Theoretically, then, so long as price is a substantial factor in the evaluation of competing proposals, the spirit of the law can be fully achieved by waiving the special paperwork requirements. But the procurement officials who write the implementing rules seem determined to maintain the status quo with all its complexity and overhead burden.

Because the military's contracting personnel are badly outranked by their industry counterparts in terms of experience and training, Congress and the Defense Department have instituted procedural "safeguards" and intricate internal review processes. Programs proceed at a glacial pace as contractors and government purchasing personnel carry out the required reviews and audits. Authority (mainly to say no) is dispersed widely among program managers, contract officers, senior military executives, auditors, and inspectors.[23] Accountability is greatly diluted in the process.

It has been estimated that approximately forty line and staff officials have veto power over some part of the efforts of the program managers. One can insist that they use certain designated military specifications in awarding the

Figure 9-1   The Military Procurement Process

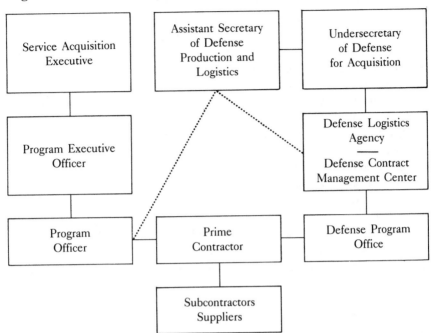

contracts. Another can impose specific reliability requirements. Yet another can impose small business and minority business requirements. None of these staff people has responsibility for the success of the program. Program managers typically spend 50-70 percent of their time "selling" or "defending" their programs at higher levels. Some report that they have to go to forty meetings to get any significant decisions made on a single program.[24] (See Figure 9-1 for a very simplified illustration of the military procurement process.)

In those cases where good people are attracted to military procurement work, the bureaucratic approach embedded in *DAR* and other procurement regulations diminishes their effectiveness—and encourages them to leave for more challenging assignments. A RAND report on this subject concluded that the imposition of detailed requirements erodes the program manager's authority and reduces the ability to conduct the procurement program efficiently.[25] That conclusion should come as no surprise to anyone familiar with the details of the military acquisition process.

Shortcomings of Defense Contractors

Perhaps the most worrisome aspect of the expansion of procurement detail is the impact on the contractors. The cumulative effect of imposing an almost endless array of bureaucratic requirements on the private enterprises that provide goods and services to the military establishment is to force them to adopt the thought processes of government arsenals. In the process, we lose the benefits of risk taking, initiative, and innovation, the key reasons for using private business in the first case. If this sounds too theoretical, merely consider the specific responses to this situation by the companies that do substantial amounts of business with the Department of Defense.

Many contractors insulate their defense work from their mainstream commercial activities. Such action minimizes criticism by government auditors of the allocation of overhead costs and so forth. It also ensures that the commercial divisions will not be "contaminated" by the bureaucratic environment of the military procurement process and thus forget what they know about cost control and fast market response.[26] However, there is an adverse by-product of this separation of military and commercial work: the insulation of the military activity makes it less likely that the government will benefit from the rapid rate of technological innovation occurring in the companies' commercial research laboratories.

Companies go to great lengths to avoid the burdens of the military procurement system: one electronics company has two divisions, one producing defense components and the other making microchips for civilian markets. When the defense division needs some microchips, the civilian division gives the chips to it without charge—in order to avoid the oversight and regulatory burdens associated with defense business. The chips are worth about $200 each.[27]

Approaches to Reform

General Principles to Guide Changes in the Acquisition Process

Both sides of the military procurement relationship—government and industry—are going to have to make a series of difficult adjustments to accord with the basic changes that are taking place in the military market. These new fundamentals include:

- fewer new weapon systems,
- reduced likelihood of a given system moving from R&D to production,
- reduced volumes of production,
- fewer companies competing for defense business, and
- greater intensity of competition among those that remain in the military market.

These trends have several implications. The tendency of the Pentagon during the 1980s to squeeze industry's profit margins in order to stay within reduced budgets does not make sense for the 1990s—not that it was good policy during the past decade. A continuation of that approach will further reduce the number of effective competitors for defense business and erode their capability. Ultimately, it would generate pressure for a new round of government subsidies to maintain the necessary minimum defense industrial base.

Also, reducing the economies of scale of defense development and production—via lower prospects for volume production as well as smaller production runs—underscores the need to curb overhead costs. It is not enough to justify ever-rising demands for congressional micromanagement of the military acquisition process by pointing to shortcomings in executive branch and contractor performance.

Broad policy groups—be they corporate boards of directors or committees of the legislature—cannot run enterprises, nor should they continually second-guess operating managements. Perhaps with the same political party in control of both the executive and legislative branches (at least for the next four years), the tremendous degree of mutual suspicion characteristic of the Reagan and Bush administrations will be reduced substantially. That mistrust has been at the heart of the tendency to increase congressional micromanagement of the entire military procurement process.

With a higher degree of mutual trust and respect, the groundwork will be laid for a badly needed dose of deregulation of military procurement and production.

Specific Suggestions for Reform

Any effort to overhaul military procurement should take account of the difference between the governmental (or legal) approach and the business (or economic) approach. The prevailing government/legal attitude is to regulate the process so closely that no errors occur, no matter how expensive the regulatory procedure becomes. Business executives and economists, in contrast, look at costs as well as benefits of rule-making. As noted by defense executive Jacques Gansler, "Trying to prevent almost all mistakes would be more efficient." [28] The practical problem that arises in the public arena is that, in writing 15 million new contracts each year, the Department of Defense would commit over 1500 errors even if its actions were 99.99 percent perfect.

In a recent analysis of the defense industrial base, the Office of Technology Assessment notes that government contracts require far greater detail in allocating costs than do commercial management information systems. OTA also reports that, because making errors in accounting on government contracts can lead to criminal charges against business executives, defense managers devote inordinate amounts of effort to matters of no economic consequence.[29]

Sometimes the obstacles to carrying out a fundamental reform of the military procurement system seem to be intractable. Perhaps foremost is bureaucracy's inherent resistance to change and its considerable ability to frustrate it. In addition, there are the intricacies and uncertainties associated with military planning, acquisition, and operations that make any systematic change in the process extremely difficult. Under the circumstances, it will take at least three major types of changes to truly reform military procurement.

The first category of reform is to streamline the regulations themselves, eliminating counterproductive restrictions and stripping out nonessential detail. The second is to upgrade the caliber of the people in the Department of Defense who administer the regulations and carry out the procurement process. The third involves the organizations and the people who actually produce the equipment. Beyond these specific actions, the essentially political character of many defense issues cannot be ignored. One must hope that the pressures of rapidly declining military budgets will strengthen the forces for greater economy and efficiency.

Streamlining the Regulations

A sweeping overhaul of the entire government procurement process is the most effective remedy for the continuing proliferation of bureaucratic detail and trivia. Richard Stubbing, a Duke University professor who worked on the military budget for many years, urges the replacement of the current 30,000 pages of military procurement regulations with "some short, simple regs ... say 100 pages or less ..." [30] That means eliminating all the socioeconomic provisions and the restrictive "micromanagement" provisions as well.

Simplifying the entire military procurement procedure is also the most direct way of responding to the perennial complaints of small firms that they are scared away from defense work because of the complexity of the procurement process.[31] Radically streamlined acquisition would also be a constructive response to the substantial erosion of the defense subcontractor and supplier base which some analysts have reported during the 1980s.[32]

Comprehensive reform also requires dividing military procurement into two broad categories: items that can be purchased readily from the private sector, and the acquisition of weapon systems. The great majority of all procurement actions—as well as a substantial proportion of the dollar volume of military contracting—covers equipment readily available from the civilian sector. These should be purchased in the same manner that civilian agencies do their buying: via sealed bids, responding to standard commercial, rather than detailed military, specifications.

To be sure, there are many borderline cases. Here the advice of a group of military policy experts assembled by the Center for Strategic and International Studies is useful: "A concerted effort must be made to accept commercial specifications when they will not affect operational requirements." The CSIS group cautioned against favoring military specifications that only marginally improve operational capabilities or that deal with the most extreme environments.[33]

Some experts urge that only performance characteristics should be specified, with the contractor having discretion on the details of the design. Some experts contend that this was the original concept of "Mil Specs."[34]

Defense expert Jacques Gansler would go further. He advocates eliminating the wall that now segregates the military and civilian industrial sectors, to allow the emergence of a single, multipurpose industrial base. To do so, he would relax Pentagon-unique accounting standards and contract requirements, as well as ease military specifications. Gansler also would allow government contractors to retain the rights to technical data.[35]

For the second category—weapons acquisition—selection should be made on the basis of prototypes produced by two or more competing firms. Mounds of paperwork are not an adequate substitute. The winner of the "fly-off" competition should receive all or at least the majority of the production business. Where it is economical to do so, the runner up would get a smaller contract, but large enough to keep its production line going. After the first production batch from each of the two contractors, the military service could alter the proportion awarded to each. Thus competition would continue throughout the production process.

The Packard Commission and others have repeatedly warned that the only consistently reliable means of getting the information needed to evaluate a proposed military system is to build prototypes and to test them. This is the "fly before you buy" policy that David Packard initiated in the early 1970s when he was deputy secretary of defense. Given the repeated shortcomings that have resulted from rushing weapon systems to premature production, we can brush aside the counterargument that prototypes are costly and time-consuming to build.

Under the present approach to military budgeting, the reluctance to subject a new weapon system to rigorous operational testing prior to making the production decision is not entirely irrational. It reflects the distorted incentives provided by "stop-and-go" military cycles. Given the vagaries of military appropriation practices, the service developing a new weapon system often is willing to rush it into production without adequate testing in order to avoid a possible new wave of budget austerity which would result in cutting back or eliminating the project. A system already in production is less likely to fall to the budget axe than one in the R&D stage. The basic change needed is to lower the peaks and raise the valleys in military spending.[36]

Upgrading the Acquisition Personnel

Virtually everyone who has examined the military procurement process has focused on the crucial role of the people who award and administer contracts. The caliber of procurement officials must be raised, and also the authority of the manager of each weapon system must be increased commensurate with the responsibility of the job. The Minuteman and Polaris strategic missile programs are often cited as examples of good acquisition practice. In both cases, small teams of highly competent people were given the responsibility and the authority to do the job, and, to a considerable degree, they were left alone.[37]

Managers of new weapon systems development and production efforts have limited authority and few tools to manage their programs. They often function as little more than briefing specialists and marketing representatives, spending much of their time seeking additional funds and continued support for their programs. At least some of the officers assigned to supervise weapon production should be persons experienced in industrial management. They should also possess the authority needed to accomplish their jobs, be well compensated, and be accountable for the results.

It is essential to improve the training of the officers responsible for making multimillion (often billion) dollar decisions. The notion of upgrading the personnel assigned to the staff function of acquisition, however, flies in the face of the traditional focus of the military establishment on line management and combat responsibilities. Nevertheless, the viewpoint of the modern military officer needs to be broadened substantially in order to carry out the multifaceted role of conducting national security programs in a rapidly changing, high-tech, global environment.

However, this is more than a matter of education and training, important as those factors are. The cumbersome staffing structure of the military procurement process must also be overhauled and streamlined. A substantial reduction should be made in the total number of acquisition personnel, bringing it closer to the levels of comparable commercial business. Military program managers are usually separated from the undersecretary of defense for acquisition by five or six administrative levels. Each layer demands a right to review all progress reports and major proposals for change. Some of these layers have an extensive horizontal structure, so that the views of several different officers must be accommodated in order to pass through a particular layer or "gate." [38]

The federal government should take a leaf out of the book of private business experience. Many large companies have gone through a painful downsizing in the course of which they have changed entrenched institutional cultures, enhanced decisionmaking, and stimulated innovation. The payoffs in terms of cost and efficiency have been so substantial that the procedure has become almost universal.

Improving Government-Contractor Relationships

Reforming regulations and upgrading procurement personnel, however necessary, are only preludes to doing a better job of designing and producing the weapon systems needed for this nation's military arsenal. It is too easy to dismiss the concern over the high cost of military procurement with the assertion that the process needs to give competition a greater role. In purchasing standard items—desks, chairs, pencils, paper—contracts have almost always been awarded to the responsible bidder who offered the lowest price.

Reviewing contractor proposals. The truly serious problems arise in buying items that are so advanced that they do not exist at the time of purchase—new generations of aircraft, missiles, space vehicles, and communication equipment. Ideally, the award should go to the company that will provide the optimum combination of high quality, low cost, timely delivery, and ready maintainability. However, it is difficult to ascertain those qualities ahead of time. The answer is not to award the development and production work to contractors who want the business so badly that they will underestimate cost substantially. Nor is it a bargain to go with a low-cost producer who will sacrifice quality, time, and readiness in order to minimize price. There is a way out of this dilemma.

In making the initial award on a new weapon system or other major item of equipment, military contracting officers should be required to take more fully into account the bidder's past record on defense work. The company's track record may be the best indication of future performance. Focusing on actual accomplishment also provides a powerful incentive for improving performance.

In this spirit, contract forms should be revised to provide larger profits for successful technical and cost performance and, conversely, more severe penalties for a poor showing. Under the existing system, given the essentially cost-plus nature of so much of military procurement, mediocre work may at times be rewarded. The system that I am advocating requires considerable forbearance on the part of Congress and of citizens generally. A contractor who has performed very well should not be criticized for receiving "unconscionable" profits. Nor should the company that does poorly be bailed out.

Under the "fly before you buy" policy of former deputy defense secretary David Packard, competing contractors were required to build and thoroughly test working prototypes before the major production contracts were awarded. This approach yielded the F-16 fighter and A-10 attack plane, two of the most successful procurement projects of the postwar era in terms of both performance and cost. Unfortunately, Packard's approach was largely abandoned when he left. It should be restored.

Simultaneously, some of the "reforms" of the military procurement process instituted in the 1980s should be reversed. Military R&D contracts should not be viewed as "loss leaders" on the part of defense contractors hungry for future business. The DoD should pay for what it gets. Trying to shift the impact of the defense budget cuts to the contractors by financially squeezing them is an unseemly process for the federal government. There is no effective substitute for just buying less.

Cures for the high cost of military production do not come easy or cheap. Much of the increase in unit prices of weapon systems is a consequence of the relatively inflexible production-line technology used by most defense contractors. Defense manufacturing today is nearly as inflexible as it was in World War II. Then it was highly successful in producing single designs in quantities often measured in the thousands over long periods of time at comparatively low unit costs. However, the Department of Defense now procures a typical new weapon system in the hundreds with much higher unit costs and with designs changing frequently in the course of the production cycle.

Current defense procurement relies on some of the oldest manufacturing plants in the United States, which helps to explain high costs. For example, the machinery used by the Grumman Corporation to produce the F-14 fighter aircraft was, on average, thirty-four years old in 1987.[39] Defense decision makers should follow the recent experiences of civilian-oriented manufacturing companies. Hard-pressed by foreign competition, many have built new production facilities. But this is a cogent example of how interrelated are the different aspects of procurement policy. Reducing the peak-and-valley budget cycles and their inevitable uncertainty will make it more likely that defense contractors will make substantial investments in new production equipment. These capital outlays tend to have limited application in commercial production, as seen by the great difficulties experienced by defense contractors when they try to diversify outside of the governmental and aerospace markets.

To provide an incentive for government contractors to use their own funds to modernize military production capacity, private investment in defense work will have to be linked more closely to profits. To a far greater extent than in the past, contractors will have to be rewarded with higher profits for work done on time, for meeting promised performance standards, and for delivering goods and services at or below contracted cost. Conversely, tougher penalties in the form of substantially reduced profits should be imposed for poor performance—including substandard work, late delivery, and avoidable cost overruns. Total earnings on defense work would not necessarily rise, but individual company earnings might shift substantially.

Under an effective incentive system, a truly successful weapon system program would yield very high profits for its producer. But an inefficient program would result in low profits or outright losses. A strategy of relying more on private investment and the profit motive would be an important step to the privatization of military procurement.

Changing the procurement package. One highly publicized way of responding to smaller defense budgets is the "roll over" approach. Under this concept, when a new weapon system is designed, only a few prototypes are produced. The Department of Defense thus pays for the development cost but avoids the far larger production outlays unless and until the end items are needed. The roll over approach is viewed as a relatively inexpensive way of maintaining progress in military technology.

Contractors, as would be expected, are dubious of this new approach. They point out the long delays that would occur between producing a few prototypes and beginning quantity production. It is likely that training production workers, obtaining components and parts, and ironing out the inevitable problems that arise in moving to full production would all be very time consuming.[40]

There are more basic limitations to the roll over concept. Because production traditionally is far more profitable than development, contractors would have the incentive to put their most creative people in the programs that they expect to move from development to production. Moreover, given the essentially contingent nature of the prototype efforts, there would be little pressure to meet deadlines. Quite the reverse, the underlying incentive would be to stretch out the work. Under the circumstances, this approach does not seem to be the way to go.

Defense conversion. Important limits should be acknowledged to any desire to provide an improved operating environment for defense companies. There is little reason to provide special subsidies to help them "convert" to civilian pursuits. The industry's dismal track record at diversification over the past forty years, however, has not dampened the enthusiasm of some legislators to propose a new array of governmental mandates requiring contractors to try to "do good."

A perennial example is the proposed Defense Economic Adjustment Act, originally developed by the late House member Ted Weiss (D-N.Y.). This bill, a prototype for many less ambitious proposals, requires every defense contractor of almost any size to set up a bureaucratic conversion planning operation. Worse yet, the plan would be triggered by the termination of the smallest defense contract despite any expansions in other business segments of the company, military or commercial. Legislative variations on the conversion planning theme have been introduced in the Senate by Connecticut senators Christopher Dodd (D) and Joseph Lieberman (D); S. 2133, the Defense Industrial Stabilization and Community Transition Act, is one example. Despite their good intentions, these bills would only add to the bureaucratic burdens that now beset defense companies.

A more realistic approach is to acknowledge that substantial excess capacity coupled with weak finances characterize the major defense contractors. Downsizing will enhance efficiency and make the survival of the key firms in the industry more likely. Mergers and consolidations will reduce the current number of players. Some of the financially weaker firms may be acquired by civilian-oriented companies. A smaller group of stronger firms will improve the long-term position of the defense industry in a post-cold-war environment.

Conclusion

The end of the cold war and the subsequent reduction in defense funding make a fundamental overhaul of the military procurement process more urgent than ever. More efficient and less burdensome acquisition of weapon systems can help the nation reach national security objectives within those smaller military budgets. Maintaining a stable and predictable level of military acquisition—which may be increasingly likely with the end of the cold war—is the most powerful incentive to great efficiency in defense development and procurement activities. It obviates the necessity for individual services to move rapidly from development to production in an effort to protect a given weapon system from the budgetary knife.

Greater efficiency in defense spending will also generate several indirect but powerful benefits; it will help restore the public support for the military establishment that was eroded by the highly publicized accounts of $100 hammers and $600 toilet seats. Of perhaps even greater importance, streamlining military procurement will remove many of the current roadblocks that inhibit the interchange of scientific and technological advances between military and civilian producers. Moreover, reducing the bureaucratic burdens imposed on government contractors will bring down their overhead cost structures and enable them to compete more effectively in commercial markets. The reduction in corporate overhead, in turn, should have a positive feedback on the military budget, reducing the expenses that are normally allocated between military and civilian production.

Appendix: Major Socioeconomic Laws
Governing Federal Procurement

Program	Authority	Purpose
Improving working conditions: Walsh-Healey Act	41 U.S.C. 36-45	To prescribe minimum wages, hours, ages, and working conditions for supply contracts over $10,000.
Davis Bacon Act	40 U.S.C. 276a-1-5	To prescribe minimum wages, benefits, and work conditions on construction contracts in excess of $2,000.
Service Contract Act of 1965	41 U.S.C. 351-358	To prescribe wages, fringe benefits, and work conditions for service contracts over $2,500.
Contract Work Hours and Safety Standards Act	40 U.S.C. 327-330	To prescribe 8-hour day, 40-hour week, and health and safety standards for laborers and mechanics on public works contracts over $2,500.
Favoring Small Business: Small Business Act	15 U.S.C. 631-647	To place fair portion of government purchases and contracts with small business concerns.
Section 8a	15 U.S.C. 637 and 13 C.R.R. 124	To allow the procuring agency to contract with the Small Business Administration, which in turn contracts with small or minority business firms.
Utilization of small business concerns	Same	To require all contractors who have federal contracts greater than $5,000 to accomplish the maximum amount of subcontracting through the use of small business.

(Continued on next page)

Program	Authority	Purpose
Small business subcontracting program	Same	To require in certain contracts greater than $500,000 the establishment of a program of subcontracting which will enable small business concerns to be considered fairly as subcontractors and suppliers.
Small business set-asides	Same	To provide preferential treatment for small business by allowing exclusive participation of small business concerns in set-aside procurements.

Favoring disadvantaged groups:

Program	Authority	Purpose
Equal employment opportunity provisions	Executive Orders 11246 and 11375	To prohibit discrimination in government contracting.
Affirmative Action Program	Same	To require a written program of specific actions in the EEO area by companies having federal contracts of $50,000 or more and 50 or more employees.
EEO compliance review	Same	To conduct on-site reviews of contractor actions in support of the affirmative action program for those contractors with federal contracts of $1,000,000 or more.
Labor surplus area concerns	15 U.S.C. 644 and Executive Order 12073	To provide preference to concerns performing in areas of concentrated unemployment or underemployment.
Utilization of labor surplus area concerns	Same	To require contractors with contracts between $5,000 and $50,000 to use best efforts to place contracts with firms in labor surplus areas.

Program	Authority	Purpose
Labor surplus area subcontracting program	Same	To require specific action of contractors with contracts greater than $500,000 which will aid in awarding subcontracts to firms in labor surplus areas.
Labor surplus set-asides	Same	To require award of partial set-asides to firms in labor surplus areas by the government.
Minority business	Executive Order 11625	To require use of minority business enterprises as subcontractors as much as possible for defense procurement.
Utilization of minority business	Same	To require the utilization of minority business enterprises to the greatest extent possible on contracts greater than $5,000.
Minority Business Subcontracting Program	Same	To require the establishment and conduct of a program to enable minority business enterprises to be considered fairly as subcontractors under federal contracts greater than $500,000.
Employment of the handicapped	29 U.S.C. 793 and Executive Order 11758	To require government contractors to take affirmative action to employ and advance handicapped individuals.
Prison-made products	18 U.S.C. 4121-4128	To require mandatory purchase of specific supplies from Federal Prison Industries, Inc.
Blind-made products	41 U.S.C. 46-48	To make mandatory purchase of products made by blind and other handicapped persons.

(Continued on next page)

Program	Authority	Purpose
Women's Business Enterprise Policy	Executive Order 12138	To provide federal awards to women-owned businesses.
Favoring American companies: Buy American Act	41 U.S.C. 10a-10b	To provide preference for domestic materials over foreign materials.
Preference for U.S. products	22 U.S.C. 2354(a)	To require the purchase of U.S. end products for the military assistance program.
Preference for U.S. clothing, fibers, and specialty metals	Public Law 95-457	To restrict the Department of Defense from purchasing specified classes of commodities of foreign origin.
Ball bearings and timing devices	Executive Order 11490	To ensure the continued existence of an industrial base for those products necessary for national defense.
Acquisition of foreign buses	Public Law 90-600	To restrict use of appropriated funds to purchase, lease, rent, or otherwise acquire foreign-manufactured buses.
Prohibition of construction of naval vessels in foreign shipyards	Public Law 91-171	To prohibit use of appropriated funds for the construction of any Navy vessel in foreign shipyards.
Preference for U.S.-flag air carriers	49 U.S.C. 1517	To require the use of U.S.-flag air carriers for international air transportation of personnel or property.
Preference for U.S. vessels	10 U.S.C. 2631, 46 U.S.C. 1241	To require a shipment of all military and at least half of other goods in U.S. vessels.
Required source for jewel bearings	DAR 7-104.37	To preserve a mobilization base for manufacture of jewel bearings.
Required source for aluminum ingot	DAR 1-327, FPR subpart 1-5.10	To eliminate excess quantity of aluminum in the national stockpile.

Program	Authority	Purpose
Restriction on R&D contracting with foreign sources	Public Law 92-570	To prohibit the entering into a contract with a foreign entity for performance of R&D on military systems which can be carried out by a U.S. corporation at a lower cost.
Protecting the environment and quality of life: Clean air and water acts	Executive Order 11738	To prevent the award of contracts over $100,000 to businesses that are in violation of the clean air and clean water acts.
Humane Slaughter Act	7 U.S.C. 1901-1906	To purchase meat only from suppliers who conform to humane slaughter standards.
Noise Control Act	42 U.S.C. 4914	To provide a monetary preference to low noise emission products in federal procurements.
Resource conservation	42 U.S.C. 6962	To mandate the procurement of items composed of the highest percentage of recovered materials.
Energy conservation	42 U.S.C. 6361	To mandate the consideration of relative energy efficiency of goods and services capable of satisfying the government's needs.
Other government purposes: Nonuse of foreign-flag vessels engaged in Cuban and North Vietnamese trade	DAR 1-1410	To prohibit contractor from shipping any supplies on foreign flag vessel that has called on Cuban or North Vietnamese ports after specific dates.

(Continued on next page)

Program	Authority	Purpose
Offset provisions	Sales agreements with foreign countries	To provide for purchases from foreign contractors by U.S. government agencies or contractors as consideration for foreign government purchases from U.S. contractors.
Geographic distribution of DoD subcontract dollars	Public Law 95-111	To require the reporting to Congress of annual geographical distribution of DoD subcontract dollars.
Privacy Act	5 U.S.C. 552a	To make provisions of the Privacy Act applicable to a system of records designed, developed, operated, or maintained on behalf of a federal agency.

Source: U.S. Congress, Joint Economic Committee, *Socioeconomic Regulations and the Federal Procurement Market* (Washington, D.C.: Government Printing Office, 1985), 59-62.

Notes

1. Harvey Sicherman, ed., *U.S. Defense Strategy for a New Era* (Washington, D.C.: American Security Council Foundation, 1992), 22.
2. See Murray Weidenbaum, *Small Wars, Big Defense* (New York: Oxford University Press, 1992), chapter 8.
3. George Sammet, Jr., and David Green, *Defense Acquisition Management* (Boca Raton: Florida Atlantic University Press, 1990), 87.
4. William E. Kovacic, "The Sorcerer's Apprentice: Public Regulation of the Weapons Acquisition Process," in *Arms, Politics, and the Economy*, ed. Robert Higgs (New York: Holmes and Meier, 1990), 105.
5. Quoted in Willard C. Rappleye, Jr., "Now, Fix Defense Procurement," *Financial Week*, June 11, 1991, 63.
6. Typically, the military item was far more complex than the commercial counterpart, or the military price tag was an artifact of standardized cost accounting. See Weidenbaum, *Small Wars*, 160.
7. The Competition in Contracting Act of 1984 expanded protest procedures. For an analysis of the benefits and costs, see Robert C. Marshall et al., "The Private Attorney General Meets Public Contract Law: Procurement Oversight by Protest," *Hofstra Law Review* (Fall 1991): 1-71.
8. The MAC Group, *The Impact on Defense Industrial Capability of Changes in Procurement and Tax Policy* (Cambridge, Mass.: MAC Group, 1988), 21; Mark L. Goldstein, "Singing the Procurement Blues," *Government Executive* (November 1991): 41.
9. John F. Lehman, Jr., *Command of the Seas* (New York: Charles Scribner's Sons, 1989), 191.
10. Cited in Richard Stubbing and Richard Mendel, "How to Save $50 Billion a Year," *Atlantic Monthly*, June 1989, 53.

11. James Blackwell, *Deterrence in Decay: The Future of the U.S. Defense Industrial Base* (Washington, D.C.: Center for Strategic and International Studies, 1989), 1.
12. See William H. Gregory, *The Defense Procurement Mess* (Lexington, Mass.: Lexington Books, 1989); Blue Ribbon Defense Panel, *Report to the President and the Secretary of Defense on the Department of Defense* (Washington, D.C.: Government Printing Office, 1970); Jacques S. Gansler, *Affording Defense* (Cambridge: MIT Press, 1989).
13. Blue Ribbon Defense Panel, *Report to the President*, 92.
14. U.S. Senate, Committee on Armed Services, *Defense Acquisition Process* (Washington, D.C.: U.S. Government Printing Office, 1989).
15. Roswell Gilpatric, "Revamp Defense Thinking," *The New York Times*, April 10, 1992, A19.
16. *Defense Procurement: Fresh Fruit Buying Practices* (Washington, D.C.: General Accounting Office, March 2, 1990).
17. U.S. House of Representatives, Committee on Armed Services, *Defense Acquisition: Major U.S. Commission Reports 1949-1988*, Vol. 1 (Washington, D.C.: U.S. Government Printing Office, 1988), 508-509.
18. Quoted in Dick Cheney, *Defense Management: Report to the President* (Washington, D.C.: U.S. Department of Defense, 1989), 26.
19. G. K. Smith et al., *A Preliminary Perspective on Regulatory Activities and Effects in Weapons Acquisition* (Santa Monica, Calif.: RAND Corporation, 1988), vii-viii.
20. *Task Force Report on the Office of the Secretary of Defense* (Washington, D.C.: President's Private Sector Survey on Cost Control, 1983), 151. See also testimony of J. Ronald Fox in U.S. Senate, *Defense Acquisition Process*, 194-200.
21. *DOD Acquisition: Capabilities of Key DOD Personnel in Systems Acquisition* (Washington, D.C.: U.S. General Accounting Office, 1986).
22. Cheney, *Defense Management*, 12.
23. Kovacic, "Sorcerer's Apprentice," 104-131.
24. Gansler, *Affording Defense*, 212.
25. Smith et al., *Preliminary Perspective*, viii-ix.
26. "Rethinking the Military's Role in the Economy: An Interview with Harvey Brooks and Lewis Branscomb," *Technology Review* (August/September 1989): 60.
27. Blackwell, *Deterrence in Decay*, 45.
28. Jacques S. Gansler, *The Defense Industry* (Cambridge, Mass.: MIT Press, 1980), 258.
29. Office of Technology Assessment, *Redesigning Defense* (Washington, D.C.: U.S. Government Printing Office, 1991), 66.
30. Quoted in U.S. Senate, *Defense Acquisition Process*, 226.
31. Lee I. Koppelman and Pearl M. Kamer, *Maximizing the Potential of Long Island's Defense Sector in an Era of Change* (New York: Long Island Regional Planning Board, 1988), 117.
32. See Blackwell, *Deterrence in Decay*.
33. *A New Military Strategy for the 1990s: Implications for Capabilities and Acquisition* (Washington, D.C.: Center for Strategic and International Studies, 1991), 43.
34. Sicherman, *Defense Strategy*, 25.
35. David C. Morrison, "End of the Line," *National Journal*, June 8, 1991, 1330.
36. See Weidenbaum, *Small Wars*, 6-9.
37. See testimony of David Packard and R. James Woolsey in *Defense Acquisition Process*, 136, 165, 178.
38. See Kovacic, "Sorcerer's Apprentice," 106.
39. Michael Rich and Edmund Dews, *Improving the Military Acquisition Process* (Santa Monica: RAND Corporation, 1986); Cynthia Mitchell and Tim Carrington, "Antique Arsenals," *Wall Street Journal*, October 8, 1987, 1.
40. Sicherman, *Defense Strategy*, 25-26.

10

Conclusions
Ethan B. Kapstein

Defense spending is falling around the world, creating a new set of challenges for policy makers in both the economic and national security communities. From an economic perspective, the decline in military expenditures must be offset by some combination of public and private investment if the factors of production once utilized by the defense sector are to find alternative employment. From a security perspective, the decisions made today by public officials with respect to personnel, training, and acquisition will determine the forces that their countries will be capable of fielding in the early twenty-first century. Overall, downsizing defense is one of the most complex policy issues of our day, and it deserves the attention not just of experts, executives, and officers, but of the general public as well.

Given the difficulties associated with "building down smartly" (to use a phrase from the Bush administration), it must be tempting for government officials to adopt a laissez-faire approach to the economic problems that are now facing defense industries. After all, with respect to many if not most microeconomic decisions it is most efficient to let the market decide. But repetition of the term "laissez-faire" must not substitute for making tough decisions.

The contributors to this volume are not of one mind about what governments should do in the face of defense cutbacks; some favor more market-oriented approaches than others, at least with respect to the defense-industrial issues associated with the problem. But all, I think, would agree that governments do have an important role to play not only as militaries adjust to new strategic conditions but also as firms adjust to changes in research, development, and procurement programs.

Ethan B. Kapstein is assistant professor of international relations at Brandeis University and codirector of the Economics and National Security Program, John M. Olin Institute for Strategic Studies, Center for International Affairs, Harvard University.

This concluding chapter, which is by no means a consensus document on the part of the contributors but is solely an expression of my personal views, has three objectives: to review the major findings of the book; to offer some thoughts concerning the implications of those findings for public policy; and to provide suggestions for future research.

Major Findings

The chapters in this book have addressed not only many of the macro-, micro-, and international-economic issues associated with defense down-sizing, but some of the prominent political questions involved in the process as well. While writing this book, monumental changes occurred in international and domestic politics which caused the editor and more than one author to throw up our hands in despair as we tried to make revisions that reflected the changing times. But that being said, it was never our intention to produce a journalistic account of the downsizing debate. To the contrary, we have tried to provide an informed examination of the fundamental issues underlying this policy challenge.

With respect to the macroeconomics of defense downsizing, Roger Brinner reminds us in his chapter that the adjustment to reduced levels of military spending will not take place overnight, but could take five-to-ten years to work their way through the economy; those regions that were highly dependent on defense activities will, of course, take the longest time to regain their equilibrium. During this period of adjustment, central banks in those countries that are coping with defense reductions will find it difficult to balance their efforts to achieve both price stability and economic growth.

As Brinner notes, the cyclical changes produced by lower defense spending include increases in unemployment and reductions in inflation. These provide a double incentive to cut interest rates, and Brinner expects gradual cuts to occur. But this alone will not translate into investment and greater consumer demand for housing and durable goods since these responses are also tied to projections about future earnings. If lower defense spending, coupled with other cuts in government expenditure, reduces economic growth and employment levels, it could take many years for consumers to regain confidence in their economic prospects and for firms to engage in new investment.

Over the long term, significant benefits are likely to result from lower levels of defense spending. To put the issue as simply as possible, the economy as a whole will gain if the same level of national security can be purchased for less money than in the past. However, two caveats can be put forward: first, there is nothing to stop investors from making unproductive investments (witness the overbuilding of commercial real estate in many countries during the 1980s); second, government-sponsored research and development may not be maintained at cold-war levels, with worrisome consequences for the defense and high-tech sectors. (Admittedly, some would argue that a reduction in defense-sponsored R&D would be beneficial to the commercial sector.)

In conclusion, Brinner argues that it is better to cut defense gradually than to make lumpy and severe cuts as a response to the politics of the moment. By making the downsizing effort predictable, firms and individuals will have time to adjust and make decisions about their future. To be sure, the predicament of these affected groups would be exacerbated by inappropriate monetary and fiscal policy responses. But if the Federal Reserve eases credit policy in line with its price stability objectives, over the long term countries should enjoy the benefits of reduced defense spending.

As serious as the monetary and fiscal policy challenges associated with downsizing are, they are perhaps more straightforward than the microeconomic questions that now must occupy decision makers and defense executives. In his chapter, David Blair poses the issue as the choice between a "competitive," or market-oriented, approach to maintaining the defense industrial base (which has been the preferred option in the United States), and a quasi-nationalized approach (as exemplified by the French). As Blair observes, defense planners today must not only think about which weapon systems they will field in the next century but also about which capital stock they wish to maintain for future crises. Once governments determine that they must make decisions about capital stock, they are engaging de facto in industrial policy.

During the Reagan and Bush years, explicit discussions of defense industrial policy rarely took place in Washington. Perhaps there was no need for them; until 1986 defense budgets were rising, and in the early Bush years there were still many "big-ticket" weapons programs on line. With the election of Bill Clinton and the appointment of Les Aspin as secretary of defense, however, the discourse changed and now industrial policy is once again an acceptable topic for policy makers, especially in the defense realm.

Aspin's recent "bottom-up" review of U.S. defense policy has made explicit the decision to preserve some companies in the event their capabilities are needed in the years ahead; these companies will continue producing weapon systems (albeit at greatly reduced rates) even though no strategic rationale exists for those systems at the present moment. Good examples of such a policy decision are provided by Electric Boat, the sole manufacturer of advanced nuclear submarines, and Newport News, the monopoly provider of aircraft carriers. According to Deputy Secretary of Defense William Perry, "You can't mothball technical talent, the brains, the know-how ... our intervention here is only to protect certain military capabilities which are unique, and it's very, very limited." [1]

Whatever the strategic merits of preserving specific defense industrial capabilities, it is unlikely that military requirements alone will be the deciding factor. As both Kenneth Mayer and Peter Trubowitz make clear in their respective chapters, Congress is likely to play a decisive role in the ongoing defense debate, and in that arena a variety of interests beyond just national security are at stake.

To begin with, Mayer suggests that the strategic debate itself remains very much open in the post-cold war era. Neither the Bush nor the Clinton administrations have articulated a vision of the post-cold war world or the place of the American military in that world that has met with universal approval; witness growing public concern over the use of American troops for "peace-keeping" operations in Somalia and elsewhere. Aspin's "bottom-up" review, for example, posits the need for American troops to be prepared to fight two regional conflicts simultaneously, with the Middle East and Korean Peninsula being the prominent locales. Many members of Congress and editorialists have already berated the administration for presenting a scenario which, to their mind, is simply unbelievable.[2] As American strategy shifts during this uncertain era, so too will the congressional debate over downsizing.

At the same time, this uncertainty may open the door to a variety of protectionist forces that will cry and sigh on behalf of "national security." During every previous downturn in defense spending a variety of special interests knocked on congressional doors in search of government assistance, and a surprising array of them were successful. Despite its free-trade ideology, the United States protects a large number of domestic industries allegedly for reasons of national security.

The industrial politics of downsizing are further complicated by regional economic questions, as Peter Trubowitz explains in his contribution. As Trubowitz reminds us, "the stakes in the current policy debate are high." The downsizing question entails a basic conflict over national priorities and the employment of scarce financial resources. Different regions view the issue according to their reliance on defense contracts. Not surprisingly, those regions with high dependence tend to support relatively large defense budgets; those with smaller defense sectors have supported sharper cuts. The politics of downsizing are thus pitting regions against one another, and in the logrolling process that normally accompanies efforts to heal such divisions we can expect that a strange mix of military bases and industries will remain alive even in the absence of a clear strategic rationale to maintain them.

John Lynch and Billy Dickens argue that regions have only limited information *a priori* about the long-term effects on local economies of cuts in defense spending. They discuss cases in which communities have actually benefited from base and plant closures, as better uses are made of the land and labor pool. They criticize the federal government, however, for the inadequacy of its community assistance programs. Oftentimes, the conversion of military facilities requires the development of additional infrastructure, such as roads and utilities. In the absence of government support to build such infrastructure, it becomes difficult for conversion efforts to succeed. Lynch and Dickens also note that while the government does provide some assistance to those who have been directly affected by military base and defense industry closures, nothing is done to help those who work in local "supporting" industries. In sum, they call for a better partnership among communities, state economic development organizations, and the federal government in assessing the impact of defense downsizing and in making attractive the alternative utilization of facilities.

Richard Minnich provides an industry perspective on the conversion issue in his chapter. He suggests that defense firms *can* transform themselves over time, but that defense plants, in general, cannot; in short, those plants that are no longer producing weapons will ultimately be closed rather than converted to some alternative production. Defense company executives, he argues, are like other executives; they seek to make profitable investments that will increase the firm's return on equity and, consequently, increase its stock price. As defense budgets decline, executives will have no choice but to seek other opportunities in the commercial sector. Driven by these market incentives, they will engage in efforts to merge, acquire, diversify, and consolidate. Not all firms will succeed in these efforts, but those that do will be stronger as a result.

In contrast to the United States, Bud Udis reports in his contribution that there has been surprisingly little discussion in Europe of defense conversion; indeed, he observes a nearly complete absence of government conversion policy. Instead, European arms producers are looking to defense exports and arms collaboration programs as a way of staying in business. At the same time, he shows that most of the major European defense firms have, over the past five years, greatly reduced their dependence on defense markets and are earning an ever-greater share of their revenues from commercial sales. Overall, however, he presents a mixed picture of the prospects of these firms. Some, he suggests, will survive the current period of downsizing, but many others will not. The corporate problem of adapting to new international conditions, he suggests, may also be exacerbated in several European countries by the rigidity of labor and management attitudes toward change.

The problems facing Americans and Europeans can hardly be compared with those now confronting Russia and the other successor states, as presented by Yevgeny Kuznetsov. Kuznetsov points out that downsizing in the Russian context is not limited to a few communities or regions but is the central issue for the nation's industrial policy. Russian industry was completely intertwined with defense production; ironically, the Soviet Union created the world's greatest "military-industrial complex." The meltdown of the Soviet Union and the concomitant drop in military expenditures have created a chaotic situation for industrial managers.

But Kuznetsov does not present an unambiguously negative picture. He suggests that, in the midst of this chaos, some entrepreneurial managers have emerged. If Russia is able to gain access to hard currency and high technology, he believes that an "economic development" model could work over time. In order for this to occur, however, political stability and an enduring system of property rights will have to emerge.

Wrapping up the volume, Murray Weidenbaum turns to the future and makes an argument for an entirely new approach to defense acquisition in the United States. The current procurement system, he suggests, is a relic of an earlier time; it is a bundle of regulations that aim to meet not just national security objectives but myriad political, social, and economic goals as well. Micromanagement by Congress, coupled with changes in Defense Department purchasing strategy, have created a defense acquisition culture that is legalistic and wasteful. In an era when defense dollars were plentiful, the country could perhaps afford to have such a system; today it cannot. If we listen to Weidenbaum, it is just possible that the United States will find a way to ensure its security in an economically sensible and responsible manner.

Policy Implications

As the contributors to this volume have amply demonstrated, the world-wide process of defense downsizing has important macro-, micro-, and inter-national-economic dimensions, in addition to a great variety of political and social dimensions at the local, regional, and national levels. It is unlikely that any single formula for downsizing exists that can serve all countries that are now grappling with the problem of how to cut their military expenditures while maintaining national security. Nonetheless, some general lessons emerge from this study that could be of value to public officials, defense executives, and concerned citizens.

Perhaps the first lesson, at least from an economic perspective, is that defense downsizing and economic conversion should be viewed ultimately as a macroeconomic process in which the factors of production leave defense work in search of alternative uses. Over time, the process is really one of transformation rather than of conversion. The economy grows in new sectors and new regions, and the factors of production eventually gravitate to these new possibilities. The United States and Western Europe have already seen such dramatic economic shifts occur during the postwar period (after the 1973 oil crisis, for example), as large population groups and capital resources moved to such areas as the Sun Belt and to the south of France.[3]

Naturally, the transformation will be hastened during periods of economic growth and will be retarded by recession. It thus behooves central banks, treasury ministries, and legislatures to adopt an appropriate mix of fiscal and monetary policies that encourage economic growth. The malignant effects of downsizing can be multiplied many times by poor economic management; for the most dramatic example, recall the response of the Federal Reserve Board to the Great Depression, and the untold misery that was created by overly restrictive monetary policies.[4]

At the industrial level, as well, downsizing is generally best seen as a transformation rather than as a conversion process. This has important public policy implications. In the United States and some other countries we already see efforts by government to encourage defense firms to convert by offering them contracts to provide new services or to develop "dual-use" technology; that is, technology that is relevant to both the commercial and military sectors. A recent report by the U.S. Arms Control and Disarmament Agency, however, concluded that "conversion efforts have rarely succeeded and none of the phasedowns in defense spending since World War II have required specific conversion legislation."[5] While this lesson will probably do little to stop members of Congress from engaging in the pork-barrel politics associated with many government contracting decisions, it should nonetheless be remembered.

This is not to suggest that governments will have no useful role to play in the downsizing. Again, from an industrial perspective, the government should assist with worker retraining, community redevelopment, and the like. Despite scarce resources, the Pentagon's Office of Economic Assistance has done an admirable job of helping communities adjust to post-military life. Public officials should not be ashamed of using resources to help those who have spent their careers serving the government, either directly or indirectly.

There is also an international dimension to the present-day decline in military spending that should not be forgotten. It is most obvious, of course, in the case of Russia, but defense industries in other countries are feeling or will soon feel the pinch as well. One thinks of such countries as Israel, which was downsizing even before the recent outbreak of peace in the Middle East, and South Africa, which will inevitably shrink a defense sector that was built up during the era of apartheid. The question arises: what are the roles of the United States, its allies, and the major international organizations in this global process?

Clearly, as the world's predominant power the United States must take a special interest in what happens to defense establishments around the world, for both economic and security reasons. In Russia, what happens economically during the process of defense downsizing will largely determine the country's medium-term growth prospects. If the released factors can find alternative uses, this should have positive implications for the country. But if the end-game for defense workers and members of the armed forces is massive unemployment, the economic and political ramifications could be devastating. The United States will want to remain actively engaged in helping Russia make the shift to a market economy, and a large part of that process will involve defense sector transformation.

In sum, defense downsizing will involve macro-, micro-, and international economic decisions, in addition to policy development at various levels of government. The process will undoubtedly become politicized, and in an era when it is difficult if not impossible for military officers and defense officials to paint a strategic picture that everyone can agree upon, decisions taken by the executive branch will be all the more subject to scrutiny. Faced with the challenge of defining policy, these officials may be tempted to respond to any question with the phrase, "let the market decide." Sometimes that will be the right answer; but sometimes governments will have to do more. The policy response to defense downsizing should make extensive use of market forces, but recognition of market failure is also needed.

Directions for Future Research

During the late 1970s and early 1980s a widespread debate emerged over the economic and strategic implications of "excessive" defense spending. Authors such as Paul Kennedy popularized the connection between defense spending and economic decline, with seemingly important lessons for the United States and, even more pointedly, for the Soviet Union.[6] Further, as the quality of weaponry in the superpowers' arsenals grew ever more sophisticated, it seemed as if their client states were also becoming more powerful, with dangerous consequences for regional security in the Middle East and elsewhere.

In the ten short years since that time the world has gone from the cold war to the collapse of the Berlin Wall and its builder, the Soviet Union. For some countries and political communities, the international system is now a more dangerous place than it was before, but for most the security environment is less threatening. Downward pressures are being placed on defense budgets, and governments are responding to those pressures. Everywhere public officials are facing the challenge of planning for future national security requirements in an uncertain environment and with greatly reduced funding.

One of the first research questions that arises from this analysis concerns how countries are responding to these similar international circumstances, and why do we observe differences across countries? What are the roles of the various political and economic interests involved in the downsizing debate, and how are they making their voices heard? We still know relatively little about the national security decision-making process in countries other than the United States, and more research in this area would be valuable.

Similar questions can be asked about industries. How are industries responding to the downsizing, and why do they respond differently one from another? What strategies are most successful for firms in this environment (for example, diversification or specialization)? Students of business administration and industrial economics have yet to provide complete answers to these and other questions of corporate behavior.

There are, of course, also important normative questions that can be raised during this era of downsizing. What should be the role of the United States with respect to Russian defense conversion? How should research and defense dollars be spent by defense ministries in this era of uncertainty? What weapons should countries buy? These questions must all be answered as we head toward the millenium.

As scholars, officials, and executives raise—and attempt to resolve—these and other issues, they will no doubt find themselves in the midst of political conflict. Increases in defense spending were certainly controversial, but at least there was plenty of money to go around. Now, military expenditures have become a zero-sum game, a classic example of "whose ox gets gored."

Few like to work in such an environment. Indeed, it would be tempting to turn away from the problems altogether. But the issues associated with defense downsizing are no less worthy of our attention than those that faced the policy makers of the early 1980s, and we hope that this volume will contribute to enlightened public debate over the dilemmas we now face.

Notes

1. Quoted in *Baltimore Sun*, September 3, 1993, 14.
2. See, for example, the editorial "Where's the Bottom?" *New York Times*, September 3, 1993, 22.
3. Ironically, some of these migrants went in search of work in the booming defense and aerospace industries of these regions. See, for example, Ann Markusen, et al., *The Rise of the Gunbelt* (New York: Oxford University Press, 1991).
4. For those who are unfamiliar with the history, the Federal Reserve adopted restrictive monetary policies even in the face of massive unemployment; government stimulus packages, of course, were also relatively small during this pre-Keynesian era.
5. U.S. Arms Control and Disarmament Agency, *Report to the Congress on Defense Industrial Conversion* (Washington, D.C.: ACDA, August 1990), 17.
6. Paul Kennedy, *The Rise and Fall of the Great Powers* (New York: Random House, 1987); for more on the debate, see Ethan B. Kapstein, *The Political Economy of National Security: A Global Perspective* (New York: McGraw-Hill, 1992).

Index